MIDDLESEX COUNTY

Endpapers: *Main Street in Cranbury was transformed into a spectacular fantasy by an ice-storm during the winter of 1892. Courtesy, Cranbury Historical and Preservation Society*

Title page: *Oil on canvas painting, "Captain Alexander Hamilton's Battery Defending Brunswick," by Charles Waterhouse (1974). Courtesy, Jane Voorhees Zimmerli Art Museum, Rutgers The State University, New Brunswick, NJ; gift of the class of 1924 on the occasion of their fiftieth reunion*

Contents page: *Thomas Edison is seen (seated seventh from the left) with a group of assistants in an upstairs room of his Menlo Park laboratory. Note that the gas fixtures hanging from the ceiling have been fitted with incandescent lamps. From the collection of the Thomas A. Edison Tower and Museum. Courtesy, U.S. Dept. of the Interior, National Park Service, Edison National Historic Site*

Note from the authors: *Lenni Lenape was accepted for many years by scholars and historians as the correct name of the Native people who lived for centuries in New Jersey and who are part of the Delaware tribe. More recently, we have come to understand that Lenape is more appropriate, as Lenni means "common people" as does the word Lenape.*

MIDDLESEX
COUNTY

C r o s s r o a d s   o f   H i s t o r y

By Gary Karasik and Anna M. Aschkenes

American Historical Press
Sun Valley, California

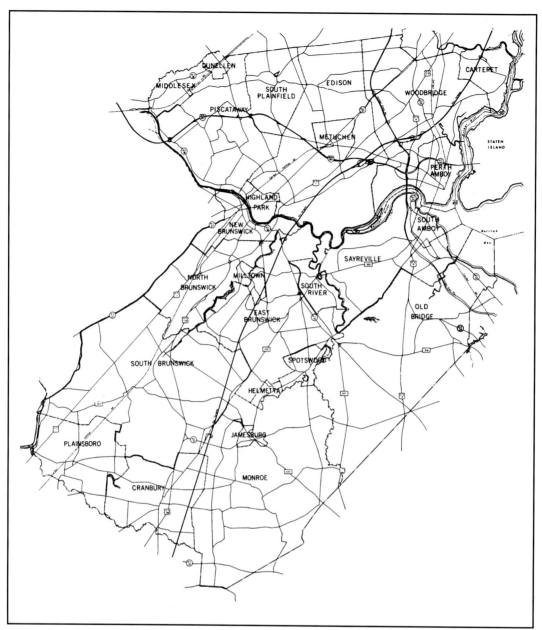

*Incorporated in 1683, Middlesex County's borders have undergone
many changes, as have the internal demarcations of the municipalities.
Middlesex is considered a transportation hub, as evidenced here in
this 1999 map of the County displaying major thoroughfares.
Courtesy, Middlesex County Department of Planning*

Library of Congress Catalogue Card Number: 99-75345

ISBN: 1-892724-06-5

Bibliography: p. 238
Includes Index

CONTENTS

PREFACE

Until recently, our sense of history—and thus our sense of ourselves—has been largely dependent upon fate; we have made assumptions about the past based upon what has been accidentally preserved. Societies routinely, and sometimes purposely, destroy their pasts or the pasts of others by discarding or burning books and artifacts. The result is a body of recorded history that is highly limited, selective, and gap-riddled.

This situation, for good or ill, is changing dramatically. With the proliferation of computers and mass storage devices, the study of history must undergo a fundamental change, requiring a battery of new skills. The historian's role will shift from preservation to selection. They will become judges, deciding what to preserve. The problem will not be *if* some bit of information exists, for it will most certainly be recorded somewhere; the problem will be where to find it. Historians of the future will be faced with a startlingly difficult task, that of selecting the important, the seminal, the significant event or report or fact from a truly astounding amount of data; they will be inundated. Ironically, the identification of the important fact will become vastly more selective and subjective than it has been in the past.

In a small way, we have been confronted with a similar problem in writing this history: it has been extraordinarily difficult to decide what not to include. A truly comprehensive history of Middlesex County would be a monumental task, requiring several more volumes than the three undertaken by haberdasher John P. Wall and collaborator Harold E. Pickersgill in their thorough *History of Middlesex County: 1660-1920.*

Therefore a deliberate effort has been made in this book to import the greatest possible amount of historical detail via the illustrations, while the text follows the main trends of area history. Illustrations that are available elsewhere, in national and state histories, have been excluded, and strict adherence to chronology has been sacrificed in the early chapters, in favor of a wealth of never-before-printed views of New Brunswick and Middlesex County communities.

Indeed, it would be easy to justify a separate volume for each of the county's 25 municipalities. Instead, the authors have chosen to follow the social, economic, and cultural trends of the County as a whole, contrasted by a more in-depth perspective on the city of New Brunswick. As the County seat and the cultural hub of central New Jersey, New Brunswick illustrates the renaissance of the American city and the renewal of the urban lifestyle. Here the synergy of public/private partnerships is evident, holding promise for the future and the next 300 years of Middlesex County.

"Under the Foot Bridge," painted in watercolors by Edward Lange during the 1870s, is from the collection of the Alexander Library. The scene is of the Raritan River, New Brunswick. Courtesy, Special Collections and Archives, Rutgers University Libraries

ACKNOWLEDGEMENTS

Despite the image of a struggling artist starving alone in a garret, no writer is an island. The process of acknowledging others —without which a project of this sort could never succeed—has always been a problem because mentioning one individual in a sense de-emphasizes the help given by others who may not be mentioned. All of the help is vital, and we have received so much from so many. Deprived of any part of that help, the final product would be diminished.

This visual and narrative excursion through the history of Middlesex County has been a work evolving. First published in 1986, it proved to be an extremely popular reference and was soon sold out in book stores. In its preparation, dozens of persons came forth to guide the narrative and to assist in the identification of images. Therefore, some of our thanks are to those who took time from their busy schedules to assist us in 1986. Among them are Ruth Marcus Patt, unstinting in her willingness to take time away from her frantic schedule to help; the reference staff of Alexander Library and the New Jersey Room, Rutgers, The State University; M.J. Babcock who shared his collection and writings with us; Delores Parent, at that time with the New Brunswick Chamber of Commerce; Leslie Bachelor, William G. Marshall and Quentin Smith. Some we have acknowledged here have moved on to other jobs or retired for a well earned rest. One or two others, such as the much loved William Kraemer, are no longer with us. But, they remain included, so as to recognize their important contributions to the original work.

As we approach the new millenium, a publication on the history of Middlesex County is more appropriate than ever, as this is a time when thoughtful consideration is being given to our past. Lay people are joining educators, philosophers and commentators in questioning—what persons or events have shaped our society? How has my community changed? What is on the horizon as we bring the 20th century to a close and embark on that journey called "future?" Thus, *Middlesex County Crossroads of History* was conceived.

Building upon the 1986 volume, this edition is more comprehensive. It contains many more and new images and provides an update on each community. Here too, we were assisted by many agencies and individuals in locating photographs and documents pertinent to the story of Middlesex County and wish to acknowledge their efforts. As with all good things, it took the hands of many, working in tandem, to create a whole that is far greater than any of the individual parts.

Lastly, we owe a debt of gratitude to the guardians of our heritage—those who have preserved artifacts and memorabilia, whose sense of history and obligation to society impel them to maintain the archives and treasure troves of the past. Without the efforts of these individuals, we would have far less understanding of our history.

Ralph Albanir, Middlesex County Parks
   Department
Ron Becker, Special Collections and Archives,
   Rutgers University
Michael Blackwell, New Brunswick Recreation
Walter Blakely, New Brunswick
Michael W. Boylan, East Jersey Olde Towne,
   Piscataway
Noreen Braman, Middlesex County Cultural
   and Heritage Commission
George Campbell, Edison Memorial Tower
Nancy Casteras, Woodbridge Township
   Cultural Arts Commission
Ruth Clark, South Plainfield Historical Society
Gary Cooper, Saint Peters Hospital, New
   Brunswick
Carol Denequollo, New Jersey Repertory
   Ballet

David Fleming, New Brunswick Cultural Center, Inc.

Ralph Genella, North Brunswick

George Street Playhouse, New Brunswick

Estelle Goldsmith, East Brunswick Museum Corporation

James Gutman, Johnson & Johnson

Janice Haraz, Spotswood Cultural and Heritage Commission

Kenneth M. Helsby, Cornelius Low House, Piscataway

Jean Holtz, DEVCO, New Brunswick

Jane Voorhees Zimmerli Art Museum, New Brunswick

Anide Jean, Crossroads Theatre Company, New Brunswick

Susan Kenen, Buccleuch Mansion, New Brunswick

Louise Kerwin, Jamesburg Historical Society

Marcia Kirkpatrick, Jamesburg Historical Society

Susan Kittredge, Middlesex County Cultural and Heritage Commission

William Kraemer, East Brunswick

Dr. Herbert Kraft, Seton Hall University

Jeanne Kolva, Highland Park Historical Society

Ruth Lewis, Middlesex County College

Edward Lingenheld, Rutgers Preparatory School

Sharon Marsh, Middlesex County Cultural and Heritage Commission

Alvia Martin, Madison Township Historical Society

Peter Mazzei, Special Collections and Archives, Rutgers University

Middlesex County Vocational Technical High School

Carolyn J. Mobley, New Brunswick Tomorrow

Reverend Dr. August Molnar, American Hungarian Foundation

New Brunswick Chamber of Commerce

Kim Nguyen, Middlesex County Cultural and Heritage Commission

Wesley Ott, Dunellen

Margaret E. Pemberton, Middlesex County Clerk, Board of Chosen Freeholders

Perth Amboy Office of the Mayor, Joseph Vas

Thomas J. Pollock, Middlesex County Planning Department

James Pulaski, Middlesex County Cultural and Heritage Commission

Barbara Rokicki, W.A.T.E.R.

David Sheehan, Edison Township Historical Society

Dorothy Silady, Spotswood Cultural and Heritage Commission

Ruth Simmons, Special Collections and Archives, Rutgers University

Ed Skipwood, Special Collections and Archives, Rutgers University

Betty Wagner, Cranbury Historical Society

Woodbridge Office of the Mayor, James E. McGreevey

Frank Yusko, Spotswood High School History Club

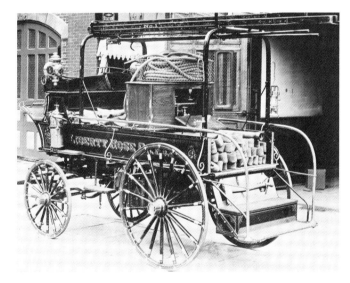

In 1802 the taxpayers of New Brunswick paid a total of $235.55 for fire protection. Two years later, the city voted to award to each fireman who fought a major fire one gallon of "spirits." By 1900, New Brunswick had acquired the best personnel and equipment, such as this apparatus belonging to the Liberty Hose Co. Courtesy, New Brunswick Chamber of Commerce.

10

Facing page: *In 1890, J.M. Macom recorded the beauty of the brook separating Middlesex and Somerset counties at the New Brunswick boundary line on Livingston Avenue. Courtesy, Special Collections and Archives, Rutgers University Libraries*

Right: *"Solitude," a miniature in watercolors, is the work of Anna Aschkenes. Printed at the request of the author*

Below: *"Winter in Old Bridge, New Jersey," by noted landscape and genre painter James Crawford Thom, is a charming depiction of the community in which Thom resided for eight years. Courtesy, East Brunswick Museum Corporation*

INTRODUCTION

The history of Middlesex County both parallels and reflects the history of the United States. As with the country, the county's beginnings were agricultural, but its real strength lay ultimately in manufacturing. Historically, the county's central location ensured that area residents played pivotal roles during the colony's earliest days and during the American Revolution. Middlesex County also played a central role in the development of the various modes of transportation from which the country drew vitality. Additionally, as the site of Thomas Alva Edison's Menlo Park, the storied place where that quintessential inventor did much of his

most important work, the county's role in the country's development expanded further. Each stage of Middlesex County's history has precisely paralleled, reflected, or augured some critical stage in this country's development.

Always, the people and places of Middlesex County seem to have been involved with the development of new and progressive ideas, whether political, commercial, medical, or social. Always, the county has been the site of and profited from innovation, especially from commercial and technological innovation. Always, there have been located here factories and plants that efficiently and

Above: *Selman A. Waksman, a Russian immigrant, studied as an undergraduate at Rutgers University. In later years he discovered streptomycin and was awarded the Nobel Prize.*

Right: *Halladay's Wind Engine was manufactured by W.R. Pease in New Brunswick in 1854. Both pictures courtesy, Special Collections and Archives, Rutgers University Libraries*

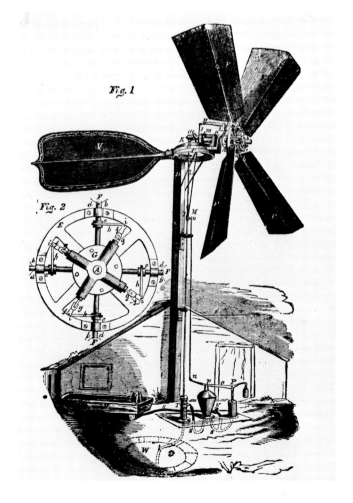

successfully manufactured the products of exciting new ideas and dramatic new technologies. The list of major corporations that have or have had facilities in the county is long indeed and consists of names famous both locally and around the world: Michelin, Squibb, Johnson & Johnson, Armstrong Cork, National Musical String, Nabisco.

There are many reasons for the county's historical eminence. The Raritan River enters into the Atlantic just south of the Port of New York, and for a time this river provided the medium of transport for much of the raw material upon which an emerging American economy and industry depended.

Location along the main route from Philadelphia to Boston via New York City ensured the county a prominent place in the country's early political and military history. And the rolling hills and fertile soil were features that attracted many individuals and corporations fleeing the constraints of the ever-more-crowded New York City area.

Transportation, politics, medicine, technology, the arts—Middlesex County has nurtured all these human endeavors. Rare is the place that can boast of accomplishments so many and varied taking place on its soil, encouraging—inspiring—its people. Rare indeed.

Dr. Solomon Andrews of Perth Amboy, a physician at age twenty-three, received patents for a barrel-making machine, fumigators, forging presses, and a padlock for mailbags used by the U.S. Postal Service. In 1863, Andrews launched the first successful lighter-than-air ship capable of controlled flight. Courtesy, City of Perth Amboy Tercentennial Committee

The Walker-Gordon Laboratory chose Plainsboro as the site for its innovative dairy farm in 1897. The "Rotolactor," put into operation in 1930, milked fifty cows in twelve and one-half minutes. Courtesy, Plainsboro Historical Society

Left: *"Boat Yard at Ayes Beach, Highland Park,"
in watercolors and pen and ink, is by W.A. Koster.*

Below: *"The Raritan River, Three Miles North of
New Brunswick, New Jersey" is an oil on canvas by
John McAvoy. Both paintings are from the collection
of the Alexander Library. Courtesy, Special Collections and Archives, Rutgers University Libraries*

Rutgers University, depicted in this 1844 etching, was founded by the Dutch Reformed Church in 1766. Today it includes seven campuses, 40,000 students, and 2,500 faculty members. Rutgers produced four governors for the State of New Jersey, as well as a secretary of state, a justice of the U.S. Supreme Court, and a vice president. Courtesy, Special Collections and Archives, Rutgers University Libraries

The United Methodist Church in Cranbury. Courtesy, Special Collections and Archives, Rutgers University

CHAPTER ONE

THE LAY OF THE LAND

In 1609, Captain Henry Hudson accepted a commission from the Dutch East India Trading Company to sail the Halve Maen westward from Amsterdam in search of a shorter passage to India. Although Captain Hudson did not succeed in this endeavor, he did report on his finding wonderful lands with majestic mountains, endless forests, abundant resources, and navigable rivers, one of which now bears his name. Another of the rivers he reported came to be called the Raritan.

Hudson returned to Holland with a cargo of furs from the inhabitants of these rich lands. As a result of his discoveries, a new trading company—the Dutch West India Trading Company—was formed. This new company was granted sole rights to develop and administer the new territory, which was to be called Nieuw Netherlands.

Samuel Seabury, the first Episcopal bishop in America, and John Croes, the first Episcopal bishop in New Jersey, preached from St. James' three-tiered pulpit. Courtesy, Edison Township Historical Society, Inc.

To begin the exploitation of the resources of their new lands, the Dutch established a trading post called Nieuw Amsterdam. The post was within the protection of the bay at the mouth of the Hudson River, on a large island. The exotic inhabitants of the new lands, whom Hudson dubbed "Indians," called the island "Manahattan." From this base, the Dutch sent explorers and surveyors to map the lands and traders and trappers to barter with the inhabitants and to gather furs for export.

Not until several years later, during the course of these explorations, did the Dutch see the potential for development and settlement of the Raritan River Valley, which Hudson had only superficially mentioned. They soon established another trading post at Pavonia (Jersey City), across the Hudson from Nieuw Amsterdam, and by the 1630s full exploration of this beautiful and desirable valley was underway.

The Dutch explored the valley thoroughly, and it has been reported that several Dutch

homesteads developed into a small community called "Hollander Dorp" (Dutch Village) along the river opposite the present site of New Brunswick. But the Dutch, to their eventual dismay and loss, concentrating too intently on immediate profits and not sufficiently on the future, failed to take the necessary steps to ensure their control over the area. The British wrested control of Nieuw Amsterdam in 1664, changing its name to New York, and that same year, the British Crown chartered all of the former Nieuw Netherlands to British proprietors, renaming these lands New Jersey. All traces of the Hollander Dorp and the Dutch occupation of the Raritan River Valley disappeared when the Proprietors took over political stewardship of the Raritan River Valley in 1670.

The settling of the area that was to become Middlesex County took place rather late in the process of European colonization of the New World, which had begun in the late 1400s. As the New Jersey settlers were beginning to clear land and build homes in what is now Piscataway and Highland Park, the Spanish were traveling north from Mexico along the coast of southern California. At the same time, the Russians had noticed the abundance of seal and sea otter pelts to be had along the coast of northern California, and the French and others were trapping pelts and trading with the inhabitants of Canada.

During and after the late 1400s, there had been an unsurpassed explosion of travel. Motivated by curiosity, acquisitiveness, arrogance, conviction, and fear of persecution, soldiers and explorers and merchants and missionaries sailed off into the unknown in vulnerable little ships toward victory and death, discovery and wealth, glory and sanctuary, claiming as they went, for God, King, Company, and Wallet, the wealth and property of all the inhabitants of all the lands through which their quests led. Not until some 150 years after all this had begun in earnest did Europeans begin settling the Raritan River Valley.

The Indians living in the Raritan Valley when the Europeans first arrived had been successfully hunting and farming for many years in the seemingly endless forests of North America's eastern seaboard. They had a huge store of knowledge about farming and hunting and about making medicines from native plants and minerals. These natives met and traded with the Europeans.

In the Raritan River and Delaware River valleys, these people called themselves the Lenni Lenape, meaning "Original People" or "True People." The colonists called them the Delaware because they were concentrated in the Delaware River Valley, although they ranged through New Jersey and southeastern New York to eastern Pennsylvania.

The Lenni Lenape of the Raritan River Valley called themselves by a name which sounded to the earliest explorers like "Rari-chons" and which became "Raritan." The Raritans did not object to the inroads of Europeans into their territories as the Incas had objected to the presence of Francisco Pizarro or as the Plains Indians were later to object to the advance of Americans. Though there are reports of isolated violence against the colonists—mostly in response to blatant provocations by the early Dutch—the Raritans did not mount an organized, violent resistance against the invaders.

When the Europeans arrived, about 2,000 Lenni Lenape were scattered throughout the lands from the Delaware River Valley to the salt marshes of the Meadowlands. As described by Van Tienhoven in 1650, the Lenni Lenape's Raritan River Valley was "the handsomest and pleasantest country that man can behold . . . with abundance of maize, beans, pumpkins and other fruits."

This lovely synagogue, Congregation Poile Zedek, was erected in 1923 and represents one of the oldest Jewish communities in Middlesex County, having been founded in 1890. The decorative structure is situated on Neilson Street, New Brunswick, on a site that was occupied by a temperance hall during the last quarter of the nineteenth century. The Jewish community is proud of its long heritage in the New Brunswick area, with records confirming residency by a Jewish family in 1756. Courtesy, Special Collections and Archives, Rutgers University Libraries

Though apparently once a warlike people, the Lenni Lenape, whose history has been traced to the far west of North America, had become gentle anglers and hunters. Living in bark hut communities of several hundred, they planted maize and even had a system of currency of polished shells, called wampum. The hospitable Lenni Lenape acted as hosts, guides, and tutors to the Europeans, providing them with shelter, showing them the best hunting and trapping grounds and trails, and teaching them about

Cranbury's Brainerd Lake is named for David Brainerd, an evangelist who preached to the Indians in 1745, reportedly with great effect. "Men, women and little children seven years of age became in great distress for their souls." Courtesy, Special Collections and Archives, Rutgers University Libraries

fertilizing farmland and storing and preserving food.

In 1679-1680, two Dutch missionaries, Danker and Sluyter, traveled across New Jersey from New York to Delaware and Maryland, via the Indian trails. Their journal tells of being received into Lenni Lenape dwellings after presenting the Indians with some fish hooks:

While we were in the house a naked child fell from its mother's lap and received a cut in its head, whereupon all who sat around that fire and belonged to that household began to cry, husband and wife, young and old, and scream more than the child, and as if they themselves had broken their arms or legs. In another corner of this hut there sat around a fire, forming another household, a

party whose faces were entirely blackened, who observed a gloomy silence and looked very singular. They were mourning for a deceased friend. The Indian guide having made himself ready took both our sacks together and tied them on his back for the purpose of carrying them, which did not suit us badly as we were very tired. He did that without our asking him, and conducted us in a direction more southeasterly to their King or Sackemaker, who lived two or three miles from there. On arriving there they immediately offered us some boiled beans in a calabash, cooked without salt or grease, though they brought us our own kind of spoons to take them out with. It was the Queen who did this, who was dressed more than the others. She gave us also a piece of their bread, that is, pounded maize kneaded

into a cake and baked under the ashes. We ate some of it, more for the purpose of satisfying her people than our appetite. Meanwhile we agreed with the Sackemaker to set across the river for three guilders in seewan. We presented fish hooks to several of them, but especially the Queen who had entertained us. The Sackemaker being ready took one of our sacks to carry and went on ahead of us; and there went this King carrying our pack, almost without any clothing on his body. He conducted us to the creek, which was two or three miles distant to the north and northeast, over a very difficult and rocky hill.

Only when seriously mistreated did the Raritans pursue any violent means of redress, once attacking a Dutch sloop and killing some hogs on Staten Island. The Dutch troops sent to avenge the act burned the Raritans' corn and killed a number of the Indians. When the Dutch offered a bounty of wampum for every Raritan head, the Long Island Indians killed a number of Raritans, which put a stop to any further active hostilities. Although there are reports that a tax was levied in 1671 among the settlers in Woodbridge to pay for war materiel, only ten pounds of powder and twenty pounds of lead were required. There is no evidence that an enterprise was ever mounted from either side. Instead of fighting with the Europeans, the Lenni Lenape traded, shared native lore, and slowly withdrew from their lands as the Europeans advanced.

The legacy of the Lenni Lenape remains in the physical development of the country. Roads followed old trails, and towns were built at or near the sites of villages. New Brunswick arose near an ancient Lenni Lenape village called Ahandewamock, and Inian's Ferry at the site of a ford where a trail crossed the Raritan.

The settlers improved these paths to ac-

To mark the occasion of its 100th anniversary, the Cranbury Press *reprinted the July 17, 1885, edition. The advertisements contain a wealth of historical detail about Cranbury. Courtesy, Cranbury Historical and Preservation Society*

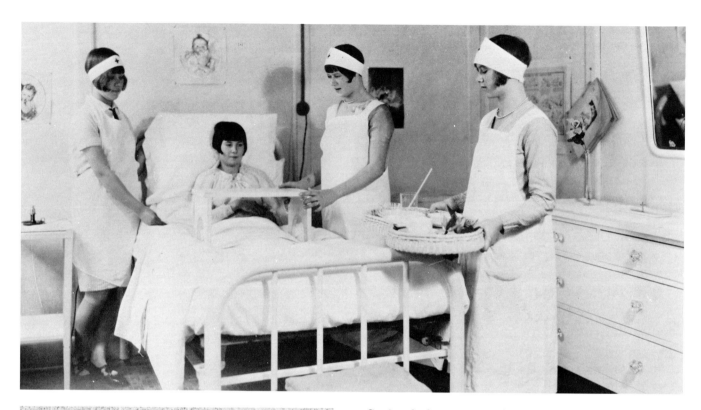

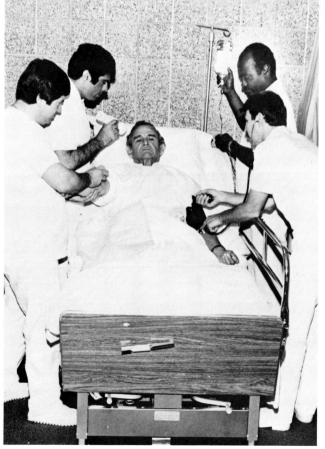

Societal change is evident in these two photographs of students in the nursing programs offered by the Middlesex County Vocational and Technical High Schools. The photo above was taken of a home nursing class in 1928. The one below was published in the early 1980s as a poster for the Practical Nursing Department. Courtesy, Middlesex County Vocational and Technical High Schools and Adult Technical Schools.

commodate heavier traffic and add more routes. The first road through New Jersey was laid out by the Dutch; roughly paralleling one of the major Lenni Lenape trails, it began at New Amsterdam, crossed the bay by ferry to a point near Elizabethtown, and traversed the areas that would become Woodbridge and Piscataway to the ford that became Inian's Ferry and later New Brunswick. There the road split, one branch going through the present site of Princeton to Trenton, crossing the Delaware and ending at Philadelphia, the other passing through the present-day township of Cranbury to Burlington and crossing the Delaware at Bristol to rejoin the first branch.

Another Lenni Lenape legacy formed the basis for a medical system that ultimately generated the first formal medical society in the New World, the Medical Society of New Jersey. Many modern drugs are derived from herbs whose medicinal properties were passed on by the Lenni Lenape to the settlers (in time of specific illness or need) and to doctors who sought out Lenni Lenape knowledge of medicine in order to record it.

Although the Europeans brought to North America their own rich history of folk medicine and a supply of medications and dried herbs, this supply was necessarily limited by the transatlantic journey, and the colonists had to learn about local plants and minerals.

Diaries of the colonists refer to "squaw" remedies and provide details on the preparation and dosages of Lenni Lenape medications. Other references note the attendance upon colonists of Lenni Lenape herbalists when European remedies failed.

The highly advanced knowledge of medicine which the Lenni Lenape taught the settlers formed the foundation for the professionalizing of medicine, and both New Jersey's and Middlesex County's proud history of advancement in the health sciences

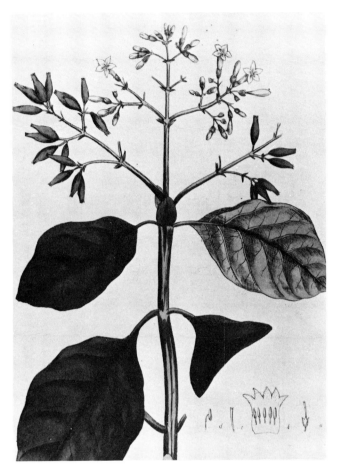

The colonists and early doctors of New Jersey owed much to the Lenni Lenape people, who taught the application of herbal remedies to the European settlers. A good number of the curative practices eventually were included in the United States Pharmacopoeia. Medicines such as quinine were prepared by apothecaries from the bark of the cinchona plant, pictured here. Courtesy, University of Medicine and Dentistry of New Jersey, George F. Smith Library, and the Middlesex County Cultural and Heritage Commission

Metuchen's first library was constructed in the 1800s on Main Street. The "Reading Room," as it was called, was relocated to its present site on Highland Avenue at the turn of the century. Courtesy, Middlesex County Cultural and Heritage Commission

Top left: *This magnificent mansion in Jamesburg, known as Lakeview, is the result of several major additions and combinations of architectural styles. The original room, located at the rear of the house, was built in the 1600s as a farm house. James Buckelew, for whom the town of Jamesbury was named, doubled the size of the structure around 1832. In the late 1800s his widow added the third story, the west wing, and the conservatory. Lakeview is now being restored by the Jamesburg Historical Association. Courtesy, Jamesburg Historical Association*

Top right: *The Hiram Market was the hub of activity in early New Brunswick. Constructed in 1814, the market stood in the middle of Hiram Street and measured 25 feet wide by 150 feet long. Farmers and merchants sold their produce and wares; travelers arriving by ferry or stagecoach stopped at Keenon's Tavern or stayed at Macom's Hotel, both in the Hiram Market District. The city scales were located here and were in use from 1822 until 1916, although the structure itself was torn down in 1866. Courtesy, Special Collections and Archives, Rutgers University Libraries*

The Ross House, one of the oldest in Metuchen, has five fireplaces and contains "bible doors," so called because of the cross made by the panels. Courtesy, Middlesex County Cultural and Heritage Commission

are a result of that legacy.

Perhaps the most significant—yet least tangible—aspect of the Amerindian legacy is the respect for and harmony with nature that the Europeans saw in the people whom they met and conquered. This relationship with nature became a fundamental part of American consciousness and ideology.

This sensibility still deeply informs the American character. It joined with the other attitudes that drew or drove Europeans to the New World—acquisitiveness and inquisitiveness, venality and adventure, nobility and fear of persecution—to form the complex, creative, often contradictory mind of the American people.

Three basic pursuits have melded to shape the development of American history: commerce, conscience, and a mystical reverence for the land, a belief that people are tied to and derive a spiritual strength from the very earth upon which they live. These three sometimes mutually exclusive needs have made America what it is and have made Middlesex County a quintessential example of the American experience.

Perth Amboy was the first important city to emerge
in Middlesex County. By 1830 Raritan Bay had become a terminus for coal, and within fifty years major manufacturing and industrial operations were
centered in Perth Amboy. As late as 1940 cargo
schooners, such as those seen in this 1920s photo,
were still traversing the waters of Raritan Bay, ser-
vicing local lumberyards and coal shipping piers.
Courtesy, W.A.T.E.R., Inc.

CHAPTER TWO

LIFE IN EARLY MIDDLESEX

In 1651, Cornelius Van Werckhoven petitioned the Dutch government for permission to plant settlements in various areas of New Netherlands. At the same time, Van Werckhoven commissioned a New Amsterdam resident, Augustine Heermans, to negotiate with the several Amerindian groups inhabiting the rich territories for the purchase of tracts in several locations, including areas of Long Island and the fertile mainland territories west of Staten Island.

Heermans' venture was among the first attempts to settle the lands of East New Jersey, and he succeeded in purchasing rights to a tract roughly seventeen miles long and thirty-four miles wide, bordered on the east by the Kills, on the north by the Passaic River, and on the south by the Raritan River. The southerly section of this large tract would eventually form a substantial portion of

On the Farrington Farm near Cheesequake Creek, seeds were planted in wooden hot-bed frames, where their growth could be controlled with the aid of a layer of salt hay. At sunset, the farmer covered the young plants with a glass sash, which together with the salt hay retained the sun's warmth and pre-vented frost damage. Once the seedlings were strong enough to be transplanted to the open fields, the salt hay was re-used as bedding for the livestock, or mixed with manure and spread on the growing fields as fertilizer. Courtesy, Madison Township Historical Society

Middlesex County.

Heermans successfully negotiated for other tracts as well, making Van Werckhoven a landowner of great importance, but complaints from other speculators prompted the Dutch to insist that Van Werckhoven develop one area only. Van Werckhoven chose Long Island, and the title to the Raritan tract reverted to the Lenni Lenape.

Shortly after the Dutch surrender, a group of English settlers who had been living on Long Island successfully petitioned Deputy Governor Nicolls for the right to settle the area that Van Werckhoven had failed to develop, and on October 28, 1664, the Long Islanders purchased the same tract of land that Heermans had already purchased once from the Lenni Lenape. The Lenni Lenape, displaying surprising business acumen, were quick both to perceive and to take advantage of this opportunity. Deputy Governor Nicolls confirmed the purchase on December 1, 1664, and the Long Islanders settled at Elizabethtown Point.

Farm scenes like this one are becoming rare because of the rapid growth of residential and corporate communities. As agriculture has decreased, Middlesex County's position as a leader in sciences and technology has expanded and will soon be enhanced by construction of four research centers. Courtesy, Madison Township Historical Society

The new settlers soon discovered, however, that the Lenni Lenape were sharp bargainers indeed, for the English had assumed that the westerly boundary of the tract was the Raritan as it curved to the north. Following the first of a long series of disputes that would rage over rights to Middlesex County lands, the English had to purchase a second tract from the Lenni Lenape to firmly establish title to the lands all the way up the Raritan to Bound Brook.

Unfortunately for the legal peace of mind of colonists involved in this transaction, Deputy Governor Nicolls had agreed on this occasion (as he did on several other occasions) to convey title to lands that were not

Above: *Harvesting salt hay was a unique and difficult task along Cheesequake Creek. As the tide rose, the land was covered with water. The farmer had only brief periods during low tide to quickly cut and load the salt hay and transport it to higher ground. Horses were fitted with oversized wooden shoes known as "mud boots."*

The hauling nets at Seidler's Beach were a common sight when crabs, fish, eels, and bottom fish were caught by nets laid along the floor of the Raritan Bay. Clams and oysters were raked or dredged, not gathered by net. Because state laws prohibited the taking of oysters during certain months of the year, oyster season was eagerly anticipated. Both photos courtesy, Madison Township Historical Society

really under his jurisdiction, for while much of the above was occurring, the Duke of York who held the royal charter, had conveyed the territory between the Hudson and Delaware rivers to the king's loyal supporters John Lord Berkeley and Sir George Carteret.

Berkeley and Carteret foresaw significant wealth to be derived from their new dominions, which they named New Jersey, after the Channel Island of Jersey, on which Carteret made his home. (Another name, Nova Caesarea, was chosen but was eventually dropped at the urging of the settlers). Berkeley and Carteret would ultimately divide their property between them, the southwesterly half (which became West Jersey) going to Lord Berkeley, and the northeasterly half (which became East Jersey) going to Lord Carteret. Carteret and those who later purchased his interests sought to repudiate Deputy Governor Nicolls' actions in disputes requiring great expenditures of time, money, and energy.

To encourage settlement of the area, Berkeley and Carteret offered extremely favorable conditions to settlers. Among these conditions were absolute freedom of worship and the right to a colonial Assembly; this Assembly was to have the sole power of taxation and a share of the legislation of the province. Similar rights, some even more liberal, had also been granted settlers by the Dutch, and colonists had become accustomed to conditions that were non-restrictive in the extreme, especially when contrasted with the conditions of life in Great Britain and elsewhere in the Old World.

This moral and administrative independence reinforced the de facto political independence enjoyed by the colonists, particularly those of New Jersey. These and other factors—including the absence of their British landlords, the unwillingness of the Crown to pay for the maintenance of significant numbers of British troops (until the French and Indian War, 1754 to 1763), the stubborn autonomy of the settlers, and the growing sense of national identity—would lead to grievances, rancor, disputes, and, ultimately, to the American Revolution.

To administer his dominions, Sir George Carteret sent a distant relative, Philip Carteret, to serve as governor of the New Jersey territories he controlled (Lord Berkeley sent Robert Coxe to govern West Jersey.) Governor Carteret, anxious to promote the growth of the colony, initially confirmed the rights granted by Deputy Governor Nicolls to the Elizabethtown settlers, going so far as to join with the settlers' representatives in the sale of a portion of the large tract to Joshua

Pierce and associates on December 11, 1666. This subdivision was to become the location of the earliest Middlesex County towns and townships of Piscataway, Woodbridge, and Perth Amboy.

Lord Carteret was to gain little from his East Jersey territories before his death. To pay his debts, his wife and executrix, Lady Elizabeth Carteret, in 1680 sold the Carteret interests in the tract for 3,400 pounds to a group of businessmen and speculators, among whom was William Penn, the wealthy Quaker who was to found Pennsylvania. The speculators initially called themselves the Twelve Proprietors, until each divided his interest in the tract with an additional associate; this latter group became the Twenty-four Proprietors.

Upon taking possession of their new lands, the Twenty-four Proprietors were greatly dismayed to find that so large a portion of their property had already been given up under grants and sales by the Dutch, by Governor Nicolls, by Governor Carteret, and by Lord and Lady Carteret. With the intent of reversing as many of these grants and sales as possible, the Proprietors began at once to legally contest all claims, and these disputes eventually became so bitter, onerous, and long-lived that the defendants ultimately petitioned King George II for relief, asserting that they were being ruined by the Proprietors' relentless litigation.

Among those tracts covered under agreements that predated the Proprietors' purchase were, besides the Elizabethtown grant, a 1,300-acre tract purchased by Thomas Lawrence that included what is now Clifton Avenue, at the end of George Street in New Brunswick; a tract sold to Lawrence's stepson, Cornelius Longfield, that extended to a line that is now the south side of Livingston Avenue in New Brunswick; and a tract that went to John Inian and associates. On his parcel, John Inian would establish Inian's

Ferry at a site where a major Lenni Lenape trail crossed the Raritan River. Inian improved and built roads in the vicinity, encouraging travel and commerce. Around Inian's Ferry would grow the city of New Brunswick.

The legal wranglings between the resident settlers and their absentee landlords lasted more than sixty years, but in the end those with legitimate prior claims to property generally prevailed. The settlers were aided in their efforts to keep their properties by disagreements among the Proprietors themselves, who by and large trusted each other less than they trusted the settlers.

Over the years, despite all the costly litigation, the Proprietors did succeed in subdividing the acreage of their tract, and the expanses of East Jersey were slowly populated. By 1683, the population of Woodbridge was 600 and that of Piscataway was 400. (Many of the early settlers brought Negro slaves, but it is not known if they were counted in these earliest population figures.) Yet even amid all these complex legal maneuverings, the disposition, settlement, and development of the new territory inevitably resulted in the formation of judicial and military districts and of counties, townships, and towns.

In 1682, East Jersey was divided into the counties of Middlesex, Essex, Bergen, and Monmouth; these were joined in 1688 by Somerset, which was formed out of territory originally contained within the boundaries of Middlesex County. In 1693, various townships were set off in the East Jersey counties. In Middlesex County, these townships were named after towns that were already established within township borders and included Perth Amboy before it was divided into Perth and South Amboy, Piscataway, and Woodbridge, among whose earliest residents is listed John Pike, of the same family as Major Zebulon Pike, who fought in the

Revolutionary War, and General Zebulon Montgomery Pike, who fought in the War of 1812 and for whom Pike's Peak is named.

Piscataway Township was originally a huge tract, comprising nearly all of southwestern Middlesex County across the Raritan as well as the lands that today comprise Piscataway proper. In 1709, Somerset County took for itself an additional section of Middlesex County, including a large portion of what was originally Piscataway; the final boundaries of Somerset County, which continued to annex parts of Middlesex, were not finally fixed until 1850.

The Proprietors lost no time in aggressively furthering the area's development; they created Perth Amboy in 1686, fulfilling the stated intention of Lord Carteret. Governor Philip Carteret and his council at first held their colonial Assemblies at various locations throughout East Jersey, but they settled upon Perth Amboy as the permanent

site after 1688. Also in Perth Amboy, and indicative of its early territorial importance, would be built Proprietary House, home of New Jersey's colonial governors, the last of whom would be William Franklin, Royalist son of American rebel, philosopher, inventor, and diplomat Benjamin Franklin. Proprietary House, an elegant and historic structure, can still be seen on its bluff in Perth Amboy.

There was general agreement that the site on Amboy Point would make an ideal setting for a city; indeed some felt a city rival-

With a population of 1,303 and a total of 140 homes, Perth Amboy was bustling in the 1840s. The road leading to the water is Smith Street, on which stood the City Hotel, formerly Hick's Tavern. Courtesy, W.A.T.E.R., Inc.

Right: *State and Smith Streets in Perth Amboy were the focal points for much of the downtown commerce, as seen in this 1926 photo. Smith Street was named for Dr. Charles McKnight Smith, founder and first president of the Middlesex County Medical Association, and a distinguished community leader.*

Below: *The ferry slip at the foot of Smith Street was the debarkation point for service to Staten Island from 1709 to 1963. The shed, which still stands today, houses a 1904 wooden drawbridge and lift mechanism that is believed to be the last of its kind anywhere in the nation. The Waterfront Association to Effect Restoration and the United States Navy Seabees are restoring the slip for use as a maritime museum. Both photos courtesy, W.A.T.E.R., Inc.*

ing London could someday develop there. In 1683, soon after his arrival, Governor Thomas Rudyard wrote:

Upon our view and survey of Amboy Point we find it extraordinary well situated for a great town or city beyond expectation. At low water round about the point are oysters of two kinds, small as English and others two or three mouthfuls, exceeding good for roasting and stewing. The Point is good, lively land, ten in some places and twenty foot above the water mark. About it are several coves where vessels may lay up conveniently; besides great ships of any burthen may all ride before the town land locked against all winds; the Raritan river runs up or rather down 50 for larger, some say 100 miles for small boats.

There was also a healthy whaling industry along the coast and in the waters of Raritan Bay that a community located on this site could both service and benefit from.

The Proprietors agreed that Amboy Point could provide excellent port facilities, and they were envious of the profits gleaned by New York from its port. So the creation of Perth Amboy was, in large part, an attempt to wrest a substantial percentage of the lucrative shipping business away from the extremely successful, profitable, and politically powerful Port of New York. The Proprietors' attempt—which in the long run would prove futile—was spiritedly resisted by the rival colony, and the commercial competition and political contentiousness between New Jersey and New York has continued to the present.

By the turn of the century, the Proprietors were having great difficulty even collecting the rents due them from their increasingly independent and recalcitrant tenants. In 1702, weary of struggling with the colonists, the Proprietors ceded to Queen Anne all

their rights of jurisdiction over East Jersey, whereupon the Queen rejoined New Jersey to New York under the administration of the arrogant and despotic Lord Cornbury (Edward Hyde). But the colonists complained so bitterly about the demands of Lord Cornbury that Queen Anne replaced him, first with Lord Lovelace, who died soon after taking office, and then with Robert Hunter, called Brigadier Hunter, who arrived in 1709. A long succession of territorial deputy governors followed until Lewis Morris, working doggedly to have New Jersey once again separated from New York, saw this redivision come to pass in 1738. Lewis Morris, appointed the first royal governor of New Jersey independent of New York, was also the first American-born governor of the province.

The desire of both the Dutch and the English governments to encourage rapid population growth of the new dominions, so as to provide greater revenues and more political stability, led them to offer extremely liberal conditions to prospective citizens. Ironically, this encouragement of freedom for some virtually mandated slavery for others. To make immigration to the colonies as attractive as possible, the Proprietors declared that they would give each freeman who agreed to settle in Nova Caesarea 150 acres for himself and, additionally, 150 for each able-bodied employee or indentured servant, and 75 acres for each "weaker" servant or slave over fourteen whom the freeman might bring.

Acceptance of the practice of slavery among the colonists was not universal, however. The Quakers of New Jersey united with those of Pennsylvania to implore their members not to employ slaves and to cease further importation of slaves into the territories. However, Queen Anne instructed Lord Cornbury to stop any movements that interfered with the traffic in slaves, in order

Saw-pit steam-driven timber operations, as seen here in Old Bridge Township, contributed to a flourishing lumber industry during the nineteenth century. The county's extensive waterways shipped raw timber, clapboards, shingles, and lumber for ship building to ports in New York, New Jersey, and throughout the eastern seaboard. Courtesy, Madison Township Historical Society

The earliest manufacturer of stoneware along Cheesequake Creek was Captain James Morgan, who established a pottery on the south shore of Raritan Bay. He created salt-glazed cobalt blue crocks, jugs, jars, and other items from approximately 1754 to 1784. His son, James Morgan, Jr., operated the concern until 1800, when he relocated and established a partnership with Jacob van Wickle and Branch Green, near the South River Bridge in Old Bridge. Courtesy, Madison Township Historical Society

quently moderate by Old World standards, which included drawing and quartering, disembowelment while alive, and partial hangings followed by beheadings. In 1535, for instance, one Englishman found guilty of treason was sentenced to be carried back to the Tower of London ". . . and from thence drawn on a hurdle through the City of London to Tyburn, there to be hanged till he should be half dead; that then he should be cut down alive, his privy parts cut off, his belly ripped, his bowels burnt, his four quarters set up over the four gates of the city, and his head placed upon London Bridge." Such inhumane sentences explain the significance of the clause that the victorious American citizens of the new nation wrote into the Constitution for their new nation, a clause prohibiting "cruel and unusual punishments."

Long before the Revolution and the writing of the Constitution, however, colonial assemblies and courts had made a conspicuous point of specifying more humane punishments. Colonial citizens who were found guilty of crimes received far less severe sentences than they would have received for similar crimes committed in the Old World, and the colonial assemblies often passed general amnesties for certain crimes at the ends of legislative sessions. But the sentences meted out to colonial slaves found guilty of crimes were often more like those in the Old World and included hanging for petty theft and burning alive for more serious crimes.

The harsh conditions of their lives occasionally led slaves in the colonies to rise against their owners, and on several occasions, slaves in Middlesex County took part in these minor rebellions, one of which occurred near the Raritan River. The participants in this uprising had determined to obtain their freedom via a general massacre, after which they intended to join with the

to ensure a steady supply and moderate prices, and despite the Quakers' efforts, slavery flourished throughout the colonies. In Middlesex County, there were slave barracks in Perth Amboy, and, with few exceptions, the labor in the homes and on the farms of white colonists in Middlesex and surrounding East Jersey counties was performed by black slaves. Beyond their physical and emotional deprivations, colonial slaves did not receive the same judicial treatment that colonial citizens reserved for themselves.

When colonial citizens were found guilty of crimes, justice in the colonies was fre-

Indians to help the French defeat the British. As a punishment, several of the ringleaders were hanged.

The census of 1800 records the number of slaves in New Jersey as 12,422. In February 1804, the New Jersey legislature passed an act that granted freedom to every child born of slave parents after July 4, 1804, to take effect when the males reached twenty-five years of age and the females reached twenty-one. Despite this, there were still slaves counted among Middlesex County's population in the census of 1840. According to the census of 1850, though, slavery in the county had disappeared.

The adventurous men and women who

The Cheesequake Creek dock often berthed steamboats such as the John B. Collins *(shown here) and the* Muddy Day, *which carried locally grown apples, strawberries, blueberries, eggplants, tomatoes, and peppers. Shipping their produce to New York, farmers marked each crate, barrel, and basket with their initials. Once the cargo was delivered, the empty containers were returned, sorted by markings, and reclaimed by the farmers. This circa 1915 photo shows Mrs. Edna Farrington Thomas, left, and Mrs. Gertrude Matthews. Courtesy, Madison Township Historical Society*

settled the Raritan River Valley were primarily, though not exclusively, farmers. They bought the goods they needed and sold the goods they produced at the two major port settlements that grew up along the Raritan River. Among the products of the Raritan Valley intended for export were grain, flour, and bread; lumber and finished wood products; beef and pork; fish; and copper and iron. These products were purchased by brokers, agents, millers, and warehouse-keepers of both these Raritan River ports, Raritan Landing and the rapidly developing port across and downriver two miles, not yet officially named New Brunswick.

The Raritan River merchants stored goods in large warehouses and loaded them from massive wharves onto rafts, flatboats, and sloops and sent them downriver to be transferred to ships at Perth Amboy; the goods would then be transported to Europe, to coastal markets in the colonies, or to the Caribbean. Goods for export were sold by their producers for cash or were traded for imports of European manufactured goods

(until colonial manufacturing facilities developed), for colonial foodstuffs, and for Caribbean rum, molasses, sugar, and Madeira wine.

Although Raritan Landing was the first port to develop, its location at the highest point of navigation on the river at high tide proved to be instrumental in its losing out in the trade battle with New Brunswick, because New Brunswick could provide deep water during both high and low tides. But for a time, Raritan Landing flourished as a milling, warehousing, and embarkation point

The Raritan River was not always kindly toward the townspeople who depended on it as an avenue of commerce. The flood of 1882 covered Burnet Street in New Brunswick, forcing some to stand atop the roofs of buggies or on first-floor overhangs to avoid the waters. Others, undaunted, rowed the crest of the flood, which exceeded twelve feet. Rowboats were paddled through the door of Macom's Hotel on Burnet Street, and then up Church Street as far as Neilson Street. Courtesy, New Brunswick Chamber of Commerce

In 1904, the Raritan River once again flooded Burnet Street in New Brunswick, but on this occasion huge frozen masses were carried with the waters into the streets, the result of an ice jam. Courtesy, Special Collections and Archives, Rutgers University Libraries

for the region's inland farmers and tradespeople.

Their low-lying locations made both Raritan Landing and New Brunswick susceptible to flooding, and Raritan Landing was severely flooded in 1739, causing many of its residents to seek higher ground for their homes. Cornelius Low, one of Raritan Landing's earliest and most prosperous residents, was one whose original home near the river was flooded. Low's newer house, of stone, was at one time considered among the finest in all of New Jersey. The Low House, as it is now called, has been restored and stands

elegantly on a bluff overlooking the Raritan at the head of Landing Lane in what is now Piscataway.

Though New Brunswick eventually eclipsed Raritan Landing as the main Raritan port, Raritan Landing thrived for many years. Except for a brief period of economic decline during the Revolution, when the hostilities disrupted river traffic and caused great hardship in both towns, Raritan Landing and New Brunswick were active ports until the mid-nineteenth century. During this latter period, however, Raritan Landing began a final economic decline from which

Albany Street, New Brunswick, was again inundated during the flood of March 1920. Although this photo was taken when the waters had already begun to recede, telltale signs of the flood's initial height can be seen. The ice-lines on the telephone poles, right, and on the truck in the center of the picture indicate the water's previous level, which measured at eight feet in some areas of New Brunswick. Nearly three days passed before the waters subsided, leaving $250,000 in damage in its wake. Courtesy, New Brunswick Chamber of Commerce

there would be no recovery; as a result of this decline, all visible traces of this once-busy port have disappeared.

Several factors in addition to the shallowness of the river at low tide caused the decline of Raritan Landing. Among these were the location of the outlet of the Delaware and Raritan Canal at New Brunswick, which encouraged the growth of that city at the cost of decreased traffic upriver; the advent of deep-draft steamboats, which could not even at high tide navigate the shallower channel at Raritan Landing; and, finally, the coming of the railroad, which bypassed Raritan Landing altogether, precipitating the settlement's demise. By 1870, Raritan Landing had been entirely abandoned. Its site was covered with shale during landfill operations in the 1930s, and today one can see only flat parkland and grass where once were 200-foot wharves and large warehouses for grain and produce.

Though Perth Amboy for a while experienced a modest success as a port and briefly enjoyed a position as the most important city in the county, it too eventually lost a considerable portion of its business to New Brunswick. Perth Amboy's eclipse occurred for many reasons, among which were competition from other ports and political machinations, as colonial governments played for advantageous legislation in Great Britain.

The major reason for the trade shift from Perth Amboy toward New Brunswick was the realization by owners and captains that heavily laden, smaller transoceanic ships

Owned at one time by the Treat family, the Spencer Hotel in the Old Bridge section of what is now East Brunswick was a favorite rest stop for many travelers, among them John D. Rockefeller. The posts in front of the building were whitewashed to prevent the horses from eating the bark. Courtesy, William Kraemer, East Brunswick

could sail directly upriver to New Brunswick and load and unload there, saving the time and expense previously incurred by loading and unloading cargo to and from smaller vessels at Perth Amboy for shipment upriver.

New Brunswick, initially called Raritan Ford, had grown quickly around John Inian's ferry. Inian also built roads and improved many of the trails in the area, thus making travel easier and encouraging commerce. Wharves soon sprang up, as did mills that could take advantage of the steadily flowing river. The city for a while was called Prigmore's Swamp, then Inian's Ferry. Henry Greenland, a medical doctor and militia captain, opened the first inn, located near the ferry, as a way station for travelers and a meetinghouse for residents.

From these modest beginnings would spring the city of New Brunswick. Greenland's inn contributed greatly to the growth of the region because travelers who stayed there spread word of the Raritan Valley's lushness. But the inn's function as a local meeting place was also of major importance, for here the area's residents could discuss political, economic, and social concerns; thus, Greenland's inn contributed both to the area's growing prosperity and to its residents' sense of regional and national identity. These factors would prove to be of fundamental value during the Revolutionary War, for during this great conflagration, Middlesex County would be a focal point.

Most of the early settlements in the county—Woodbridge, Piscataway, Perth Amboy —were founded either by groups of settler families or by the direct design of the Proprietors, as was the case with Perth Amboy. Though large groups of settlers did arrive in New Brunswick from time to time, the city grew primarily from a steady influx of individual migrants and families who came and built homes, businesses, churches, and

Top: *George Herzog purchased this tavern in 1918 and renamed it the Farmers Hotel. Prior to his ownership, it was known as the Cheesequake Hotel. The dirt road in the foreground is now Route 34; the apparatus to the right of the doorway is a scale used by farmers to weigh produce and salt hay to be transported to market. Courtesy, Madison Township Historical Society*

Bottom: *Journeying from Virginia to New York City for his inauguration as president in April 1789, George Washington stayed the night at the Cross Keys Tavern in Woodbridge. Courtesy, Special Collections and Archives, Rutgers University Libraries*

schools, creating a particularly diverse early population that included, in addition to the slaves, English, Dutch, Scotch, Irish, German, Italian, French, and Asian settlers.

The town rapidly became a regional center for religious activity and trade. The Dutch Reform and Presbyterian churches were among the first to establish active congregations in New Brunswick, and the town's location on a wide and navigable river in the fertile heart of one of the colonies' most important grain producing regions provided commercial revenues upon which to build a city. There were no fewer than six gristmills in New Brunswick by the 1730s, and farmers from all over the area brought their grain here for milling, storage, sale, and shipment.

So rapidly did the town grow and so important did it become commercially and politically that by 1730 its first charter was issued, incorporating the City of New Brunswick and bestowing legal authority to regulate its own affairs. It is unclear precisely when the name New Brunswick first began to be used, though some sources indicate use of this name as early as 1716. The importance to the townspeople of the Raritan

Above: *The State Bank of New Brunswick issued this 1860 one-dollar bill, which is engraved with images of the area's chief industries. To the right, corn and other produce in a field can be seen with a farmer's wagon and tools. On the left, a train traverses a railroad bridge overlooking a Raritan River barge and a farmer feeding hay to a cow. Courtesy, Frank W. Phillips, Santa Paula, California*

Facing page: *It is believed that David Carnegie, Lord Rosehill, sponsored the petition to King George III that resulted in the grant of a 1770 charter for the establishment of St. Peter's Episcopal Church, Main Street, in Spotswood. The charter appointed two wardens, Lord Rosehill and John Lewis Johnstone, who is credited as the first settler of the community. Both men were from Scotland, as were many of the settlers of Spotswood. Johnstone was from a clan known as Spottswoode (Spottiswoode, Spotswode). Courtesy, Spotswood Cultural and Heritage Commission*

as the conduit for the economy of the area can be inferred from the original seal of the new city. The seal displays, in the foreground, a sloop riding at anchor on the river along with a sheaf of wheat next to a pair of scales; the town itself can be seen only in the background.

New Brunswick was described in 1748 by a Swedish naturalist, Peter Kalm, as

a pretty little town in a valley on the west side of the river Raritan. On account of its low situation it cannot be seen coming from Pennsylvania before arriving at the top of the hill which is close to it. The town extends north and south along the river . . .

The wooden Albany Street Bridge, New Brunswick, constructed in 1794, charged tolls at the following schedule of rates: man on foot, two cents; man on horse, seven cents; man with wheelbarrow, four cents; hogs and sheep, two cents each. The crossing was replaced by a stone bridge in 1844, which was also subject to tolls. In 1875, however, the Middlesex County Board of Chosen Freeholders purchased the bridge for the sum of $58,000 and for the first time permitted free passage. Courtesy, New Brunswick Chamber of Commerce

The town has only one street lengthwise, and at its northern extremity there is a street across. Both of these are of considerable length. One of the streets is almost entirely inhabited by Dutchmen who came hither from Albany, and for that reason they call it Albany street. On the road from Trenton to New Brunswick I never saw any place in America, the towns excepted, so well peopled.

The chartering of New Brunswick gave Middlesex County the distinction of being the only county in America to have two chartered municipalities—the other being Perth Amboy—within its limits.

After the establishment of Inian's Ferry and the improvements of the road by Inian, this route became the most popular in the province (though it did not lack competition, since many other roads were opened immediately thereafter). During the early eighteenth century, the number of roads through the territory grew dramatically: from 1705 to 1713, thirty-five roads were established within Middlesex County alone. One important road traveled along the Raritan, branching from the main highway at Piscataway and running west of present-day Metuchen through New Market to Bound Brook and into Somerset County. Many other roads, strictly local in character, were laid out to link smaller communities to the more important early towns of Raritan Ford (New Brunswick), Woodbridge, Piscataway, and Perth Amboy.

Scheduled stage wagons and freight lines for hauling passengers, produce, and, later, mail were instituted during the first decade of the eighteenth century, and these were soon joined by "stage boats" that combined the two modes of transportation. As these conveyances became more sophisticated and reliable and as the roads improved, the stage lines began to take over more and more of the mail-carrying duties that had been entrusted first to friendly Amerindian runners and later to riders.

The development of the postal system was slow, however. In 1754, Benjamin Franklin took over duties as colonial postmaster, bringing great improvements. Still, for many years, the only post offices in New Jersey were in Burlington and Perth Amboy, these communities being on the route from New York to Philadelphia; as late as 1791, New Jersey had only six post offices.

Until scheduled steamboat traffic became widespread in the early 1830s, water transportation was often unreliable and dangerous, as a result of unpredictable and violent winds and storms that could arise without warning. Benjamin Franklin was once delayed while attempting the relatively short journey from Boston to Philadelphia when his stage boat was blown across New York Harbor; he reported that he was finally able to reach Perth Amboy only after thirty hours on the water.

There were three major transportation routes within New Jersey, all crossing through Middlesex County: the Amboy-Burlington route, which was the shortest lived, though it was popular for a time; the Amboy-Bordentown route, which was an instant success; and the New Brunswick-Trenton route, which in time became the most popular of the three. Travel and service on all these were irregular in winter because of the condition of the roads and the unpredictable weather on the water legs of these journeys. Even with the most favorable conditions, the voyage between Philadelphia and New York, a distance of just over 100 miles, required five days. Through the middle of the eighteenth century, the network of roads and the resulting social and commercial interaction from the passenger, mail, and freight lines inseparably tied Middlesex County and New Jersey to

Top: *In 1927 Middlesex County Vocational School #2 was opened in Perth Amboy. It became but one of the milestones in a long list of successes for the Vocational and Technical High Schools and Adult Technical Schools of Middlesex County, which are ranked among the finest in the nation. Courtesy, Middlesex County Vocational and Technical High Schools and Adult Technical Schools*

Bottom: *This etching shows the Eagleswood Military Academy, noted for both its education and military training of young men. Prior to the founding of the school, Eagleswood was the site of a utopian community for intellectuals, artists, and abolitionists in Perth Amboy. Founded by Marcus and Rebecca Spring, the community was visited by Henry Thoreau, Louis Comfort Tiffany, Horace Greeley, Ralph Waldo Emerson, and William Cullen Bryant. From 1861 to 1867 the famous landscape artist, George Inness, lived and painted in a stone studio on the grounds of the estate. Courtesy, Special Collections and Archives, Rutgers University Libraries*

the other colonies. Politics and commerce became tightly interwoven with a developing sense of "American" interests separate from "British" interests.

The colonial economy became stronger as agriculture and manufacturing expanded along with religious, social, and educational interests. Two of the world's oldest, best-known, and most respected universities—the College of New Jersey (which would become Princeton) and, in New Brunswick in 1766, Queen's College (which would become Rutgers)—were founded during this period, indicative of a deep concern for public education that continues to the present.

A vital culture was developing. The colonists, who had always thought of themselves as intellectually independent, began more and more to think of themselves as politically independent, as Americans rather than as British. Meanwhile the British just as stubbornly refused to think of the colonists as anything but colonial subjects who had rights only at the sufferance of Parliament and the Crown.

As the 1700s progressed, the Raritan Valley area became quite prosperous. The colonies in general were developing successfully, and as they showed signs of increasing wealth, Britain became increasingly eager to share in this wealth. The colonists, with a long tradition of not paying taxes, saw little reason to begin. Hadn't the colonies already patiently submitted to enough regulation by Parliament? And, the colonists asked, hadn't Britain benefited directly and substantially from the colonies' success through the goods Britain sold there and elsewhere within their North American sphere of influence?

The British would discover just how broad the gulf between them and their subjects had become when, after 1754, Britain demanded colonial support in the French and Indian War.

France formed an alliance with disgrun-

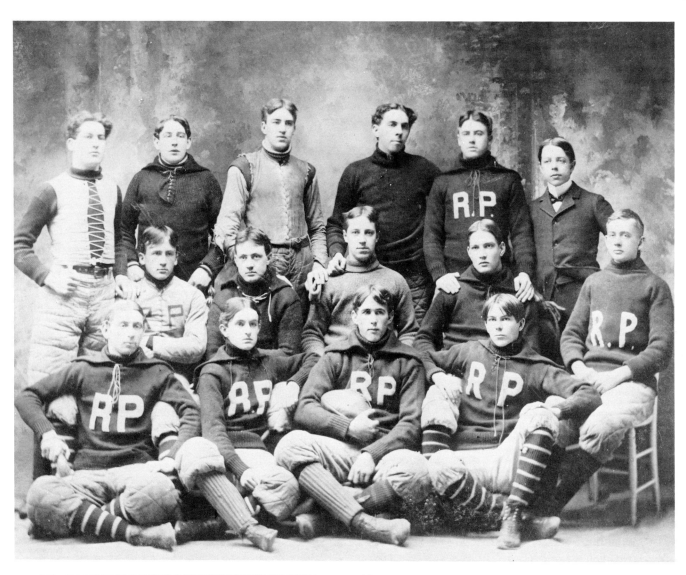

Above: *Rutgers Preparatory School, chartered in 1766 by King George III, was originally part of Rutgers University, New Brunswick. This photograph, taken during the 1890s, is particularly interesting as one notes the padded knickers as the only protection for the football team. Rutgers Prep is located in an area now known as Franklin Township, Somerset County. Courtesy, Rutgers Preparatory School*

Left: *Birchall School on Main Street was the first public school constructed in Spotswood. Although now in private ownership, the school served for a time as the headquarters for the Spotswood Board of Education. Courtesy, Spotswood Cultural and Heritage Commission*

Notice of Sale.

The undersigned, EXECUTORS of SAMUEL DALLY, Deceased, will sell at

PUBLIC AUCTION

by virtue of the Last Will and Testament of said Deceased, on

Thursday, Dec. 9th,

1897, at the hour of half-past **TWO** in the afternoon, at the Woodbridge Hotel, in the Village of **WOODBRIDGE, N. J.**, the following valuable real estate, situate in the **VILLAGE OF WOODBRIDGE**, County of **Middlesex, N. J.**, viz.:

FOUR BUILDING LOTS, 50x130 feet, on Main Street, adjoining Demarest Avenue.

FOUR BUILDING LOTS, 50x130 feet, and ONE LOT, 25x130 feet, on Grove Street, at its junction with Demarest Avenue.

ONE LARGE HOUSE AND LOT on the South side of Main Street, known as the C. M. Dally House. Size of Lot, 85x130 feet.

CONDITIONS made known on Day of Sale.

EPHRAIM CUTTER,
C. W. DRUMMOND,
Executors.

Dated December 1st, 1897.

The Woodbridge Hotel was the site of a public auction in 1897, to sell the local holdings of Samuel Dally. Such sales were common and, in this case, consisted of four lots on Main Street, Woodbridge, others at Grove Street and Demarest Avenue, and the house and lot known as the C.M. Dally House. Courtesy, Special Collections and Archives, Rutgers University Libraries

tled Amerindian tribes in an attempt to drive the British out of the colonies. To protect their interests, the British for the first time dispatched large contingents of troops to North America and thus incurred the enormous expense of supporting an overseas army. Parliament and the Crown felt that the colonials should help with the expenses of an effort that was, after all, intended to protect the colonists from the greedy French and savage Indians. Parliament and the Crown let it be known that they expected the colonists to serve with British troops and to quarter British soldiers in colonial homes. Though many colonists were loyal to the Crown and welcomed the British troops, others were slow to agree to these conditions. Murmurs of resentment were heard.

After the war, heavily in debt, the British turned to the colonials—the prosperous subjects for whom the British had lately sacrificed so much. The British need for revenue to pay for the war was pressing. Moreover, Parliament and the Crown desired to reaffirm their sovereignty over their increasingly disrespectful subjects. Parliament passed regulations and taxes upon colonial trade and commerce.

Until these developments, the citizens of Middlesex County had been enjoying great prosperity. Early hardships had been overcome, and many colonists felt that this period of relative ease was a just reward for their many long years of hard work. Though there were, to be sure, many colonists who remained fiercely loyal to the Crown, a steadily growing number of colonists saw no reason to suffer indignities at the hands of the British who, after all, had for many decades been enjoying the fruits of colonial labors without having suffered the great physical hardships or risks.

By the mid-1770s, the gulf between the British and their "subjects" had grown wide indeed, and in 1776 a copy of the Declaration of Independence was brought from Philadelphia to New Brunswick, where Colonel John Neilson read the document to an assembly of citizens.

Thomas Paine, whose writings enflamed the American colonies' desire for independence, found refuge from the British while he stayed at the home of Henry Guest, a New Brunswick whaler and tanner. Courtesy, New Brunswick Chamber of Commerce

CHAPTER THREE

THE REVOLUTION IN MIDDLESEX COUNTY

William Franklin, Benjamin Franklin's illegitimate son, was appointed royal governor of the province of New Jersey in 1762. When he arrived in New Jersey in 1763 to take up his responsibilities, he found a split colony—East and West Jersey—with two capitals, one in Burlington and another in Perth Amboy.

Franklin and his wife Elizabeth at first rented a residence in Burlington. But the Proprietors of East Jersey wanted to bring the royal governor (along with the prestige and the commercial advantages of being the active provincial capital) to Middlesex County's Perth Amboy, the city they were determined to develop into the "London of America." Two years earlier, the Proprietors had agreed to purchase land and to build quarters suitable for a royal governor.

It would be more than a decade before the house, called Proprietary House,

A
BILL
IN THE
Chancery of *New-Jersey*,

AT THE SUIT OF

John Earl of *Stair*, and others, Proprietors
of the Eastern-Division of *New-Jersey*;

AGAINST

Benjamin Bond, and some other Persons of *Elizabeth-Town*, distinguished by the Name of the *Clinker Lot Right* Men.

WITH

Three large MAPS, done from COPPER-PLATES.

To which is added,

The PUBLICATIONS

OF

The Council of Proprietors of *East New-Jersey*,

AND

Mr. NEVILL's Speeches to the General Assembly,

CONCERNING

The *RIOTS* committed in NEW-JERSEY,

AND

The Pretences of the Rioters, and their Seducers.

These Papers will give a better Light into the History and Constitution of NEW-JERSEY, than any Thing hitherto published, the Matters whereof have been chiefly collected from Records.

Published by SUBSCRIPTION:

Printed by *James Parker*, in *New-York*, 1747; and a few Copies are to be Sold by him, and *Benjamin Franklin*, in *Philadelphia*; Price bound, and Maps coloured, *Three Pounds*; plain and stitcht only, *Fifty Shillings*, Proclamation Money.

Facsimile of Title of Lot 281.

This 1747 broadside announced the availability of a publication which would "give better light to the history and constitution of New-Jersey." Published by James Parker, the notice advised that a few copies would be sold by Benjamin Franklin. In 1765 James Parker published the Constitutional Courant *newspaper at Parker Press in Woodbridge. Courtesy, Special Collections and Archives, Rutgers University Libraries*

could be completed. The governor initially asked that Proprietary House be purchased, since some of the citizens of the province were averse to their governor living in a house rented from the Proprietors, against whom there was a good deal of resentment. But the necessary funds were never appropriated and eventually the governor leased the stately house for sixty pounds per year. The house was decorated to Franklin's fastidious and expensive tastes, and in 1774 Governor Franklin and his wife took up residence.

During the period between Governor Franklin's arrival in New Jersey and his settlement in Proprietary House, relations between the colonies and Great Britain steadily declined. And as the diplomatic relations between the two political entities worsened, so did the once-close relationship between the younger Franklin and his famous inventor/writer/freethinker father.

Benjamin Franklin visited his son's family and likely stayed at Proprietary House while traveling on business for the Post Office Committee during the last days of August and first days of September in 1775. During this nine-day visit, which was to be the next-to-last between the two men before the Revolution, father and son debated at length. The son argued for patience, continued loyalty to the Crown, and conciliation between the contending parties; the father, more and more discouraged by what he saw as the son's intransigence, argued for more radical countermeasures. The debate became heated, and the two men soon realized that their political, intellectual, and emotional positions were irreconcilable.

At their next and final meeting, the father would refuse to stay longer than a day with his son and would refuse to discuss the issues over which they had split. The elder Franklin referred to the governor's home as "that Tory house."

The governor had for some months been secretly sending local newspaper accounts of provincial revolutionary activities and long reports of the activities of the Continental Congress to England. With these packets, he also sent offers to mediate between the two sides, and he urged the British to make concessions to the colonists. His former friend William Alexander, whom the governor had removed from the Provincial Council, requested and received permission from the Provincial Congress to seek evidence of what he regarded as Governor Franklin's "treason"; one of these packages of reports and newspapers was intercepted and forwarded to the Congress, which directed that the royal governor be arrested.

The governor later wrote that on January 8, 1776, "About two o'clock that Night . . . I was awaked with a violent knocking at my Door, which alarmed my Wife so much that I was not without Apprehensions of her Dying with the Fright. Looking through the Chamber Window I perceived that a Number of armed Men had invested the House."

Governor Franklin was placed under house arrest for five months, during which time he stubbornly proclaimed his rightful authority to govern New Jersey in the name of the King of England, despite the presence of more than 1,700 American troops encamped in Perth Amboy. In June 1776, just before the issuance of the Declaration of Independence signaled the formal break between the colonies and England, Governor Franklin called into session the old Provincial Assembly.

Although his purpose was to propose a plan for reconciliation with Great Britain, Governor Franklin's action was perceived as

Cochrane's Tavern was the New Brunswick headquarters for General George Washington from November 29 to December 1, 1776. Located at the corner of Neilson and Albany streets, the tavern is also said to have been one of the hiding places, in 1779, of Lieutenant Colonel John Graves Simcoe, credited as one of the finest and cleverest field commanders in the British army, notorious for his burning and looting of the Raritan Valley. Courtesy, Special Collections and Archives, Rutgers University

direct defiance of the Provincial Congress, which ordered a second arrest. Thus, New Jersey's last royal governor, the duly appointed representative of the King of England, was taken to Connecticut and imprisoned.

While the governor was in prison, often in solitary confinement, he was refused permission to visit his wife Elizabeth on her deathbed. Upon his release from prison, the embittered Franklin did not return to Perth Amboy but went directly to England, from which he would never return; he died in 1813.

In June 1775, George Washington passed through Middlesex County on his way to Cambridge, Massachusetts, where he was to take command of the Continental Army. Washington had been through Middlesex on several previous occasions, traveling the main route from Philadelphia to New York. General Washington would pass through Middlesex many times more as the war raged on in this area that would come to be called—with reference to the bloody arena of cockfights—the "Cockpit of the Revolution."

Early in the war the American troops had notable and surprising success, but when the British realized how determined the colonists were, they began to take the revolutionaries more seriously, sending better commanders, better troops, and more supplies. In July of 1776, soon after the issuance of the Declaration of Independence, a huge British fleet appeared in New York Harbor. Under the command of Admiral Howe, the fleet carried an army of nearly 30,000 men under the command of the admiral's brother, General Howe. The British intended nothing less than a quick and complete quelling of the Revolution.

Until this point, there were also many colonists who had not yet begun to take the war seriously. The third public reading of the Declaration of Independence in New Brunswick on July 8, 1776, and the arrival of the large British force combined to stir patriotic feelings in Middlesex and in the province.

The following entry is from the July 27, 1776, minutes of a Queen's College literary club, the Athenian Society: "General Howe with the British fleet arriving at Sandy Hook, all of the members of the Athenian Society who were able to bear arms immediately marched to oppose the enemy. Matters being thus in confusion, July the 27th, the college was suspended till the 21st of October." Though sessions and meetings would resume, the college, founded just ten years previously, would be again suspended through much of the long and harsh British occupation of New Brunswick.

In November 1776, Washington's full-scale retreat took him and his men through New Jersey to New Brunswick. They camped briefly at New Brunswick from November 30 to December 1, when redcoats were reported immediately across the Raritan. To cover Washington's retreat, the young artillery commander Alexander Hamilton fired on the British and Hessian troops from a bluff overlooking the Raritan, and Washington and his dwindling army were able to escape safely into Pennsylvania.

Washington's retreat from New Brunswick left New Jersey for a short time in the possession of the British, who had occupied Perth Amboy on December 1. On the night of December 25, Washington and his troops recrossed the Delaware and, in the ensuing battles for Trenton and Princeton, forced the British to abandon these towns. As a result, the Americans won back control of a large portion of the territory. Following these victories, Washington and his troops went into winter quarters at Morristown.

The British and Hessians occupied the Middlesex County townships and towns of

John "Corn King" Borrowes, Sr., purchased this house in 1760. His son John (married to Margaret Forman, a sister of Mrs. Philip Freneau) was a major during the Revolutionary War and trained a company of militia on the grounds of the mansion. On June 3, 1778, a British regiment invaded Matawan, then known as Middletown Point, doing considerable damage. They entered the Borrowes' house looking for the major, but he had escaped through a rear window. Today, musket shot holes in the stairway ceiling attest to the attempted capture. In 1904, Benjamin F.S. Brown, publisher of the Matawan Journal, *acquired the home. It was purchased by the Borough of Matawan in 1974 and now serves as a museum for the community. Courtesy, Matawan Historical Society*

For eight generations the Parker family lived in the house known as the "castle" on Water and Front streets in Perth Amboy. The stone section was constructed in 1670, and the large wooden addition, at right angles, was erected in 1760 by Captain James Parker, a seaman, one-time mayor of the community, and delegate to the Provincial Congress. The residence has since been demolished. Courtesy, Special Collections and Archives, Rutgers University Libraries

Perth Amboy, New Brunswick, Piscataway, and Woodbridge through June 22, 1777. The viciousness and callousness these troops showed toward the colonists here and elsewhere in the colonies was so offensive that, even in relatively conservative New Jersey, many formerly neutral or pro-British colonists came over to the side of the rebels or at least stopped lending the British open or even clandestine support.

The contending British and American

armies almost completely destroyed Perth Amboy; at one time during the war, St. Peter's Church was used to stable cavalry horses. Of the devastation wrought on Proprietary House, an Anglican preacher, the Reverend Joseph Bend, would write:

Yon ruined mansion view; observe it well,
There wit and mirthful glee were wont to
    dwell,
Prudence and courage, manly sense refined,

The Georgian style Buccleuch Mansion was built by Anthony White in 1739 for his wife Elizabeth, the daughter of Lewis Morris, royal governor of New Jersey. During the American Revolution, while the British occupied New Brunswick, the Enniskillen Guards of Northern Ireland were quartered in the house, where sabre cuts and spur marks are still clearly visible in the floorboards. Deeded to the city of New Brunswick in 1911 by Anthony Dey, the mansion is now an historic site administered by the Jersey Blue Chapter of the Daughters of the American Revolution. Courtesy, Special Collections and Archives, Rutgers University Libraries

With every great endowment of the mind.
There by his proxy Britain's Monarch
  reigned,
Unshaken loyalty its court maintained.
The sad reverse, the mournful prospect see,
And yield submission to the stern decree,
Defaced, the glory of the neighboring plain,
Its naked, ruin'd walls alone remain,
A sad memento they shall ever stand,
And find no friendly, no assisting hand,
Remorseless foes shall on its ruins jest,
And screech-owls, toads and snakes the
  walls infest.

With nearly 5,000 troops encamped in New Brunswick—a town of perhaps 1,000 people before the occupation—this was a time of great hardship in the Raritan River Valley. The British took what they needed from the farmers and tradesmen and destroyed the rest so that the American troops could not benefit from it. Hunger and suffering were widespread among the colonists who did not collaborate with General Howe and the British troops.

Because the colonists were able to harass the British on land, the main British supply routes went by water, and the Raritan served as the major route for provisions to the British garrison in New Brunswick. But the colonists soon developed an offense on water. A number of private citizens who owned boats fitted them out with small cannons and sailed their smaller, quicker vessels against slower-moving merchantmen and even warships.

Though some of the privateers were little better than pirates, most preyed on British shipping only and were thus patriotic pirates. Every British supply ship whose cargo did not reach the British seriously undercut the enemy's war effort, and as a result, these privateers substantially enhanced the effectiveness of the meager American navy.

Perhaps the most colorful and successful of these privateers was Adam Huyler. Huyler had emigrated to the colonies in the early 1750s, a young man not yet twenty years old. Twenty years later, he had become Captain Huyler, the prosperous owner of several sailing ships that berthed at New Brunswick. When the War for Independence came, Huyler took the opportunity as a private citizen to serve his adopted country by attacking British shipping on the Raritan River and Bay, sometimes ranging into New York Harbor.

Much of Huyler's success derived from the sheer bravado he and his well-drilled men displayed, often attacking far larger ships carrying more men and heavier weapons. On one occasion, Huyler and his tiny fleet and small crew attacked five British merchantmen—guarded by a large, heavily armed British man-of-war—anchored inside Sandy Hook. Huyler and his crew rowed his two whaleboats to the merchantmen, boarded and looted four of them, and then set them afire; they spared the fifth because they found women and children in one of the cabins. On another occasion, Huyler and his men blew up a British warship after removing large stores of ammunition and supplies. These and numerous other daring (and lucrative) exploits by Huyler and other privateers greatly damaged the British and aided the colonial military.

While harassed by Huyler and other privateers on the water, the British in New Brunswick and Middlesex County were also being harassed on land by Washington's troops. On several occasions, the British attempted to draw Washington into a major confrontation, hoping to defeat his small army and rid themselves of the nuisance of the Revolution in one blow. These attempts failed, and General Howe, finding it increasingly difficult either to provision his New Brunswick garrison or to defend the surrounding territory against Washington's

The "George Washington Tree," in front of the Neil-
son House on Burnet Street, New Brunswick, was so
called in deference to the common but mistaken be-
lief that General Washington used it as a hitching
post. Ironically, the British flag was flown from this
sycamore during the Revolutionary War when Lord
General Howe was quartered in the Neilson House.
It was cut down in 1913. Courtesy, Special Collec-
tions and Archives, Rutgers University Libraries

repeated forays, began to think it more profitable to deploy his troops elsewhere.

Howe made one last attempt to draw Washington out, advancing as far as Milltown. But Washington did not engage him, and Howe withdrew. As the British, preparatory to evacuating New Brunswick, returned toward that town, Washington perceived an opportunity to attack the retiring army's rear, and he dispatched a detachment of troops led by General "Mad Anthony" Wayne to pursue them, which Wayne and his men did with great vigor and success.

General Howe and the British garrison finally left New Brunswick on June 22, 1777, with the forces of General Wayne in hot pursuit. Wayne wrote the following letter about a week after the British withdrawal:

I have but this moment returned to camp. We have been out ever since last Sunday week on which day we made a triumphal entry into New Brunswick after pushing the Britains from redoubt to redoubt and at last into Amboy where they now lay; but in all probability before this reaches you they will not have a single inch of ground in . . . New Jersey.

The following winter, General Washington and his troops camped in the freezing cold of Valley Forge, again taking the field against the enemy in the spring. After their success at the Battle of Monmouth on June 28, 1778, Washington offered his weary troops a much needed rest; he marched them back toward New Brunswick and encamped there beside the waters of the Raritan, near the present site of Johnson Park. On July 3, 1778, the eve of the new country's second anniversary, he gave his men these orders:

Tomorrow, the anniversary of American independence will be celebrated by the firing

of thirteen pieces of cannon and a feu de joie of the whole line. The Army will be formed on the Brunswick side of the Raritan at five o'clock in the afternoon on the ground pointed out by the quartermaster. The soldiers are to adorn their hats with green boughs and to make the best appearance possible. The disposition will be given out in orders tomorrow. Double allowance of rum will be served.

On the Fourth, Washington and his army crossed the Raritan and observed America's second birthday in New Brunswick itself. The following is one witness's joyful account of that event:

After his Excellency with his suite had rid round the lines and returned to his quarters, on a signal given from thence, thirteen pieces of cannon were fired at the park, which were followed by a running fire of musketry and artillery beginning on the right of the front throughout the whole of both lines. After this, three huzzas to the perpetual and undisturbed independence of the United States of America. The same round was performed the second and a third time and exceedingly well executed every time. My situation being high and at a convenient distance in front afforded me a complete view of the whole and presented by far the grandest sight I ever beheld.

The route to the victory that would finally break the back of the British forces in America was surveyed by a Queen's College graduate, Simeon DeWitt. On August 29, 1781, Washington wrote a letter from New Brunswick to DeWitt, who had become Washington's Geographer General:

Sir, immediately on receipt of this you will begin to survey the road to Princeton, thence to Head of Elk through Darby,

New Brunswick, as the county seat, provided the site for the old courthouse, built in 1840. Prior to 1793, Perth Amboy and New Brunswick were rivals for the designation of county seat. Perth Amboy, in its bid for the honor, offered to transport by ferry, free of charge, anyone involved in litigation from as far away as South Amboy. New Brunswick countered with an offer of 300 pounds toward the construction of a courthouse. After a controversial vote, New Brunswick was selected. Courtesy, New Brunswick Chamber of Commerce

Chester, Wilmington and Christianna Bridge. At the Head of Elk you will receive further orders. I need not observe to you the necessity of noting towns, villages, and remarkable houses but I must desire that you will give me the rough traces of your survey as you proceed on as I have reasons for desiring this as soon as possible.

Washington's reasons consisted primarily of his daring plan to join with French troops in a dash toward Virginia, there to trap, defeat, and capture the forces of General Cornwallis. Washington's plan was a success, and Cornwallis, who was in a vulnerable position within the Yorktown peninsula, was soundly defeated.

Shortly after the Revolutionary War, General Washington resigned his commission as Commander of the Continental Army and in December 1783, after saying goodbye to his officers at Frances' Tavern in New York City, left for his beloved Mount Vernon. His route would once again take Washington through New Brunswick; this time he was on his way home for what he intended to be a long and peaceful rest.

At New Brunswick, Washington was greeted by a grateful populace. In response to this warm greeting, he characteristically asked for compassionate and generous treatment for the soldiers who had fought so long and hard:

I receive with perfect satisfaction the address of the citizens of New Brunswick, and acknowledge with great sensibility, that their sentiments of my character and services are favorable beyond my fondest expectation. If anything could add to my happiness at the present auspicious period it would be the testimony of esteem and veneration which you gentlemen have exhibited toward those worthy and deserving men who have so eminently contributed to the glorious termination of the war . . .

Top: *Middlesex County women organized a demonstration through downtown New Brunswick in support of the suffrage movement. Women had the right to vote as early as 1776 under the constitution of New Jersey. It was not until 1807 that state voting laws were changed to exclude women. Courtesy, New Brunswick Chamber of Commerce*

Bottom: *The first black voter in the United States was Thomas Mundy Peterson. On March 31, 1870, the day following the adoption of the Fifteenth Amendment to the U.S. Constitution, Peterson cast his vote in a local Perth Amboy election, just shortly after news of the Emancipation Proclamation reached the residents of Middlesex County. Peterson, a former slave, was the first custodian of School Number One in Perth Amboy. He was buried in St. Peter's Cemetery.*

Facing page: *With its roots in the Revolution, Middlesex County has often been in the vanguard of progressive politics. The popularity of Theodore "Teddy" Roosevelt was evident by the large crowd he attracted while campaigning in New Brunswick in 1912. Courtesy, New Brunswick Chamber of Commerce*

General Washington was not to enjoy that retirement so soon, however; his grateful fellow citizens asked him to be the country's first leader, a position that would have made him a New Brunswick resident if the plan of Azariah Dunham and several other citizens of New Brunswick had succeeded.

In 1788, President Washington appointed a committee to recommend a site for the new nation's capital. Azariah Dunham, New Brunswick's first mayor after independence was won, petitioned Congress and the site-selection committee to consider New Brunswick. New Brunswick's petition read:

Let the place speak for itself. Let impartial men declare its beauties and point out its defects; your addressers will be silent upon this occasion . . . [If] the banks of the Raritan be looked upon as eligible ground, its inhabitants will deem it a distinguished privilege and a singular felicity to live within their jurisdiction, and under their immediate government.

It is recorded that "men from all over the country joined with those of New Brunswick in presenting to Congress the advantages of the banks of the Raritan and urged the national fathers to investigate before going elsewhere."

Though eventually Congress selected another, less suitable city, Mayor Dunham's proposal received a great deal of support.

Dealers came from throughout the area to the Lehigh Valley Railroad coal docks in South Plainfield, considered the largest such facilities in the east. Courtesy, South Plainfield Historical Society

CHAPTER FOUR

WATER AND IRON,
BLOOD AND STEEL

The end of the war brought a period of euphoria during which the young nation, though beset by problems, happily ignored them. In time, however, the new states came to recognize their need for an effective central government to permanently bind them and arbitrate disputes.

On May 25, 1787, with representatives from nine states attending, the Constitutional Convention was officially opened. Representing New Jersey at the Constitutional Convention was a delegation headed by William Livingston, the governor who had succeeded William Franklin, and who had guided New Jersey throughout the Revolution. Representing Middlesex County as part of this New Jersey delegation was William Paterson, an attorney then living in New Brunswick. Paterson was to play a major role in the development of the new Consti-

Middlesex County was prosperous in the 1880s and fashion was not overlooked, as the Standard Fashion Gazette *indicates. All the garments seen here were offered in patterns by the Singer Manufacturing Co. on Church Street in New Brunswick, along with a full line of sewing machines.*

The Gazette *advertised four sizes of patterns for misses, ages ten to sixteen, and offered most patterns for ladies in eight sizes. Boys' blouses, window curtains, and slipper cases could also be made from patterns. Courtesy, Special Collections and Archives, Rutgers University Libraries*

tution; his was to be an active voice during the convention. And long after the convention, Paterson would continue to play a significant public role in the affairs of New Jersey and of the United States.

On June 15, 1787, the New Brunswick attorney introduced to the convention a set of nine resolutions. These resolutions came to be known as the New Jersey Plan, one of the major constitutional alternatives debated by the delegates. The New Jersey Plan differed from the Virginia Plan in that the former provided for only one legislative branch and several executives instead of the Virginia Plan's two legislative branches and single head of state. Though the New Jersey Plan was not adopted, it did form the basis for a compromise out of which the present United States Constitution grew.

On December 17, 1787, New Jersey became the third state (after Delaware and Pennsylvania) to ratify the Constitution. William Paterson became one of New Jersey's first two United States senators, which position he resigned after a year to become governor of New Jersey. Governor Paterson was also to serve for a number of years as associate justice of the United States Supreme Court, a position to which he was appointed by President Washington.

With the ratification of the Constitution and the subsequent economic and social unification of the states, prosperity began to return to New Jersey and, especially, to Middlesex County. For the next two centuries and up to the present day, Middlesex County's favored location and natural endowments would keep it in the vanguard of political, educational, social, technological, medical, and economic development.

Middlesex County owed much of its vitality to the continued development within its borders of the most modern and innovative transportation techniques. This would prove true particularly in the nineteenth century, during the acme of the industrial revolution, when industries and fortunes rose and fell on the availability of transportation facilities to get products to growing markets at home and abroad.

Implementing new technologies—transportation and otherwise—was always a talent that Middlesex County displayed matchlessly. From the county's earliest days, as soon as new techniques for the building and improvement of roads and bridges were developed, these techniques were applied in Middlesex. The improvement of roads and bridges permitted one of the country's first successful stagecoach lines—begun by a New Brunswick citizen—to pass through Middlesex County on the much-travelled route between New York and Philadelphia.

Somewhat later the Delaware and Raritan Canal, incorporating the very latest in locks and mechanical devices, was put into service carrying coal and grain between those two extremely important American rivers. This canal would give Middlesex County and New Brunswick national importance.

The railroads, too, established an early and strong presence. The Camden and Amboy Railroad, the first steam-powered railroad to operate successfully in the United

A major industry in Jamesburg during the late 1800s and early 1900s was cutting ice from the frozen waters of the Manalapan Lake. Blocks of ice were first marked or "curfed," then cut with saws pulled by teams of horses or mules. In the icehouse, the blocks were preserved with salt hay. To prevent contamination, ice skating was prohibited until the ice cutting operation was completed. Courtesy, Jamesburg Historical Association

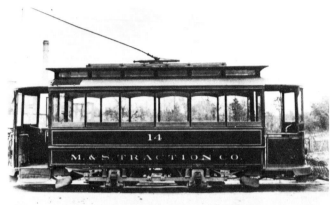
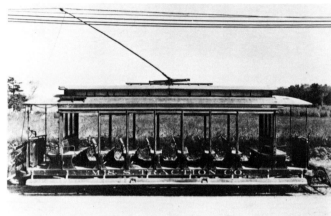

The Brill company built trolley cars that ran along the Middlesex & Somerset Traction Co. lines in Milltown: (lower right) a double-truck work car #0103; (lower left) a double-truck 15-bench passenger car #37; (upper right) a single-truck 10-bench open car, often used for summer excursions; (upper left) a single-truck closed car #14, a model that today is most commonly associated with trolleys. Courtesy, Special Collections and Archives, Rutgers University Libraries

This 1907 photo, taken at Washington Avenue in Milltown, shows a single-truck plow used by the Middlesex & Somerset Traction Co. to free the tracks of snow and debris. Courtesy, Special Collections and Archives, Rutgers University Libraries

The Bellona Hotel on Burnet Street in New Brunswick was run by Mrs. Cornelius Vanderbilt. Records from 1822 indicate that Sophia Vanderbilt was solely responsible for the operation of the hotel, which was named for the steamboat that her husband ran between New Brunswick and New York City as an employee of lawyer T. Gibbons. One story holds that Mrs. Vanderbilt gave her husband a considerable sum of money which she had saved, so that he might purchase a steamboat of his own. From these meager beginnings, he became Commodore of steamboats, a major investor in the railroads, and a millionaire. Courtesy, Special Collections and Archives, Rutgers University Libraries

States, had a terminus within the county at South Amboy.

And just as soon as steam-powered boats became practical, they could be found plying the waters of the Raritan River and the canal carrying both freight and passengers and linking with stagecoaches to provide regular passage between distant cities. "Commodore" Cornelius Vanderbilt began to build his huge fortune by providing steamboat transportation for goods and passengers on the Raritan River. (Many of Vanderbilt's passengers undoubtedly stayed at the New Brunswick inn that was owned and operated by Vanderbilt's wife.)

Toward the end of the nineteenth century, the inventions of Thomas Alva Edison (using copper wire produced in Perth Amboy and other places in the county) flooded out of his laboratories in Middlesex County's Menlo Park and sparked the electrification of the Northeast. Electricity was a great improvement over both water and steam as a means of propelling the wheels of commerce and industry, and the electric grid expanded outward at a rapid pace.

Within a relatively short time the electrification of the region was complete. Frank Sprague, an associate of Edison, promoted the idea of electric railways, and this in turn encouraged the production and implementation of electric trolley lines. These, too, spread out for miles into the countryside, creating still more growth and development. As science and technology advanced, these trolleys would become the enormous electrically powered railroads that would so perfectly complement Middlesex County's available transportation resources.

Later, with the growing availability of the automobile (many of which undoubtedly were driving on Middlesex County- produced rubber tires) and with the increasing number of miles of improved roads, the county's population and economy sped ahead at a dizzying pace: in 1790, the population of the Raritan Valley was approximately 5,000; in the census of 1800, the total was nearly 16,000; by the end of the nineteenth century, the population of Middlesex County had reached 80,000; and by 1930, the population was well in excess of 200,000 and was climbing rapidly.

Each development or innovation in transportation altered the nature of the social, economic, and political life of Middlesex County. The ease of transport of people, raw materials, and finished products played a significant role in the decisions of industrialists as to where to locate factories—and therefore jobs, housing, and the supporting services that large populations and industries required. The continuing development of transportation facilities would also deter-

mine where—and whether—various Middlesex County communities would thrive or wither (the once-prosperous Raritan Landing being a case in point).

Clearly, many industrialists found the county a hospitable place. Within its borders, one could find manufactured products as diverse as shingles and barrel staves, bandages and tires, pills and cigars, piano strings and carriages, textiles and rubber shoes (at one time, the county ranked second to Akron, Ohio, in the manufacture of rubber products), sewing needles and chemicals, bricks and glass, terra cotta tiles and leather goods, fruit jars and iron, asbestos and copper—the list is virtually endless. All these were produced and processed within Middlesex County and moved to market via county transportation facilities.

Wars also increased development of Middlesex County industry. The several seacoast blockades by the British during the War of 1812 encouraged the development of the county's textile industry. The Civil War created a nearly inexhaustible demand for manufactured goods of many kinds. The Civil War caused political division in Middlesex County as well, for New Jersey's large contingent of soldiers in the Union army brought vociferous complaints from many county manufacturers and shippers, who were fearful of alienating the South, one of their major markets.

The First World War encouraged the expansion of facilities for the production of medical supplies, drugs, chemicals, and, particularly, explosives. Soon after America entered the war, Middlesex County became the largest producer of munitions in the world.

By the beginning of the twentieth century, Middlesex County was a manufacturing and shipping center of national importance. New Brunswick alone had nearly forty factories and 20,000 people living and working within its boundaries.

The county's commitment to transportation facilities resulted in secondary and tertiary social and economic benefits, not only for the county but also for the nation and world. Improvements in transportation technology spurred development of products that had no direct connection with transportation, products that would feed and improve the lives of millions. Of the three transportation milestones in Middlesex County history—the Delaware and Raritan Canal, the Camden and Amboy Railroad, and the steamboat—the canal was the first to have a major effect.

A navigable waterway across the "waist" of New Jersey had long been considered desirable. As early as 1676, a group of speculators that included William Penn authorized surveyors to examine the feasibility of digging a canal that would link the Delaware River and New York Bay. No action was taken on this proposal, although interest in the project remained high.

In 1816, a route for the canal was again surveyed, and there was mounting political support for the project's construction. To this end, the New Jersey Delaware and Raritan Canal Company was incorporated by the legislature in 1820, but this company failed. The legislature granted a charter to yet another hopeful company, the Delaware and Raritan Canal Company, on February 4, 1830. The Camden and Amboy Railroad and Transportation Company was chartered the same day. Ground was broken, and construction began on the canal a short time after.

The railroads provided the canal with its major competition, and they would eventually bring about its demise. As if to warn the canal about what was to come, the opening of the Trenton-to-Kingston portion of the canal to local traffic in 1833 actually followed the opening of the Bordentown-to-

Amboy portion of the Camden and Amboy Railroad in 1832. The official inauguration of full canal service from Bordentown on the Delaware River to New Brunswick on the Raritan River did not come until 1834.

Upon completion, the main canal extended forty-three miles in a generally northeasterly direction from the Delaware to the Raritan. When opened, it provided the first direct water route between New York City and Philadelphia, and it was a major link in the inland waterway that joined the northeastern with the southern states. It was seventy-five feet wide at the surface, and it ultimately was dredged to a depth of eight feet. The main canal was built with fourteen locks that raised and lowered vessels nearly sixty feet over the length of the waterway.

The canal's water supply came from a navigable feeder-canal system that began at

Bull's Island, 22.5 miles up the Delaware from Trenton. This feeder canal had just three locks, of which only one—at Lambertville—raised the water level. The other two locks were guard locks that helped control the current and flow of water in the feeder, which was sixty feet wide and six feet deep.

The availability of the canal and the railway immediately opened up the markets of the Atlantic coast and Europe to the coal miners and farmers of the interior of Pennsylvania. The canal also provided these miners and farmers with the ability to inexpensively and quickly import products from these coastal and European markets. This, in turn, contributed to the nation's development westward into the fertile Ohio Valley.

Some of the farthest-reaching effects of innovations in transportation were secondary. On a visit to England to raise capital,

The Delaware and Raritan Canal, completed in 1834, was dug in the valleys of the three rivers it connects— the Raritan, the Millstone, and the Delaware. As a result, a narrow strip of land separates the canal from the riverbeds, and it was on this strip that mules once trod towing barges. Courtesy, Middlesex County Cultural and Heritage Commission

In it's heyday, the Delaware and Raritan Canal is reputed to have carried more tonnage than its more famous, cousin, the Erie Canal of New York State. In fact, the D & R Canal as it is commonly known, and the commerce it enabled, were responsible, in part, for the demise of Raritan Landing. This port city could not compete with the economy of the canal. Shown here is the last lock of the Delaware and Raritan Canal and the locktender's cottage, as they appeared in 1922, New Brunswick. In recent years, the locktender's cottage was demolished, but it and the lock are being restored by the City of New Brunswick. Courtesy, Special Collections and Archives, Rutgers University Libraries.

Tugboats on the Delaware and Raritan Canal pulled barges laden with cargo, replacing the mules that once toiled at this purpose. Completed in 1834, the Canal was an engineering marvel, running 44 miles south through central New Jersey to New Brunswick, where it emptied into the Raritan River. The main canal was 75 feet wide and seven feet deep. Courtesy, Trenton Public Library

canal company president Robert F. Stockton learned of John Ericsson's development of the screw propeller and commissioned Ericsson to design a screw-powered steamer to operate on the canal. In 1839, the *Robert F. Stockton,* later renamed the *New Jersey,* became the first iron-hulled vessel to cross the Atlantic and the first commercially suc-

cessful propeller-driven vessel in the United States.

As a tertiary benefit, the significance of agricultural goods to the county's and the state's economic well-being encouraged the creation of the Rutgers Agricultural Extension Program. Experimentation here would produce new and higher yielding forms of common crops (tomatoes), better products (milk), and many improved farming techniques, which were necessary to feed rapidly growing national and world populations.

Other canal-related technological advances include one of the earliest telegraph installations in the United States, which expedited traffic and water control through the canal. Incidentally, this communication system also enabled canal operators to catch vessels exceeding the canal's 4.5-mile-per-hour speed limit. Later, as more speed along the canal became desirable—more vessels meant greater revenues—the canal company

began offering incentives for moving faster through the waterway.

The Delaware and Raritan Canal ranked for many years among the most important commercial waterways in the United States, and its contributions to the economic and social development and history of Middlesex County cannot be overestimated. Because the canal's Raritan terminus was at New Brunswick, the merchants of that city could build thriving service industries. Wharves lining the river near the city could load and unload ocean-going ships directly, and much revenue was therefore kept from the port of Perth Amboy at the mouth of the Raritan.

Logistically, the easy access to Pennsylvania coal via the canal and later the railroad contributed to the county's desirability as a location for factories, which used that fuel for steam-powered operations. During 1866, the canal's most productive year, 2,857,233 net tons of freight were carried, 83 percent of which was Pennsylvania coal. Many manufacturers chose locations on or near the canal or the railroad right-of-way to be near the source of materials and finished products. In the same manner, manufacturers would later locate alongside superhighways and near commercial airports.

After 1866, the tonnage carried via the canal began to decline. More and more, the coal was carried by rail, which steadily became faster and cheaper. This improvement in rail service in comparison with canal service was largely due to the more rapid improvement of the technology and equipment available to railroads.

During its century of operation, the canal also carried thousands of pleasure boats and yachts, including that of Cornelius Vanderbilt, whose business interests had by then expanded well beyond carrying passengers up the Raritan to stay at his wife's inn. These pleasure boaters often preferred the protected inland route provided by the ca-

Top: *Passing through the New Brunswick lock of the Delaware and Raritan Canal in 1899 was a captured Spanish gunboat. The 100-foot vessel had been seized by American troops at the Battle of Santiago during the Spanish-American War. Courtesy, Special Collections and Archives, Rutgers University Libraries*

Bottom: *Hundreds of people lined the New Brunswick and Highland Park banks of the Raritan River to watch world-class swimmer Gertrude Ederle swim the Raritan in the early 1900s. Anticipation was soon replaced with disappointment as this much publicized feat was never accomplished. Ederle, claiming the river was unbearably salty, halted her attempt. Courtesy, New Brunswick Chamber of Commerce*

The Raritan Yacht Club, one of the oldest in America, was established in 1865. Its clubhouse is a familiar sight to boat owners along the Raritan Bay in Perth Amboy. The fleet associated with the club is mostly sail and continues to grow each year. Members compete both nationally and internationally and sponsor the annual Red Grant Regatta, which attracts participants from states throughout the East Coast. Courtesy, W.A.T.E.R., Inc.

nal to the sometimes violent vagaries of weather that might be encountered on a voyage along the Atlantic coast.

Though the canal developed the use of steam-powered vessels for use as tow boats, mules along the tow paths also provided motive power for both pleasure boaters and commercial vessels until the canal's last days. Teams of two to four tow mules could be rented.

The Delaware and Raritan Canal played a direct role during two of the United States' wars. During the Civil War, a flotilla of steam-powered canal transports carried New Jersey troops and equipment south to defend Washington, D.C. And during World War I, the federal government took over the canal's operation and stationed security troops along the length of the canal to guard strategic points. The government then used the canal to move torpedo boats, gunboats, and other military vessels and also to transport war materiel—airplane parts and munitions—as well as to convey large ship's boilers and other naval equipment from the naval yard in Philadelphia to its counterpart in Brooklyn.

But several factors legislated against the continued survival of the canal: the inherently slow process of moving goods along the canal, which compared poorly against rail travel and, later, truck transport; the extreme cost and difficulty of enlarging and extending the canal so that it could serve larger vessels and new areas; and the closings in January and February, when the canal froze. These factors brought about the loss of the canal's economic viability.

Traffic declined steadily and in some years precipitously after the peak year of 1866; the canal began to lose revenue, then to operate at a deficit. By 1931 freight traffic on the canal had declined to 41,801 tons. In 1933, exactly one hundred years after its official opening, the canal was officially abandoned by its last owner, the Pennsylvania Railroad. Ultimately, the canal would rise in importance once again, as a source of recreation for county residents.

The chartering by the legislature of the Camden and Amboy Railroad and Transportation Company was the result of persistent efforts by John Stevens of Hoboken. Stevens had spent years attempting to convince skeptics that steam-powered overland transportation was superior to animal-powered overland transportation and to wind- and mule-powered overwater transportation. Heated competition had arisen between these various interests. Finally, a compromise was reached, and the legislature granted charters to both the railroad and canal companies to build competing transport routes between the Delaware and Raritan rivers.

Born together, the two companies became

From the mid-1800s to just after World War II, Jamesburg was considered a railroad town. Its facilities included three stations (two of which are seen here), extensive freight yards, and a roundhouse. Lower Jamesburg Station (top) was on the Jamesburg and Freehold Agricultural Railroad. Upper Jamesburg Station (bottom) was part of the Camden and Amboy line. The meeting of the two lines created "Jamesburg Junction." Courtesy, Jamesburg Historical Association

Above: *The extensive Runyon coal stockyards were located off Bordentown Avenue in Old Bridge Township (formerly known as Madison Township). Coal was brought from Pennsylvania by railroad to the South Amboy docks where barges then carried it via the Delaware and Raritan Canal as far as Bordentown. The coal proceeded again by rail to the Runyon stockyards. Courtesy, Madison Township Historical Society*

Left: *Among the buildings comprising the Old Bridge Railroad Station were the passenger and freight terminals and the telegraph office, which contained six-foot-high levers attached to cables that would switch the tracks. The historic village of Old Bridge is now part of the township of East Brunswick. Courtesy, William Kraemer, East Brunswick*

Above: *An episode of the "Perils of Pauline," one of America's most popular adventure series, was filmed at the Parlin Railroad Station. Courtesy, William Kraemer, East Brunswick*

Right: *The Dunellen business district was centered around the North Avenue railway station, seen here two years before most of the area was destroyed by fire in 1875. Courtesy, Wesley Ott, Dunellen*

Top: *The famous "John Bull," manufactured in England, arrived at the Bordentown docks in August 1831. Many came to greet the ship bringing this locomotive, the first in the U.S. Much to their dismay, packing crates were unloaded—the "John Bull" was in pieces! Isaac Dripps had the monumental task of assembling the engine, without aid of drawings or blueprints. On November 12, 1831, the locomotive ran for a short distance near Jamesburg. It was put into service in 1832 and was making the trip to Camden by 1834 on the Camden and Amboy Railroad. Courtesy, Jamesburg Historical Association*

Bottom: *This Baldwin ten-wheeler, one of 255 built between 1868 and 1873, was a wood-burning engine of the Pennsylvania Railroad; it was fitted with an air-brake in 1887. The photo was taken at George and Somerset streets, New Brunswick. Courtesy, Special Collections and Archives, Rutgers University Libraries*

further entwined on February 15, 1831, when the legislature permitted their stock to be consolidated. The new company was called the Delaware and Raritan Canal and Camden and Amboy Railroad and Transportation Companies—often shortened to the Joint Companies. The intent of forming the new company, which as a result of the merger had a state-sanctioned regional monopoly on transport, was to have the canal carry freight and the railroad carry passengers. But as the railroad developed, it became the mode of choice for many of the region's freight producers, especially the coal miners.

The actual builder of the railroad was John Stevens' son Robert, who was an engineer of great ingenuity. Among Robert Stevens' most important contributions to the success of railroading in general—and therefore to the development of the nation—was the design of the T-rail, which became the standard shape for train rails. The younger Stevens was also involved in the design and modification of the *John Bull,* the first steam locomotive to operate commercially in the United States. (It is still in operating condition more than 150 years after its construction and is now part of the permanent collection of the Smithsonian Institution in Washington, D.C.)

The citizens of New Brunswick lobbied for a connection to the vital new rail line, and on March 2, 1832, an agreement was reached with the railroad to implement a route between New Brunswick and Spotswood. Consideration of this line was eventually dropped in favor of a line from New Brunswick to Trenton. Five days later, New Brunswick received a promise of additional rail service with the incorporation by the legislature of the New Jersey Railroad and Transportation Company, which agreed to provide a spur line through Newark to Jersey City.

The arrival of railroad service in New Brunswick, combined with the canal's eastern terminus there, brought an end to Raritan Landing, across the river. Raritan Landing had survived floods and burning by the British, but it could not survive this.

By 1840, both lines of the Camden and Amboy Railroad were operational. With the completion of the Trenton-to-Philadelphia rail link, through-traffic could move swiftly from the Hudson River to Philadelphia. Eventually, the New Brunswick-to-Trenton portion of the rail line became more important than the Camden-to-South Amboy portion, which was then relegated to local traffic. In 1864, partly to accommodate the movement of troops in the Civil War, the double-track main line between Trenton and New Brunswick was completed.

The bulk of railroad revenue during these earliest years derived, just as the management of the Joint Companies had intended, from passengers. And the development of passenger lines, including spurs to smaller communities, made it possible for commuters to work in cities in which they did not live. Thus, as the railroads (and, later, the automobile) stimulated the explosive growth of the suburbs, the patterns of American life were to be radically altered.

In 1867, the Delaware and Raritan Canal and Camden and Amboy Railroad and Transportation Companies merged with the New Jersey Railroad and Transportation Company and became the United Canal and Railroad Companies of New Jersey. But the Joint Companies had, during the intervening years, been acquiring stock in other transportation companies, including turnpikes, bridges, and other railroads. Among these other railroads were the Philadelphia and Trenton Railroad and the Camden and Burlington County Railroad. In 1871, all these companies, with the Camden and Amboy at their head, formed the mighty and

The South Plainfield Railroad Station was a good place to observe the variety of locomotive designs traversing Middlesex County tracks. Above, a gas/electric model waits beside the station house. Also taken in 1939, the photo at the right shows the streamlined, yellow "Asa Packer" pulling up to the water tower. Compare the "Lehigh Valley" on the next page. Courtesy, South Plainfield Historical Society

influential Pennsylvania Railroad system.

The merging of these transportation facilities gave Middlesex County and all of New Jersey's major cities access to a complete transportation grid, and these facilities tied the state together and gave it an economic strength and vitality that would otherwise have been impossible to sustain.

The Camden and Amboy cum Pennsylvania Railroad linked the United States' two most important cities, New York and Philadelphia, and as such became a major influence on area politics and policies. Its monopoly status excused it from paying many local taxes, giving it relative autonomy from the concerns and demands of local governments. By the same token, the capital amassed from huge railroad profits permitted the company to underwrite other

ventures, giving it further influence and power. The business and industry it fostered created demand for labor, which encouraged further immigration. The railroad itself was a major employer. As success followed success, its influence spread.

The flow of goods into and out of Middlesex County, once a healthy stream that flowed into and depended upon the Raritan, was becoming a broad river. But as county-produced and -purchased goods were to travel more and more by rail, the Raritan would come to be less and less important to the economic strength of the region. As it headed into the twentieth century, Middlesex County, near the geographical center of all this growth and power, would influence and be influenced by state, national, and world events.

Above: *Once only a rural section of Woodbridge Township, where some of the earliest settlers of the area had lived, the town of Port Reading grew and took its name from the major contributor to its growth—the Reading Railroad. The establishment of a coal depot at the water's edge of the Arthur Kill and the construction of the Reading Railroad Terminal in 1890 created a need for workers, along with housing and services to support the laborers' families. By the hundreds, Italian immigrants came to fill the newly created jobs, and this population gave rise to the community. Courtesy, Woodbridge Township Board of Education*

Facing page: *The "Lehigh Valley," also known as the "John Wilkes," brought an art deco look to the South Plainfield station. It was one of the first trains to sport fluorescent lighting in its coaches. Courtesy, South Plainfield Historical Society*

*One of the earliest horseless carriages in Woodbridge
Township was often seen at the Colonia Country
Club in Colonia. Notice the positioning of the seats:
two passengers faced forward and two faced the rear.
Lanterns were affixed to either side of the "coach."
Courtesy, Special Collections and Archives, Rutgers
University Libraries*

CHAPTER FIVE

ANNIHILATING SPACE

"The multiplying of the railroads soon brought the outmost limits of Middlesex County in touch with a common center; within its area the lines of two great railroad systems traversed its surface. This, with the development of the interurban lines of trolleys and jitneys, brings the citizens of any portion of its limits within ready communication with each other. The days of steamboating and coaching are at an end, the whirling steam and electric conveyances annihilate space; intercourse of communication travels with lightning rapidity, by the use of the electricity of the air, the telegraph key, and the word of the human mouth transmitted by telephonic connections" (from History of Middlesex County, New Jersey, 1664-1920 *by John P. Wall and Harold E. Pickersgill).*

As the nineteenth century drew to a close and technological marvels exploded

upon human consciousness, the profound influence that technology would impress upon the shape of Middlesex County probably could have been predicted by the insightful observer. Still, through the end of that century, even with the tremendous rate of growth in both industrial development and transportation facilities, the primary commercial activities within the county remained farming and fishing, with the then-still-pristine river supplying abundant populations of fish and shellfish.

By the late 1820s, the wholesale trade for the area consisted mainly of fish, salt, and dry-goods funneled through New Brunswick. Into the 1840s, New Brunswick served as the entry/exit point for many New Jersey and Pennsylvania products and was the chief source of supply for New Jersey and Pennsylvania. In addition, the city was the chief source of supply for New York agriculture.

As the nineteenth century matured, many new industries began to line the banks of the Raritan, its feeder brooks, and the Delaware and Raritan Canal. Major industries settling in and around New Brunswick were the New Brunswick Hosiery Company—the largest in the country—at Neilson and Hamilton streets; Janeway and Carpender Wallpaper Establishment, at Water Street and the canal; Consolidated Fruit Jar Company, which employed 325, on Water Street; a cut-nail factory—at the time the largest in the country—on Neilson Street; a tobacco factory on Church Street; and coachmakers on Albany Street.

As the 1800s drew to a close, major industries and national and international corporations—such as National Ironworks, the New Brunswick Carpet Company, and many others—were attracted to and set up operations within the city or county. Other industries would develop out of the county's natural resources and grow to national

Left: *The Sayre and Fisher Company of Sayreville manufactured front enamel (a decorative item) and fire brick. Clay bricks were laid in the sun to harden before being fired in a kiln. If rain was anticipated, the clay was covered with hay to keep it dry.*

Bottom: *Founded by James R. Sayre and Peter Fisher, Sr., the company eventually extended nearly two miles along the Raritan River and included thirteen separate yards. Schooners, such as the one seen loading at the company's east wharves, could accommodate a cargo of 50,000 bricks. Both photos courtesy, Middlesex County Cultural and Heritage Commission*

Right: *The Atlantic Terra Cotta Company plant in Perth Amboy, shown circa 1907, produced 28,000 tons of light-reflective tiles in polychrome yellow, blue, green, and sienna for the 1913 construction of New York's Woolworth Tower. The Perth Amboy facility, with 700 workers and 25 kilns, was famous for its research and development laboratories and for the noteworthy sculptors it employed. Courtesy, W.A.T.E.R., Inc.*

Above: *An abundance of water (supplied by the city works), inexpensive land, and navigable waterways provided a fertile environment for industrial growth and the establishment of numerous companies, among them the Janeway and Carpender Wallpaper Company on Schuyler and Paterson streets, New Brunswick. The firm was destroyed by fire, however, when a Pennsylvania Railroad collision caused flames to run down into the sewer and ignite the structure. Courtesy, Special Collections and Archives, Rutgers University Libraries*

Top: *A popular shore resort area, the Sewaren section of Woodbridge Township attracted many vacationers to Boynton Beach and the Sewaren Hotel. From 1880 to 1900, during the summer season, a steamboat from New York arrived daily. Boynton Beach was a delightful playground with bathhouses on the beach, a rollercoaster, picnic grounds, a shooting gallery, and a dance pavilion. Courtesy, Middlesex County Cultural and Heritage Commission*

Middle: *An unusually cold winter caused the waters of Raritan Bay to freeze in 1918. By January 6, the bitter cold had resulted in ice so thick that thousands came to frolic on the bay, and at least four automobiles made the trip to the lighthouse and back. Two adventurous gentlemen were reported to have played a game of golf on the frozen waters. Courtesy, W.A.T.E.R. Inc.*

Bottom: *During the 1800s Seidler's Beach, between Laurence Harbor and Cliffwood Beach, was the site of Salt Water Day, held on the second Saturday in August. Beginning at sunrise, farmers and their families made the trek to the beach with wagon loads of food for the day's festivities. During the 1920s, Seidler's Beach was the site for Farmers' Day activities, including entertainment and dancing, coordinated by the Department of Agriculture in New Brunswick. Courtesy, Madison Township Historical Society*

prominence. One such was the terra cotta industry, which developed from the special quality of clays found in Middlesex soil and became a nationally important enterprise. Evidence of the products of this industry— brick, tile, and statuary—can still be seen in the walls, roofs, and decorations of many county buildings and homes.

As the twentieth century dawned and then developed, major changes began to take effect. In New Brunswick, the George Street area shifted from a residential to a retail, banking, and commercial center. During this period, not only did the number of county industries grow, but also the size

In February 1887 the roller skating rink at the corner of Livingston Avenue and Morris Street, New Brunswick, was transformed by the Ladies' Auxiliary of the Y.M.C.A. to include booths, kiosks, and flags from around the world. All of this was in preparation for a "Bazaar of All Nations" fund-raising event. Courtesy, Special Collections and Archives, Rutgers University Libraries

New Brunswick was considered a cultural center when the Opera House opened in the newly constructed Masonic Hall on the southwest corner of Albany and George streets in 1871. The building also provided office space for numerous groups and businesses. It was destroyed by fire in 1896. Courtesy, Special Collections and Archives, Rutgers University Libraries

of individual businesses grew: the Bayuk brothers employed over 1,000 at their cigar and cigar box works; U.S. Rubber Company employed 1,500; Wright Aircraft employed 1,500 in peacetime and more than 8,000 during World War I.

Entertainment facilities were necessary to entertain all these people. In New Brunswick, Middlesex residents could find vaudeville, concerts, stage shows, and, ultimately, Thomas Alva Edison's moving pictures at the Empire, Rivoli, Bijou, and State theaters. There were full houses to view opera and classic theater at the 1,200-seat Opera House, and after the shows, theatergoers

Top: *Maintaining a sense of community was important to the early Hungarian immigrants. Social clubs, such as the theatrical group of St. Joseph's Byzantine Catholic Church of New Brunswick, seen here in the 1930s, helped American Hungarians preserve their language and customs, while fraternal societies were formed to provide the community with low-cost life and health insurance.*

Bottom: *Jozsef Cardinal Mindszenty of Hungary visited the city of New Brunswick in 1973 for the re-dedication of St. Ladislaus Church on Somerset Street. Cardinal Mindszenty came to symbolize the Hungarian struggle against communism after having spent eight years in solitary confinement and another fifteen years of self-imposed confinement within the American embassy. The banner reads "Welcome our Cardinal." Both photos courtesy, American Hungarian Foundation*

could get a dinner or late snack at restaurants such as Schussler's, Graham/McCormick's, Walker's, and Scheidig's Cafe. Zimmerman's Beer Garden combined a restaurant and dance hall.

The immense demand for workers during the rapid industrialization of the Raritan Valley provided employment for a flood of immigrants from all over the globe. As with the first waves of immigrants to the New World, these latter arrivals came in search of political, religious, and economic freedoms and in search of opportunity. But unlike the first immigrants, who found a vast and sparsely populated land that they could sculpt to their designs, the new immigrants found a developing land with a unified and chauvinistic populace into which these new arrivals needed to fit, to which *they* had to adapt.

Among other groups who came through or to Middlesex County were, in alphabetical order, Afro-Americans, Armenians, Belgians, Byelorussians, Chinese, Circassians, Copts, Croatians, Cubans, Czechs, Dutch, Egyptians, Estonians, Filipinos, Finns, French, Germans, Greeks, Hungarians, Irish, Japanese, Italians, Jews, Latvians, Lithuanians, Luxembourgers, Palestinians, Poles, Puerto Ricans, Russians, Serbs, Spanish, Swedes, Swiss, Syrians, Turks, and Ukrainians.

Hungarians, especially, populated Middlesex County—particularly New Brunswick—and contributed to its growth, well-being, and culture. Although there was only one Hungarian living in New Brunswick in 1880 (according to the U.S. census), by 1915 there were 5,572 Hungarians in the city population of just over 30,000. Many of these Hungarians came to Middlesex County to work for Johnson & Johnson, where at one time nearly two-thirds of the employees were Hungarian. In 1956-1957, thirty thousand Hungarians, political escapees from the Hungarian revolution, were processed

Right: *Having fled the turmoil of the Hungarian Revolt in 1956, refugees arrived at Camp Kilmer and were assisted by members of the Red Cross, the U.S. Army, and thousands of volunteers from the New Brunswick area. In the months following Hungary's struggle to free itself from Soviet domination, New Brunswick and the Hungarian Escapee Program helped to resettle 30,000 people. Of this number, 1,000 chose to make New Brunswick their home. Courtesy, American Hungarian Foundation*

Facing page, top: *Johnson & Johnson began in New Brunswick in 1886, as Robert Wood Johnson joined with his brothers James Wood and Edward Mead Johnson to produce improved surgical dressings containing medicinal compounds mixed in an adhesive. At the beginning, the company employed fourteen people and was located on the fourth floor of this small building, previously a wallpaper factory. Courtesy, Johnson & Johnson*

Facing page, bottom: *As the company grew, more than half of the women employed in Johnson & Johnson's sewing room were Hungarian immigrants. Some were skilled workers from such regions as Vas and Veszprem; many were from agricultural families. Nearly 90 percent of the Hungarians arriving in Middlesex County, and especially New Brunswick, found employment in industry. Courtesy, American Hungarian Foundation*

through Middlesex County's Camp Kilmer. Of this total, approximately 1,000 settled in New Brunswick.

Hungarians established six churches and one synagogue in New Brunswick. They also founded newspapers and social clubs, and Hungarian builders built significant areas of the city. Currently, the Hungarian community is active in the efforts to preserve and revitalize New Brunswick's neighborhoods—some of which they built.

New Brunswick attracted industry for a myriad of reasons, not the least of which was the availability of water. And most convenient was a location right on the river or canal. An on-the-water site was convenient for a factory for a number of reasons: it permitted the direct and relatively inexpensive transport of raw materials into the plant; it permitted easy access to the pure water necessary to the manufacture of increasingly complex chemicals, the smelting of metals such as lead and copper, and the refinement of petroleum; it permitted easy dumping of the liquid wastes of the manufacturing pro-

cess; and it permitted the direct and relatively inexpensive transport of finished products out of a plant.

Unfortunately, in addition to the waste products generated by manufacturing processes, there was the sewage generated by the growing populations that came to work and support the new industries. The Raritan River—seemingly ever new and forever capable of sweeping waste products into the unimaginably vast and forgiving bay and ocean—presented the obvious answer. And for a time the river was able to keep up with the requirements of the increasing population.

Damage to the river was not the only concern. Although the World War I demand for munitions and medical supplies was a significant plus for the county's economy, the processes and by-products of these industries posed a many-sided threat to the county's once-pleasant-and-healthful environment. And long-term environmental damage was not the only hazard: occasionally, munitions plants blew up catastrophically, in some cases taking many lives and causing showers of shell and shot and shrapnel to rain about a wide area.

By the end of the first year of the war, munitions manufacturers in the Raritan Valley had increased their production capacity to half-a-billion pounds of smokeless powder a year. Populations increased even more rapidly, and the amount of industrial and human waste increased in direct proportion to the activity.

There reached a point beyond which the river could no longer keep up with the demands placed upon it; the factories and workers necessary to the area's economic health were gradually overwhelming the river's ability to freshen itself. By the 1920s, the pollutants had begun to present a serious problem. The fishing industry suffered as fish populations declined, and new industries that required pure water were no longer being tempted into the Raritan Valley by the increasingly impure Raritan.

The process of cleanup did not begin until the 1930s, when the federal government, under the aegis of President Franklin Delano Roosevelt's New Deal, began to construct sewage-treatment plants. In one respect the slowdown in industrial activity caused by the Depression was beneficial, in that reduced industrial waste allowed the sewage-treatment efforts an interval during which to make up some time.

The environmental concerns that had been awakened in county residents during and after World War I (the exhaust from some of the chemical plants had begun to strip the paint from nearby houses) quickly faded with the United States' entry into World War II. There followed another dramatic buildup of manufacturing facilities to produce arms and munitions for that new war. Subsequently, further damage to the river was compounded by significant damage to county lands and landfills as well. Throughout the county and state, water supplies were being endangered by toxic chemicals leaching into the soil.

By the 1950s, concerned citizens had spearheaded a major governmental effort to clean up the general county environment and, particularly, the Raritan River. With the formation of the Regional Sewerage Authority, significant progress began to be made that, ultimately, included the return of fish populations to the Raritan and the gradual clearing of the waters. This progress, however, is being stymied in the late 1980s by the tidal entrance into the Raritan River of pollution from Newark Bay and New York Harbor.

To exemplify the spirit of Middlesex County in its imaginative and practical aspects, one has to consider Thomas Alva Edison, arguably the most important and

Since 1910, when the Boy Scouts of America were officially incorporated in the United States, young men have had the opportunity to "Be Prepared." Left to right, Roland B. Hentz, William P. Kelly, Edwin Ruth, Charles Shoemaker, Francais Shoemaker, and David Kelly demonstrate the scout salute, May 2, 1913, on the steps of Rutgers Preparatory School in New Brunswick. Courtesy, Rutgers Preparatory School

IN MEMORY OF THE UNIDENTIFIED DEAD
WHO GAVE THEIR LIVES
WHILE IN THE SERVICE OF THE
UNITED STATES OF AMERICA,
AT THE MORGAN SHELL LOADING PLANT
IN THE EXPLOSION OF
OCTOBER 4 – 5, 1918.

unquestionably the most prolific inventor of the modern era. Edison transformed our lives as no one has before or since. And not coincidentally, many of Edison's most important inventions—including the incandescent bulb—were created and/or perfected while the inventor worked within Middlesex County during one of his most fruitful periods.

Though not a native of Middlesex, Edison's family history traces back through the area's early times. Edison's family arrived in New Jersey from Holland around the year 1730 and subsequently farmed a large tract of land near present-day West Orange, where Edison would one day erect one of his research facilities.

Even as a very young man, Edison quickly ·established a reputation as a shrewd businessman. Among his earliest inventions was the stock ticker, a device subsequently used for many years by the stock exchange. He sold this invention and with the proceeds of the sale set up facilities to manufacture this and other products in Newark.

Edison moved to Middlesex County from Newark when the success of his earlier products had begun to take time away from the creation of new products. To boost his own and his staff's creativity and productivity, Edison—who is reported to have often slept only three-to-four hours per night and whose staff acquired the nickname "the insomnia squad"—set the following goal for his Middlesex County research operation: a minor invention every ten days, a major one every six months.

For more than ten years, from April 1877 (three years before he forever brightened the course of history by perfecting the first, practical incandescent electric light bulb) through November 1887, Edison maintained his now-legendary research-and-development laboratory—the world's first such institution—at Menlo Park in the present-day

This monument in the Madison Park area honors those who perished in a tragic explosion at the Morgan Shell Loading plant in 1918. The effects were far reaching as properties were damaged in South Amboy, Morgan, Cliffwood, and the Raritan Bay area. Gunpowder and other munitions were manufactured by the T.A. Gillespie Loading Co., Hercules and Dupont, and the California Loading Co. Collectively they were responsible for nearly 75 percent of the shell loading during World War I. Courtesy, Madison Township Historical Society

township of Edison.

Though the idea now seems a commonplace, the research laboratories in Menlo Park were themselves an experiment. Up to this time, the process of inventing things had been the solitary quest of isolated individuals pursuing singular goals. Edison conceived a different way: an organized institution wholly and solely dedicated to creation and invention.

In fact, though unpatented, the research laboratory would be among Edison's most important contributions. At Menlo Park, he provided an organized facility where a trained staff could work as a team with the intention of making ideas concrete. With Edison's large staff of well-trained assistants performing much of the time-consuming detail work, the results of this experimental collaboration were truly incredible, even by today's jaded, high-technology standards.

During the period of work on his incandescent bulb (which he illuminated on October 21, 1879, and which lasted for forty hours), Edison also was developing and improving the system for generation and distribution of the electric power necessary to light it. This included inventing or improving dynamos, conductors, fuses, switches, meters, sockets—virtually every component necessary to the successful and practical transmission of electric current.

Of Edison's 1,093 United States patents—by far the largest number ever granted to an individual (Edison also received hundreds of foreign patents)—356 involved the production and distribution of electrical power. On December 31, 1879, Edison presented a demonstration of his electrical lighting system to the public gathered in the streets and buildings of Menlo Park.

Though there had been other attempts at creating workable incandescent bulbs and workable electrical-distribution plans, Edison's was the first practical scheme for

Top: *Thomas Edison conducted research over a ten-year period in Menlo Park. In this artist's rendition, the buildings surrounding the main facility are: the office (front right); the carbon house (far left); the L-shaped machine shop (far right); the glass house (angled in front of the machine shop). Edison's electric rail car can be seen to the right.*

Bottom: *The tiny electric train was a favorite attraction for visitors to Thomas Edison's Menlo Park facility. Powered by a dynamo in Edison's laboratory, the railway extended through neighboring woods toward Pumptown Corners, in the direction of a water tank at Dismal Swamp in Metuchen. Both photos from the collection of the Thomas A. Edison Tower and Museum. Courtesy, U.S. Dept. of the Interior, National Park Service, Edison National Historic Site*

In 1890, the Edison Electric Manufacturing Company could regulate the amount of electricity going to various parts of the city of New Brunswick. The photo shows the switching station just prior to the installation of new gear and a monitoring board. Courtesy, Special Collections and Archives, Rutgers University Libraries

the widespread distribution of electricity. Actually, Edison's genius may reside in this word *practical* more than any other. He had a great gift for seeing and making real the day-to-day products that people wanted and needed.

Practicality played an extremely important part in Edison's business philosophy. It was a principal requirement for every one of his products; he insisted that there be a market for the inventive output of his and his staff's genius and hard work. And what could be more practical than a supply system for the electricity that would power his many other inventions?

In 1877, Edison introduced the first practical carbon telephone transmitter, a device which made Alexander Graham Bell's telephone functional. In this year, too, Edison developed what would remain his favorite invention: the phonograph.

In 1880, he began operation of the first passenger electric railway in the United States. This was a product that would subsequently develop into the highly successful electric trolleys, buses, and railways that have been transporting people and products ever since.

In 1883, Edison discovered and thereafter publicized the "Edison Effect." Edison found that if he placed an independent wire or plate between the legs of the filament of one of his incandescent lamps, he could regulate the flow of current. Upon this seemingly simple device rests the whole of the modern science of electronics.

In 1885, Edison received patents on systems that permitted wireless communications between moving trains and railway stations and between ships and shores. Later he would assign these patents to Guglielmo Marconi, who would use them in his further development of wireless telegraphy; this led in turn to the wireless broadcasting of sound and voice.

At the Edison Lamp Works in Menlo Park, employees posed for a group photo in 1880. At his nearby laboratory, Thomas Edison perfected the incandescent lamp and developed a system of electrical generation and distribution to bring electrical power to the people. From the collection of the Thomas A. Edison Tower and Museum. Courtesy, U.S. Dept. of the Interior, National Park Service, Edison National Historic Site

During Edison's ten-plus years in Middlesex County, he took out well over 300 United States patents. He is as well-known as the source for the quote, "Genius is one percent inspiration and ninety-nine percent perspiration." Another Edison quote derives from his conversation with a colleague, who was commiserating with the inventor about the failure of several thousand experiments. Edison replied, "Failures? Not at all. We've learned several thousand things that won't work."

Henry Ford, for whose automobiles Edison would design an electric self-starter, considered his close friend Edison to be the greatest genius the world has ever known. In the late 1920s, Ford had every board of Menlo

Park dismantled, moved, and reconstructed at Ford's Greenfield Village in Dearborn, Michigan. Ford even moved to Dearborn a large amount of the red Middlesex County clay upon which Edison's pioneering research laboratory stood.

Controllable lighting on demand; recorded music; motion pictures; the electronics that bring us radio, television, computers; the instruments that allow jetliners to land safely during bad weather—all these products are direct or indirect descendants of the brain of this one-time resident of Middlesex County.

In his insistence on the practical applicability of his creations, Thomas Alva Edison exemplified the traditional spirit of Middlesex County, for the county has ever excelled in the creation and manufacture of successful products that make practical use of new ideas and technologies. And if Edison's many inventions did, in fact, help propel the county into the forefront of the industrial development of the United States, it is important to remember that it was, in large part, the numerous positive qualities and resources Edison found already existing in the county that contributed to Edison's locating those incredibly productive research facilities in Middlesex County in the first place.

Not the least of these inducements was the abundance of copper and copper wire, which Edison needed to make his electrical products work. Copper, discovered in New Jersey in the 1700s, was refined in great quantity in the Raritan Valley. In fact, Middlesex County could account for approximately one-third of the United States' copper refining at the end of World War II.

The development of a practical power-distribution system naturally encouraged the spread of electric power throughout the county (and, of course, throughout the nation and the world). In turn, this early electrification of the county further encouraged

This vehicle can be likened to contemporary telephone line repair trucks, except that it was equipped to service trolley wires, which were still in use in 1925. The trolley gave way to "trolley buses," and eventually the tracks were removed and the metal was donated to World War II scrap drives. Courtesy, Wesley Ott, Dunellen

Rutgers Preparatory School has graduated many of Middlesex County's most illustrious citizens, among them poet A. Joyce Kilmer. Born in New Brunswick, he was the author of "Trees," Summer and Love, *and* Main Street and Other Poems. *Kilmer stands in the top row, center, with members of his class in May 1901. Courtesy, Rutgers Preparatory School*

broad-based industrialization that would, eventually, transform Middlesex County.

Ultimately, the inventiveness and drive of Edison and others changed the once-pastoral county from a rural into a metropolitan region, from an economy based primarily on tilling the earth and fishing the river to one based primarily on paving the earth and harnessing the river for industry.

Middlesex County has always infused its natives, its adoptive residents, and its visitors with a sense of fruitfulness and creativity. And this has been the case not only in the fields of science and technology but in other important fields as well. Middlesex County has both pioneered and excelled in medicine, politics, education—as witnessed by the presence of Rutgers University, among the oldest and most respected universities in the world—and, most notably, the arts.

Among the most celebrated of Middlesex County's natives was poet Alfred Joyce Kilmer (he dropped the Alfred as an adult), who was killed in action on a French battlefield during World War I. Kilmer, the Irish, Scottish, and English son of Fred B. and Anna Kilburn Kilmer, was called America's "soldier poet," and his family name can still be seen on streets and businesses throughout the county.

Fred B. Kilmer was himself a writer of some note—of scientific and medical literature. The elder Kilmer served for forty-five years as the scientific director of New Brunswick's Johnson & Johnson, which pioneered the then-revolutionary idea of using sterile bandages after surgery or to dress a wound. Joyce Kilmer's mother, Anna, was a talented New Brunswick musician.

Joyce Kilmer was born in New Brunswick in a house at 17 Codwise (now Joyce Kilmer) Avenue on December 6, 1886. He attended Rutgers Preparatory School, then spent two years at Rutgers College and two

years at Columbia University. As a college sophomore, he became engaged to Aline Murray, step-daughter of Henry Mills Alden, editor of *Harper's* magazine. Though his ambition was to be a writer, Kilmer's first job was teaching Latin in Morristown High School.

Anxious to further his literary career, he left the teaching profession after a year and moved his family to New York City. There, while working at various sales, journalistic, and editorial jobs, he began to have some consistent success publishing his poetry. Eventually, Kilmer obtained a position at the *New York Times* and, by age twenty-five, was listed in *Who's Who.*

Less than three weeks after the entry of the United States into the First World War, Kilmer enlisted in the army as a private. At his request, he was transferred to a combat regiment and ultimately was involved in the bloody campaign at the Marne River.

A man of deep religious faith, the boyish-looking Kilmer concluded his poem "Prayer of a Soldier in France" with the following lines:

Lord, Thou didst suffer more for me
Than all the hosts of land and sea.
So let me render back again
This millionth of Thy gift. Amen.

On July 30, 1918, while on patrol to locate enemy machine-gun emplacements hidden in the woods near the Ourcq River, Kilmer was killed by a shot through the head. Sergeant Joyce Kilmer was buried at the edge of a small copse by a river near the French village of Seringes.

In the first verse of "In Memory of Rupert Brooke," a poem to an English poet who had died earlier in the war, Kilmer wrote the following words, which apply equally well to Kilmer:

In alien earth, across a troubled sea,
His body lies that was so fair and
* young.*
His mouth is stopped, with half his
* songs unsung;*
His arm is still, that struck to make
* men free.*
But let no cloud of lamentation be
Where, on a warrior's grave, a lyre is
* hung.*
We keep the echoes of his golden
* tongue,*
We keep the vision of his chivalry.

At the time of his death, at age 31, Kilmer was one of the best-known literary figures in the United States. He was a popular and celebrated writer who wrote uncommon thoughts in the words of common people.

Today, however, only one of his works is popularly remembered. But that one, Kilmer's twelve-line poem "Trees," numbers among the most-famous, most-quoted, and most-beloved of American verses.

The automobile brought a change in Middlesex County life that was rivaled in the profundity of its effects only by electrification. Between World Wars I and II, the number of cars in America exceeded thirty million, and those autos needed roads. A major paving of Middlesex County began that has continued unabated until the present day.

In the 1920s, Route 1 brought drivers over the Pulaski Skyway to the Holland Tunnel while plans were being discussed for the George Washington Bridge and the Lincoln Tunnel. New highways were added to the county's transportation grid throughout the 1930s and into the 1940s, when, to relieve the worsening traffic congestion, work was begun on the Garden State Parkway and the New Jersey Turnpike, both of which crossed through Middlesex County.

TREES
by JOYCE KILMER

I think that I shall never see
    A poem lovely as a tree.
A tree whose hungry mouth is pressed
    Against the earth's sweet flowing breast;
A tree that looks at God all day
    And lifts her leafy arms to pray;
A tree that may in summer wear
    A nest of robins in her hair;
Upon whose bosom snow has lain;
    Who intimately lives with rain.
Poems are made by fools like me,
    But only God can make a tree.

"Trees," published in 1914, won national recognition for Joyce Kilmer. Educated at Rutgers College and Columbia University, Kilmer was on the staff of the New Standard Dictionary *and contributed to various periodicals. Killed in France during World War I, the poet was honored in his native city of New Brunswick by the renaming of the street where his historic home is situated, Kilmer Avenue. Courtesy, Joyce Kilmer Authority*

"We get what U want when U want it" was the motto of the New York and New Brunswick Auto Express Company Inc., a trucking firm founded in 1917. Although primarily a hauler of cargo, the company regularly carried children from the New Brunswick area to Kaufman's Farm, located at the corner of Franklin Boulevard and Hamilton Street, Somerset. Driver James Anderson poses by one of the firm's vehicles, decorated for a YMHA picnic. Courtesy, New Brunswick Chamber of Commerce

The new roadways provided access to the southern sections of the county for people who worked in the New York City metropolitan area but preferred to live in Middlesex County's more-rural setting. The county became popular for its open space, as seen in the development of suburban "bedroom communities."

Between 1930 and 1950—reflecting, among other things, the rapid spread of industry and supporting services, and the rapid expansion of the county as a sanctuary from the work-a-day pressures of New York City—county population doubled, eventually reaching 400,000. These people needed shelter, and home construction fast became one of the county's major industries.

As the county's population continued to increase through the 1970s, growth in the number of service jobs steadily outpaced growth in the number of manufacturing jobs. This trend has continued well into the 1980s, as the county's population nears 600,000—the number predicted in 1930 by planner Russell Van Nest Black.

To provide recreational areas sufficient

Above: *This circa 1914 photograph shows South River's first drug store, located on Ferry Street and owned by Samuel Kaufman. South River had progressed considerably since 1823, when there were only ten homes in the area. By 1866, the South River Brick Company and the American Enameled Brick and Tile Company, among others, provided employment and helped the town to grow, so much so that for a time South River was referred to as "Bricktown." By the 1900s the community was typical of many in the county, bristling with shops along the main thoroughfares.*

Facing page: *By 1913 Cochrane Tavern was no more, as Public Service moved in and constructed its offices. The commercial office, on the corner of Albany and Neilson streets, served as headquarters for the company.   Both photos courtesy, Special Collections and Archives, Rutgers University Libraries*

for the county population he predicted—accurately, as it turned out—Black outlined a plan to purchase for public use a large number of then-inexpensive tracts for parks and wildlife areas. His suggestions were not heeded. Now the enormous pressure from county residents to acquire these lands is countered by the huge outlay of funds necessary to pay for and develop these new park lands.

Perhaps the major challenge facing Middlesex County as the 1980s draw to a close and the twenty-first century rises on the horizon is the challenge of maintaining the delicate balance between developing the economy and the quality of life. Pessimists see an irreconcilable conflict between a) the necessity to provide jobs that supply salaries and tax monies and b) the maintenance and improvement of the environmental quality that allows people to enjoy the leisure and recreation that their jobs make possible. So far, inventive and practical residents of Middlesex County have been able to find ways to prove that the conflict is, in fact, only seemingly irreconcilable.

The steamboat Robert W. Johnson *was a common sight on the Raritan River in 1910. Johnson & Johnson's new corporate headquarters, recently constructed in New Brunswick, reflects the continuing commitment to the city by this and other leading corporations. Courtesy, Johnson & Johnson*

CHAPTER SIX

REBIRTH OF THE FUTURE

If the history of Middlesex County
parallels and reflects the history of America, then the history of the county
seat, New Brunswick, parallels and reflects the history of the county.

There are, to be sure, other cities and townships in Middlesex County with
fascinating histories. Perth Amboy is a case in point, evolving from the colonial
Proprietors' attempts to compete for New York's port business, beginning a ri-
valry whose repercussions are being felt to this day. Perth Amboy was, and re-
mains, a vital port, and it played a central role during the Revolutionary War
and during subsequent war efforts.

Yet after a brief flurry of commercial activity and success, Perth Amboy be-
gan to lose business to New Brunswick as the upriver port grew and as an in-
creasing number and volume of products were brought via the Delaware and

Top: *Ease of travel between Sayreville and Perth Amboy was made possible by the completion in 1940 of the Edison Bridge, which spanned the Raritan River. The link via Route 9 was considered an engineering marvel, and its success was credited to Morris Goodkind, the chief engineer.*

Bottom: *The dedication of the Edison Bridge marked the completion of a vital part of the county's transportation system. Attending the ribbon cutting ceremonies were, beginning second from left, James Logan, Donald Stirmer, Mrs. Thomas Edison, and Morris Goodkind. The structure was named in honor of Thomas Edison. Both photos courtesy, Special Collections and Archives, Rutgers University Libraries*

Raritan Canal to New Brunswick's mills and wharves for transshipment direct to faraway ports.

South Amboy, too, was important to a young nation, and the location there of one terminus of the Camden and Amboy Railroad helped to generate the rail boom that tied America into a cohesive political entity.

Piscataway, Woodbridge, Highland Park, and other cities and townships in the county have long and distinguished histories crucial to the development of our American story. But as more and more business was done in New Brunswick, it became the focal point for and eventually the hub of commercial and social development within the county. New Brunswick is, in many ways, the quintessential American city, the real "Middletown." This chapter focuses on New Brunswick as that city reflects the history of the American city.

New Brunswick is of special importance because of the national significance of the current revitalization efforts within the city, efforts that have met with substantial success. Revitalization is being accomplished only because of great individual dedication, great individual sacrifice, and great cooperation among city residents from all walks of life. But why does the American city require revitalization in the first place?

Although New Brunswick never suffered the extremes of decline that can still be found in areas of many American cities both major and minor, the broad social movements that resulted in those declines can also be traced here. Much of the history of America's rise to world prominence can be traced through the history of the American city, and cities and our sense of them still inform our sense of ourselves as a nation. Yet for several decades, we allowed our cities to deteriorate. For several decades we sat and watched the city in America change from an entity that modeled and celebrated

Three views of the George Street and Livingston Avenue triangle, New Brunswick, reflect the changing times from World War I to World War II. Following the Armistice, the triangle was crowded with people waiting to welcome home the soldiers and sailors who fought in World War I. For this special day, flags and banners were proudly displayed and a victory arch was constructed, under which Middlesex County's heroes passed. As residents returned to normal daily life, the intersection of George Street and Livingston Avenue, with the United Methodist Church in view, presented a pleasant scene. The grass triangle with wrought iron and wooden benches along the walkways was a favorite resting spot. By 1942, war had returned and sign boards encouraged the purchase of defense stamps and defense bonds, so "that we may never know the bonds of tyranny." Courtesy, Special Collections and Archives, Rutgers University Libraries

the best aspects of human culture—communality, creativity, civility—to one that sometimes modeled the worst. The aging of cities is not an inevitable process but the result of human choice. Beginning in the 1920s, and increasingly during the Great Depression, many people began to choose *not* to replace buildings or to renew capital equipment in American cities. The signs of aging began to be seen in cities all over America, and New Brunswick was not immune to the effects of this process.

But because New Brunswick has reflected each and every stage of American development, changing from a small agricultural market town to busy port, then to railroad center and industrial and manufacturing power, its responses to the changes of the last several decades are significant to anyone wishing to understand the societal changes of the past sixty years.

It was not just cities that were decaying: there is a further, intriguing parallel between the decline of American cities and the decline of American heavy industry, of "smokestack" America. Since many American cities grew up around, and were dependent upon, certain large industries, such as steel, the health of many cities' economies was inextricably entwined with the health of particular industries.

Observations of New Brunswick during this period reveal several factors that reflected the process as it occurred on a national scale. The increasing popularity of the automobile encouraged a kind of social decentralization, a growing disinterest in communality; it became fashionable to live outside the city rather than within it.

This movement perfectly complemented the American dream of land and home for every individual and family. Inexpensive automobiles and fuel and a network of highways made it possible for young, upwardly mobile families to settle in uncrowded sub-

During World War II, Middlesex County once again contributed its full share to support the troops. Here workers exit through the Hamilton Street gate of Johnson & Johnson, New Brunswick, in 1942. As a safeguard to a company vital to the war effort, the street had been closed off by the War Department. Courtesy, Special Collections and Archives, Rutgers University Libraries

Left: *New Jersey Bell Telephone established a center at Camp Kilmer in New Brunswick with personnel to assist the soldiers who wished to call their friends and families. Camp Kilmer was a temporary home for millions of soldiers en route to Europe. Courtesy, Special Collections and Archives, Rutgers University Libraries*

Below: *After the war, machine shop workers in South Plainfield—brought in on a Sunday for a painting job—paused with big smiles for the camera. In the center of this 1946 photo is Mary Mazepa. Posted on the door at the left was a sign welcoming veterans back to their jobs. Courtesy, South Plainfield Historical Society*

Left: *Captain Henrik (Kurt) Carlsen, skipper of the* Flying Enterprise, *has been a resident of Woodbridge for more than forty years. True to the traditions of the sea, Captain Carlsen remained with his ship under life-threatening conditions, while at the same time assuring the safety of his passengers and crew. For his heroic deeds, he was commended by President Harry S Truman, knighted by King Frederick IX of Denmark, and honored with a ticker-tape parade in New York City. In 1985 the Township of Woodbridge dedicated a slip on Ferry Street to the captain. Courtesy, the family of Captain Henrik Carlsen*

Below: *South Plainfield answered the call for volunteer blood donors during 1946. The building seen to the left, constructed in 1912, belonged originally to the Spicer Corporation. Spicer and another South Plainfield company, Harvis Steel, brought an influx of workers to the area, many from Poland, England, and Italy. Courtesy, South Plainfield Historical Society*

urbs, giving rise to the explosive growth of East Brunswick and Woodbridge and other county townships and communities.

The movement out of the city also depleted the cities' supplies of young families and of skilled wage earners. The "bedroom community"—the suburb—began to supplant the farm in the American consciousness.

The increasing popularity of the auto and growing use of the freight truck contributed to the decline of the railroads, which had always lived symbiotically with the cities, by cutting into both passenger and freight revenues. With declining revenues, once-lucrative and fashionable railroad companies began to delay maintenance at every level and to cut both freight and passenger service. This delay in maintenance resulted in shoddy conditions for rail passengers, exacerbating the decline in traffic.

The rise of the suburbs also encouraged the relocation of many corporations from within cities to industrial parks outside of the cities, where large tracts of inexpensive land free of city taxes could be purchased. There were many other advantages that such relocations would bring to a corporation as well: easier ingress and egress for raw materials and finished products; more pleasant surroundings for corporate executives and employees; less expensive utilities; more political influence over an area. Manufacturing facilities within the cities were in many cases simply abandoned, contributing to an increasingly pervasive atmosphere of decay.

Older, less expensive housing left behind in the cities by young, mobile families combined with social programs to encourage large numbers of the poor and unemployed to move to the cities where jobs might be found.

Physical aging caused major problems also as city facilities needed to be main-tained, enlarged, or replaced during periods of extreme inflation. The costs of city services increased dramatically at the same time that the cities' tax bases were eroding precipitously. City maintenance and capital improvements were delayed, further contributing to the atmosphere and psychology of decline. Mass transportation facilities declined. School facilities suffered, offering a further reason for more financially secure families to leave.

With much of the capital going out of an area, fewer inner-city dwelling units were built or rebuilt. In many American cities, conditions worsened as many older housing units filled with the socially disenfranchised—the elderly, the disadvantaged, the alien—who could not afford rent increases.

Without rent increases, landlords said, they could not afford to make repairs; maintenance and improvements were delayed and diminished. Real estate moguls could be assured of better returns on their investments outside the cities, and this is where investment capital went. As the physical condition of housing deteriorated, more and more young, educated families fled.

Certain social phenomena contributed as well and can be identified in a general way. When America was a predominantly agrarian society and a large proportion of the population lived isolated lives on farms and in villages, the city was a symbol of civilization and progress, a magnet for individuals wanting to see and feel the forces of change and the best that society had to offer.

During the 1800s, when rail was the prime mode of transportation and the cities were the depots, people would look forward to visiting cities like New Brunswick *because* they were crowded. The crowds of people and autos were a celebration, a cause of wonder; they offered a passing parade, and farmhands and country families went to town to be part of that parade.

Facing page: *Three scenes of the railroad depot in New Brunswick, prior to 1985, illustrate one area of the city that remained relatively unchanged for more than 100 years. The oldest image (above left) looks toward the Raritan River Bridge, circa 1870, before the tracks were elevated. The photograph of the Pennsylvania Railroad Station (above right) was taken in 1905, when the structure was considered one of the finest stations between New York and Philadelphia. The last image (bottom) shows the station in 1985, more than 80 years after its construction. Courtesy, Special Collections and Archives, Rutgers University Libraries*

But if rivers and canals and rails always led *to* the cities, the highways built for automobiles and trucks began more and more to lead *away* from the cities. A growing segment of the population wanted newer, single-family homes, a situation that became particularly acute when millions of young married couples took advantage of government-subsidized mortgages after World War II; they could find those homes only in the inexpensive tracts of the rapidly growing suburbs.

As American society had become more and more highly industrialized, cities depended upon industry for their livelihood. But the waste products of those industries made life increasingly unpleasant and sometimes dangerous. American society began to perceive cities differently. The passing parade had become traffic.

Wealthier, newer suburbs with no appreciable social-welfare costs could afford bond issues that paid for better schools and newer facilities that required less—and less expensive—maintenance. Zoning could limit industry to specific areas, decreasing pollution both visible and invisible. The inexpensive, mass-produced automobile, abundant fuel, and good highways made it possible to commute from the suburbs to work (even if that job was still in a city) in far less time and with far greater comfort and convenience than was possible on public transportation even within a city.

Because of the auto, affluent populations spread over relatively large areas could support—in fact, demanded—large suburban shopping malls that could and did provide convenient access and parking in new, air-conditioned facilities. Such capital-intensive projects further drained funds from inner-city projects (and drained business from inner-city businesses) while continuing to make suburban living more attractive.

City businesses contended with aging fa-

cilities, the huge expense of new construction on limited acreage, lack of parking space and access for customers and employees, declining populations of affluent consumers, and declining educational levels in the immediately available work force.

The children of the owners of long-established businesses often did not wish to take over a business in the inner-city area. The original owners of fashionable shops aged along with their businesses; in the absence of a family member to leave the business to, many small businesses simply closed. As more businesses closed, foot traffic declined. All this combined to encourage the closing of more and more upscale businesses that once drew the affluent to the downtown area. Fashionable stores closed and were often replaced by bars, fast-food franchises, and video arcades. Given these and other national trends, the process of urban decline accelerated through the 1950s and early 1960s.

Contributing also was a wave of immigration. Political and economic refugees from all over the world came to and settled in cities. Often they arrived poor and initially depended upon strained city services. But where earlier immigrant groups had arrived during times of seemingly limitless employment and wealth for new arrivals, the groups that arrived more recently came at a time of economic contraction, of "less is more."

It is impossible to determine qualitatively if these groups suffered worse discrimination than the immigrant groups that arrived before them, but it can be shown that there was far less economic opportunity to help these later-arriving groups overcome the problems of establishing cultural beachheads. And difficulties in the American economy as a whole worsened the plight of the urban poor, especially during the 1960s, which led to the eruption of rioting and violence.

Top: *P.J. Young's Dry Goods Store on George Street in New Brunswick was advertised in the 1920s as being "stocked with highly desirable merchandise. Carpets and household goods are found in the basement, while the main floor shows a comprehensive demonstration of the latest conceptions of the master designer's world."*

Bottom: *Thirty years later P.J. Young's Dry Goods Store continued to utilize behind-the-counter merchandise cases. However, as the pace of modern shopping quickened, the wooden counters with chairs for customers were replaced by glass counters displaying cosmetics, handbags, stationery, umbrellas, soaps, jewelry, and handkerchiefs. Both photos courtesy, Special Collections and Archives, Rutgers University Libraries*

Above: *Paul Robeson was educated at Rutgers University where he became the first black All-American football player, graduating in 1919 as a Phi Beta Kappa. As an actor he received critical acclaim in* The Emperor Jones. *His career later declined due to his outspoken criticism of racial injustice in the U.S. Today he is remembered as an honored figure for his staunch advocacy of equal rights for black Americans. Courtesy, Special Collections and Archives, Rutgers University Libraries*

Facing page: *When the State Theater on Livingston Avenue in New Brunswick was at its height as a movie palace, Bela Lugosi made a personal appearance in a live horror and magic stage show to promote his film* They Creep in the Dark. *The State Theater was host to other Hollywood stars as well, among them Hedy Lamarr, Gary Cooper, Bob Hope, and Jane Wyman. This poster was discovered when renovations were begun on the interior of the structure. Courtesy, New Brunswick Cultural Center, Inc.*

In some areas, a worsening American economy was accompanied by an intensifying racism. The presence of the children of the poor in inner-city schools fueled confrontations over the volatile issues of school integration and forced busing. This, combined with the overall decline in the quality and physical condition of inner-city school systems, caused further "white flight" to the suburbs.

Politics, too, contributed to the decline of the cities as the wealth and relative political conservatism of the suburbs began to influence the policies of county, state, and federal governments. Political "clout" spread to the suburbs in proportion to their wealth while the cities lost proportionate voice. Often, tax revenues produced in the cities were not returned to the cities proportionately, going instead for highway funds and new government projects outside the cities.

Conditions in New Brunswick never approached the extremes that many other cities suffered, but the city had its share of serious problems. So many factors legislated against the viability of cities like New Brunswick that it is remarkable that they survived at all in any recognizable form.

New Brunswick survived because, during the late 1950s and early 1960s, a number of residents began to realize that only individuals working hard in concord could hope to reverse the changes that had occurred. And slowly, but persistently, the efforts of these people have begun to show results, results that bode well for the future of New Brunswick and the American city.

Traditionally, urban renewal in the United States has been simple in concept: bulldoze the old, build the new, and banish the displaced. But in New Brunswick, a different kind of urban renewal that seeks to do more than simply raze and replace old buildings has begun.

Urban planners have learned to take into

Top: *Opened in 1921, the design of the State Theater was the work of famed architect Thomas Lamb. It was first a vaudeville house and then a movie palace. In recent years, celebrities performing here included Itzak Perlman, Marcel Marceau, Molly Picon, Yo-Yo Ma, and Ella Fitzgerald. The facility is now part of the New Brunswick Cultural Center, and its restoration is part of a multi-million-dollar revitalization effort for the city of New Brunswick. Courtesy, Special Collections and Archives, Rutgers University Libraries*

Bottom: *After many years of neglect and little or no use, the State Theater was given a new lease on life. It was designated as the cornerstone in a multi-million-dollar revitalization of the downtown section of New Brunswick known as Monument Square. Initial restoration phases of the Theater brought tens of thousands of visitors to the city, to enjoy world class performances. Current and future restoration plans are seen here, as prepared by Princeton architects, Ford Farewell Mills and Gatsch. The State Theater is far left, replete with a marquee reminiscent of its original. George Street Playhouse is the structure in the center, as is the new addition or infill building that will house an elevator core. Lastly, far right, is Crossroads Theater, the nation's most influential and well-known, African American Theater company. The three theaters and other performing and visual arts organizations comprise the New Brunswick Cultural Center. Courtesy, New Brunswick Cultural Center, Inc.*

account more than just traffic flow. People have begun again to see cities as resources instead of drains on society's resources. New Brunswick and other American cities have begun to realize that a city's major business is the quality of life of its residents.

New Brunswick has become fashionable once again. Young professionals have begun to buy old buildings and, instead of bulldozing them, are rebuilding them, saving and restoring them for their architectural beauty and character, turning them into townhouses and boutiques. In the process, the city becomes increasingly livable.

Already there have been significant successes in the drive toward revitalization, supported by both public and private funding. The Hyatt Regency Hotel chain situated a luxury conference and hotel complex on the banks of the Raritan. Rutgers, The State University completed the Center for Arts and Planning, that houses a high tech communications center, the Edward J. Bloustein School of Planning and Public Policy, and the Mason Gross School of the Arts. Johnson & Johnson constructed their worldwide headquarters in the heart of the city. Unlike many corporations which moved away from their original roots once growth necessitated an expansive headquarter building, Johnson & Johnson remained true to its origins. Well planned residential development assured that the city would continue to support all classes of people, as exemplified by upscale Riverwatch apartments, prestigious Hiram Square Townhomes, the middle income Renaissance Station Townhouses and the Providence Square/Livingston Manor Senior Housing. Commercial properties provided the business locations that generated jobs and local tax revenue, among them: Golden Triangle, Kilmer Square, Albany Street Plaza The Raritan River has been and is being cleaned up and the river side Boyd Park renovated. The logistics of such efforts are difficult and only accomplished with the good faith efforts of many. New Brunswick has such citizens and groups in abundance.

New Brunswick also has the same physical attributes that made it successful originally: an attractive location; good transportation

facilities, the river (although it is now of more importance recreationally than commercially), and Rutgers University, located largely within the city. A report by the American Cities Corporation, commissioned to evaluate New Brunswick's potential for a successful revitalization, concluded that the city offered the following advantages:

1. *location advantages and transportation access unsurpassed by any city or region of comparable size anywhere;*
2. *a fundamentally sound economic base in the city and the region;*
3. *an excellent base of health and educational institutions far beyond those of any comparable region;*
4. *governments at all levels that are resources and not impediments to New Brunswick in its efforts;*
5. *employment opportunities because of its position as county seat; and*
6. *the Raritan River.*

Less tangible but equally important assets are the changes in American attitudes toward cities and industries. In the boardrooms of corporate America, there is a renewed dedication to becoming internationally competitive. The tendency toward short-term profit taking, which hastened the decline of our smokestack industries, has begun to reverse itself within the last few years.

Corporate executives have begun to repudiate the business philosophy that led to the dearth of reinvestment in new capital equipment, the lack of maintenance of old equipment, and the wholesale shutting down of marginal factories when minimal efforts could have made them productive once again. Americans are working toward the rebuilding of our industrial capacity and the husbanding of our resources.

Americans are turning away from policies and attitudes that have caused the steady

Top: *Middlesex County College offers a two-year degree program that is among the finest in the country. Its facilities, located on 220 acres in Edison, are outstanding. Among them are the newly built Instructional Resource Center depicted here, the Institute for Management and Technical Development that includes an "earn while you learn" program with area corporations, a professional Performing Arts Center, and the Division of Corporate and Community Education. Courtesy, Middlesex County College*

Bottom: *A recent restoration project improved the ecological and recreational resources in Roosevelt Park, Edison. Here the dam and outlet structure were replaced and the nine acre lake dredged in order to restore the depth to an average of eight feet. Courtesy, Middlesex County Department of Parks and Recreation.*

deterioration of our cities and toward their rebuilding, toward communality and civilization; we are turning away from the mistakes of the past and toward the future once again.

No history of New Brunswick and Middlesex County would be complete without a note about the extraordinary, recent contributions to the area's vitality made by locally based corporations. In the 1980s in New Brunswick, it was Johnson & Johnson's courageous decision to remain in a declining city that began the corporate rebirth. In the 1990s, much credit is given to the New Brunswick Development Corporation (DEVCO), with a goal to physically combat urban blight. They did so through land banking; commercial, residential and office development; and projects that improve the social, cultural and physical environment of the city. This public/private partnership is actively restoring New Brunswick's economic vitality, factoring human issues and stockholder accountability into the business equation.

The revitalization of New Brunswick continues to go forward. Future projects address the various economic and social elements required of a thriving city and turn strategies into reality.

If efforts to revitalize New Brunswick are significant bellwethers of change in American attitudes toward cities and toward American society, they are also encouraging signs for the economic and social health of Middlesex County. A thriving New Brunswick will provide cultural benefits, jobs, and other economic advantages both for city residents and for the expanding populations of virtually every township in the county.

A vital New Brunswick will be an example for more conservative corporations waiting to see the results there. There is too much tradition and history in the Amboys, too much human energy, too many resources, talents, hopes, and dreams in the Bruns-

Above: *Many of Middlesex County's older structures have undergone adaptive re-use plans. The Rice home on South Adelaide Avenue, formerly the residence of Christopher Meyers, now functions as the YMHA. Courtesy, Special Collections and Archives, Rutgers University Libraries*

Facing Page: *The New Brunswick streetscape combines the past and present. Here the steeple to the Christ Church Episcopal is framed by office complexes including the Golden Triangle, top right, and the Hiram Square Townhomes in the foreground. Courtesy, New Brunswick Development Corporation.*

wicks, Metuchen, Edison, Woodbridge, Piscataway, and throughout Middlesex County, to be ignored.

New Brunswick has been designated the "health care city." Such an identity bears witness to the size, strength and technological capabilities of the health services community located here. In 1996, the Cancer Institute of New Jersey opened as a world-class treatment center. Funded in part from a grant provided by the U.S. Department of Energy, the Institute is one of only 19 nationally-certified clinical cancer and research facilities. It is the result of a unique collaboration among three note-worthy institutions: the University of Medicine and Dentistry of New Jersey (UMDNJ); Robert Wood Johnson University Hospital (RWJUH) and St. Peter's Medical Center.

Robert Wood Johnson University Hospital is an academic medical center, and a core teaching hospital. It also is a "level one" trauma center. Other components of this impressive facility address heart specialties, and clinical neurosciences. RWJUH includes a Children's Hospital and a Center for Alternative and Complementary Medicine.

St. Peter's Medical Center is an acute care facility and a teaching hospital. Sponsored by the Diocese of Metuchen, St. Peter's is the regional referral center for high risk pregnancies. It also contains the Hospital for Women and Children, a Regional Child Abuse Center and the largest neonatal intensive care unit in the state. The Medical Center specializes in diabetes, asthma and allergy care.

New Brunswick is home to the eighth-oldest institute of higher learner in the nation—Rutgers, The State University. In 1997, *Money Magazine* ranked Rutgers as the 14th best college value, when compared to more than 1,100 four-year colleges and universities. Rutgers Advanced Technology Centers were created to meet the growing needs of U.S. businesses that require integration between technology and

application. For instance, its AgBioTech Center deals with molecular biology as it relates to the environment and agriculture. Similarly, cutting-edge technologies are clearly at the forefront of Rutgers Center for Biomaterials and Medical Devices; Center for Ceramic Research; Center for Discrete Mathematics and Theoretical Computer Science; Center for Advanced Food Technology and, lastly, the Fiber-Optic Materials Research Program.

New Brunswick is well on its way to success, and the future of Middlesex County looks bright indeed. Development in the county proceeds at a controlled and thoughtful pace: it is spurred onward by the same entrepre-neurial spirit that homesteaded the county in the beginning; it is infused with the idea that individual identities must be expressed; and it is tempered by the need for environ-mental controls to protect the quality of life to be enjoyed by present and future genera-tions. These three often conflicting drives—the drive for profit, the drive to ensure indi-vidual expression, and the drive to ensure the quality of life—have characterized the American experience from its inception and are present in the very roots of the American psyche. Their frequent opposition has generated a kind of neurotic, but ultimately creative, tension within the American consciousness that has resulted occasionally in great blunders, but more often in great successes.

These drives have been manifest in the area now known as Middlesex County since its earliest days. Bringing two of these philo-sophic strains were the Europeans: those who came to seek their fortunes and those who came seeking freedom of individual conscience. These strains merged with the third, the harmony with nature displayed and passed on by the Lenape. And thus the nucleus of the American character was formed and nurtured in places like Middlesex County—vast and open American spaces.

Left: *Oscar Martin (left) is seen here circa 1850 with his son Forman, who held office as a Freeholder of Middlesex County. Forman Martin owned a cider mill, located on Old Post Road in Piscatawaytown, a section of Middlesex County now known as Edison. Courtesy, Edison Township Historical Society, Inc.*

Below: *State and federal agencies have designated many of the programs and services of Middlesex County government as models of innovation and cost-effective management. The County is under the leadership of the Board of Chosen Freeholders. Standing, left to right, are H. James Polos, Camille Fernicola, John Pulomena, Christopher D. Rafano, Jane Z. Brady and Stephen J. Dalina who serves as the Freeholder Deputy Director of the Board. Seated is the Freeholder Director, David B. Crabiel. Courtesy, Middlesex County Clerk to the Board of Chosen Freeholders*

South River was served by the Brunswick Traction Company, one of the trolley lines that flourished in Middlesex County from the mid-1890s to the mid-1930s. A first anniversary celebration of electric-powered streetcar service was the occasion for these 1894 photos. Above is Albany Street near George Street, New Brunswick; at the left is the intersection of Albany and Burnet streets. Courtesy, New Brunswick Chamber of Commerce

This nine room mansion was built in 1791 by Cornelius Low, a merchant, attorney and surveyor, and the most powerful member of the Raritan Landing port community. Located on River Road in Piscataway and now functioning as the Cornelius Low House/Middlesex County Museum, the facility is owned by the County of Middlesex and administered by the Middlesex County Cultural and Heritage Commission. The public may tour the grounds or engage in the outstanding interpretive exhibitions that focus on timely New Jersey history topics. Photo by Ken Helsby. Courtesy, Middlesex County Cultural and Heritage Commission.

Above: *The Old Queens College Building of Rutgers University, constructed in 1809, now houses the offices of the president of the university. Queens College, the eighth college in the colonies, was founded under a charter by Governor William Franklin in 1766. Sixty years later, it was renamed after Henry Rutgers, a New York tycoon who gave the college interest on a $5,000 bond and contributed the bell for the new cupola of this building. Photo by Jim Padilla. Courtesy, Middlesex County Cultural and Heritage Commission*

Left: *Kirkpatrick Chapel, on the New Brunswick campus of Rutgers University, was designed in the 1860s by Henry J. Hardenburgh, a descendant of one of the founders of Queens College, Reverend Doctor Jacob Hardenburgh. Photo by Ralph Genella, North Brunswick*

The First Reformed Church in New Brunswick was established in 1812. In 1834, the wooden steeple was added along with the historic town clock, which marked the hours for the merchants and buyers in the Hiram Market District of the town. The sandstone church has brownstone quoins (corners) with chips of stone embedded in the mortar, a construction method known as galleting. Photo by Jim Padilla.

The magnificent rose window in the gallery of the Barron Arts Center, Woodbridge, is known for its brilliant color and rich detailing. Five feet in diameter, the window was the creation of Joseph Baker. Formerly the Barron Library, the Romanesque Revival style building was constructed in 1877 by the family of Thomas Barron who had willed $50,000 for the purpose of constructing a free public library for the people of Woodbridge. Courtesy, Leland Cook, Colonia

148

Right: *Buccleuch Mansion is furnished as a house museum, with period rooms reflecting the years 1739-1912. It has undergone extensive restoration, in part with a grant from the New Jersey Historic Trust. The rich colors are indicative of the bright and intense color schemes of the Colonial period. Once the residence of Colonel Joseph Scott, Buccleuch refers to the Scott ancestral home in Scotland. Open to the public, the museum is in New Brunswick. Courtesy, Buccleuch Mansion, Jersey Blue Chapter, D.A.R.*

Below: *The Eureka Fire Museum on Main Street, Milltown, contains early firefighting equipment, including a 1921 American LaFrance fire engine, a hand-drawn hose cart, and fire extinguishers and fire company gear such as helmets and patches. The museum is open to the public for tours of their permanent collection and rotating exhibits. Photo by John Kaczorowski, Spotswood*

Facing page, top: *The annual New Jersey Folk Festival is coordinated by students in the American Studies Department at Rutgers University, under the direction of Professor Angus K. Gillespie. The festival is a celebration of the regional folk culture strongly in evidence throughout Middlesex County and the state. Ethnic music, dance, and food contribute to the atmosphere of the festivities held at the Eagleton Institute of Douglass College in New Brunswick.*

Facing page, bottom: *Traditional crafts are featured at the folk festival. Shown here are examples of decoy carving and whittling. Both photos by James Moise. Courtesy, New Jersey Folk Festival, American Studies Dept., Rutgers The State University, New Brunswick*

Above: *"Light Dispelling Darkness," produced in honor of Thomas Edison, is a colorful twelve-foot fountain located in Roosevelt Park, Edison, by artist Waylande Gregory. Residing most of his life in New Jersey, Gregory lived and worked for a time on a farm in the Metuchen area, producing oversized, outdoor ceramic pieces through an arrangement with the Atlantic Terra Cotta Company of Perth Amboy. Courtesy, Blakely/Sapone Production, New Brunswick*

Above: *Helmetta is the smallest municipality in Middlesex County, encompassing 0.8 square miles. It was named for Etta Helme, the daughter of George W. Helme, who founded the G. W. Helme Snuff Mill District, a company town built on 220 acres. For his workers and company executives, Helme constructed 105 homes, five brick factories (one of which is seen here), a church, schoolhouse, and general store. The company continued to flourish into the 1980s as a subdivision of the General Cigar & Tobacco Co.*

Left: *Perth Amboy today remains a port city, bounded on the south by the Raritan River and on the east by the Arthur Kill. These two bodies of water meet to form the Raritan Bay, across which lies Staten Island. Deep water shipping facilities are found on the bay, with a channel depth of thirty feet at mean low tide. Around the tip of Perth Amboy is a waterfront park that looks out onto the Raritan and the Atlantic Ocean. Adjacent to the park are marinas and seafood restaurants. Both photos by Ralph Genella, North Brunswick*

Above: Scenes such as this picturesque horse farm continue to delight passersby in Monroe Township, but are becoming less common with the rapid growth of residential communities and corporate parks. As agriculture and animal husbandry decrease, Middlesex County's position is rising in high technology and health care industries. Photo by Mark Nonestied. Courtesy, Middlesex County Cultural and Heritage Commission

Middlesex County ranks first in potato acreage in the state, third in the growing of nursery stock and eighth in overall agribusiness. Some of the nation's best sweet corn, spinach, tomatoes, blueberries and cabbage are grown in Middlesex County. Photo by Mark Nonestied. Courtesy, Middlesex County Cultural and Heritage Commission

Left: Woodbridge has always recognized and remembered its veterans. The Soldiers and Sailors Monument stands at the base of Main Street, dedicated in 1916. In the background is the former Woodbridge Town Hall, also constructed in memory of those who gave their lives while serving in the military and naval services. It no longer exists, having been replaced with a gleaming, state-of-the-arts facility, constructed as part of an award winning, Main Street revitalization project.

Below: *Begun in 1713, City Hall in Perth Amboy has been ravaged by two fires and has undergone numerous changes, renovations, and additions, yet it remains the oldest public building in continuous use in the United States. Although modest in appearance, the structure has an impressive history. It served as the county courthouse until 1793; the State Assembly met here when Perth Amboy was the capital of East Jersey. Within these walls, the vote was taken by which New Jersey became the first state to ratify the Bill of Rights, and it was here that T.M. Peterson became the nation's first black voter. Both photos by John Kaczorowski, Spotswood*

Right: *With the completion of structure restoration and improvements to the grounds in 1997, the East Jersey Olde Towne Village is fully accessible. Railings guide visitors with mobility restrictions to each building; a specially constructed wheelchair lift in the Runyon House permits access to every floor; the structures are barrier free; and materials are printed in large type and Braille. Photo by Mike Boylan. Courtesy Middlesex County Cultural and Heritage Commission*

Bottom: *The tradition of learning and performing the regional dances of Hungary has been passed down from generation to generation through youth groups such as the Hungarian American Athletic Club Folk Dance Group, seen here in 1995. Each year, in June, they perform for the public during the Hungarian Festival that takes place on Hamilton Street in New Brunswick. Other annual festivals in the county include celebrations of Polish, Italian and Latino cultures and the heritage of the Raritan River. Courtesy, Hungarian American Athletic Club.*

Above: *Under the tutelage of Ms. Chin-Wen Chao, this Chinese folk dance group from Edison has perfected the movements of centuries old, traditional dance, and has performed in concert throughout central New Jersey. Courtesy, Chin-Wen Chao*

Below: *The award-winning American Repertory Ballet is seen here performing the* Rite of Spring, *choreographed by Salvatore Aiello. As performing artists and administrators of the Princeton Ballet School, the organization is a resident company of the New Brunswick Cultural Center. Photo by Eduardo Patino, New York City. Courtesy, American Repertory Ballet 1999-2000 Season*

Facing page: *Recently established in Middlesex County, the Alborada Spanish Dance Theater performs flamenco and classical dances, many of which evidence Romany and Indian influences. The rich and colorful esthetics displayed by this company have made them among the County's most popular professional dance troupes. Photo by Elisabeth Koch. Courtesy, Alborada Spanish Dance Theater*

From 1860 to 1950, Negro League baseball was played throughout New Jersey, including Middlesex County. The players were role models for many young African Americans, and heroes admired by all of society. Among them was John Henry Lloyd, considered one of the best shortstops to ever play the game. He is remembered as a gentle giant by those who nicknamed him "Pop" and for his career that spanned more than a quarter century. Mural of John Henry Lloyd, painted by artist Vern Smith, for the Cornelius Low House exhibition on black baseball. Courtesy, Middlesex County Cultural and Heritage Commission

Left: *Proprietary House in Perth Amboy is the only extant Colonial governor's residence, having been occupied by William Franklin until his arrest by the Continental Army in 1776. Subsequently, the mansion became the headquarters for British General William Howe. In 1809, with the addition of the third floor and south wing, Proprietary House became the Brighton, a resort hotel. It later functioned as a retirement home for Presbyterian ministers and as a rooming house. Owned by the State of New Jersey, part of the property was developed by a private firm and made into commercial, rental offices. The remaining portion, under the Proprietary House Association, has been subject to restoration and will be further restored in the future. Courtesy, Proprietary House Association*

Below: *The doors and portals of Cranbury's historic homes are inviting indeed. This magnificent entryway is at the home of John S. Silvers, who owned the J.S. Silvers Bros. and Co. spice mills. Cranbury residents take great pride in the numerous well-preserved homes on the State and National Registers of Historic Places. Courtesy, Cranbury Historical and Preservation Society*

Above: *Founded in 1970, the University of Medicine and Dentistry of New Jersey, located in Piscataway, was established to consolidate all of New Jersey's public programs in medical and dental education. A second campus is in Newark. Photo by Ralph Genella, North Brunswick*

Right: *St. Peter's University Hospital is a multi-specialized acute care and teaching facility for the University of Medicine and Dentistry of New Jersey/ Robert Wood Johnson Medical School. Its neonatal intensive care unit, as seen here, is the largest such facility in the State of New Jersey, attracting some of the best medical practitioners in the east. Middlesex County has an extensive network of care facilities, among them: JFK Medical Center with 1,200 beds, cancer institute, imaging center and facility specializing in sports medicine; the Raritan Bay Medical Center with complexes in Perth Amboy and Old Bridge; and the Memorial Medical Center in South Amboy with a division for behavioral medicine, providing treatment and counseling for addictions and mental illness. Courtesy, St. Peter's University Hospital.*

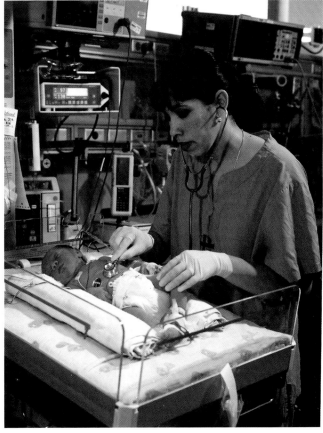

Innovation and artistry combine to create this majestic sculpture. Entitled A Bright Future Through Excellence in Vocational Education, *it was crafted by students in the Production Welding Program. Courtesy, Middlesex County Vocational and Technical High Schools.*

The Barron Arts Center in Woodbridge, formerly the Barron Library, was constructed in 1877. This historic landmark is distinguished by its ornamental cornices, stained-glass windows, delft-tile fireplace, and massive clock tower. The elegant structure was designed by J. Cleveland Cady, architect of the origi-nal Metropolitan Opera House in New York City. The thriving Barron Arts Center offers exhibits of nationally prominent artists, "First Friday" concerts, and a literary series entitled "Poetswednesday." Photo by James Padilla. Courtesy, Woodbridge Township Cultural Arts Commission

The Providence, *a 110-foot replica of a Revolutionary War sloop, was the first ship commanded by John Paul Jones and the first vessel ever commissioned by the Rhode Island Navy. She sailed into Perth Amboy during the summer of 1997 and remained in port for a week, providing workshops for young people during the day and sailing opportunities for adults in the evening. The project was sponsored by the City of Perth Amboy and the Middlesex County Cultural and Heritage Commission. Courtesy, City of Perth Amboy, Office of the Mayor*

CHAPTER SEVEN

MIDDLESEX TO THE MILLENNIUM

Middlesex County is the heart of New Jersey. It pulses with abundant opportunities and continues to beckon people from all over the world. Where 20 years ago, a Metuchen Baptist Church was converted into the first Hindu Temple, today five temples serve residents within a 30 mile radius of New Brunswick. The faces of Middlesex County reflect the global nature of the economy and the area's historical ability to attract new populations. One can shop in an Asian grocery, or in a bodega. Stores offer hand crafted Judaica or antiques from Mongolia and Vietnam. One can taste the foods of Italy, Israel, Portugal and India, or enjoy the cuisines of Mexico, Ethiopia, and Japan. The dress, language, food, music and culture of the world's people comingle here, taking root in the communities and spilling out into the streetscape.

New Brunswick is an excellent example. Walking in its neighborhoods one hears dozens of languages and cultural sounds and is enticed by the fragrance of

Plays-in-the-Park is known throughout the state for its presentation of Joseph and the Amazing Technicolor Dreamcoat, performed each December holiday season at the State Theater in New Brunswick. Plays-in-the-Park performs during the summer months, at the amphitheater in Roosevelt Park, Edison, which has been named in honor of former Freeholder Director, Steven J. Capestro. Courtesy, Middlesex County Department of Parks and Recreation

exotic foods. As the location of the third largest university in the country, New Brunswick has students and faculty from throughout the United States and from the major world centers of learning. And, this is the "health care city," attracting the finest visiting and permanent medical professionals and scientists, who pass on their knowledge in New Brunswick's teaching hospitals and conduct research in the city's technology facilities.

New Brunswick is a cultural hub, having made the extraordinary decision to center massive revitalization efforts around the creation of a cultural district, at a time when others failed to see the economic engine of the arts. Today, the downtown district is anchored by the New Brunswick Cultural Center and the lively restaurant and service trades that have grown up around it.

Middlesex County is in the forefront of change, exhibiting a unique ability to blend the old with the new, to incorporate tradition with high tech innovation. It seeks to institutionalize the factors which build a strong and viable infrastructure, while providing the tools for growth. Yet Middlesex County acknowledges that change must be managed and development must be measured.

The Waterfront

The strength of Middlesex County is found in its willingness to adapt, to embrace new concepts and new populations, to facilitate innovative planning and development, and to do so without neglecting the elements that made the county great. Nowhere is this more evident than in the extensive waterfront development occurring in communities with coastal boundaries. Throughout the county there are visible signs of progress and a renewed vitality.

Perth Amboy
In Perth Amboy, *FOCUS 2000* and a newly-created Perth Amboy Redevelopment

Agency embody this drive toward the future. One of the nation's oldest cities, Perth Amboy was settled more than three centuries ago by persons who were attracted to the prime location of the city. Located along the Raritan Bay and the Arthur Kill waterway Perth Amboy was known as "Portus Optimus" or the greatest port. But as often happened in older cities, the port was allowed to deteriorate. By the mid-1970s, it no longer carried its cognomen with pride. The evolution of the Perth Amboy waterfront, over the last two decades, is therefore extraordinary. Where only remnants of a glorious past could be seen, now exists the heart of a revitalization effort continuing into the 21st century. Perth Amboy once again capitalized upon its proximity to water and its superb location.

The *FOCUS 2000* plan envisions Perth Amboy with

• a world class waterfront, suitable for recreational activities, boutique shopping and fine dining;

• an industrial park with warehouses, distribution centers and high technology

Restoration of the Tottenville Ferry Station was completed in 1998, in part with funds from a federal historic preservation grant. The project will allow the reinstatement of daily ferry service to Staten Island and weekend service to New Jersey shore recreational communities. Courtesy, City of Perth Amboy, Office of the Mayor

facilities, attracting business enterprises to its unparalleled residential amenities such as a performing arts center, cultural museum, retail shopping, sports and recreational activities.

Already the city has built an extensive marina, added decorative landscaping along the water's edge, installed brick walkways along the harbor and added several fishing piers. The armory, once a naval installation, has been transformed into a premiere restaurant and a restaurant cruise ship began operations in 1999.

Perth Amboy was the site of ferry service for nearly 300 years. From the late 1680s to 1953 when a fire destroyed the ferry wait-station, passengers and produce were transported from various locations along the Perth Amboy waterfront to New York City and Staten Island. During the 20th century, the ferry which embarked daily from the city was called the Tottenville Ferry.

It should be noted that early on the city demonstrated its interest in ferry trade. On the fourth day of July 1737, it proclaimed:

. . . that there is a Ferry settled from Amboy over the Staten Island which is duly attended, for the conveniency of those that have occafion to paff and repaff that way. The Ferriage is fourteen pence Jerfey currency, for Man and horfe, and Five pence for a single paffenger.

The music of Mariachi d'Oro greeted participants to El Dia de los Muertos—Day of the Dead—festivities in Perth Amboy. Although primarily a Mexican tradition, similar celebrations are found in other Latin American countries. Courtesy, Middlesex County Cultural and Heritage Commission

Today the city's interest in a viable ferry service has resulted in the restoration of the Tottenville Ferry Slip. Located at the foot of Smith Street, the slip underwent a $1 million restoration in 1998, with funds received from the New Jersey Urban History Initiative of the National Park Service/Department of the Interior. The structure has been restored to its appearance at the turn of the century. Considered to be one of the most identifiable landmarks in the city, the slip will berth a ferry making daily trips to New York City, with excursions on the weekends to the Atlantic Highlands and Atlantic City.

With such magnificent scenery along the water's edge, and renewed shipping and recreational activity on the Raritan Bay, the harbor is attracting residential development, too. The largest of the city's private, housing developments is being built on the waterfront. Harbortown, in the east end of the city at the foot of High Street, is intended to contain 1,654 housing units, once all three construction phases are completed. Harbortown, coupled with the assisted living facilities and the siting of new low-cost housing throughout Perth Amboy proper, will assure an affordable and livable city with a broad-based economy.

Perth Amboy's population is as diverse as its economy. With approximately 50,000 residents, the city is predominantly Latino, representing the cultures of Puerto Rico, Mexico, Dominican Republic, Cuba, Peru, Bolivia, Argentina, and other Latin American countries. These rich communities join the older African American neighborhoods of the city, and the more established ethnic enclaves where families trace their origins to Hungary, Italy, Poland, Germany, Greece, Spain, Portugal, Russia, the Ukraine, Czechoslovakia and other Slavic countries. These populations have maintained their centuries old traditions. They have given rise

El Dia de los Muertos is a period for communication with one's ancestors, and a time when the living welcome the souls of the dead who "return" for a few brief hours to enjoy some of the pleasures they once knew in life. These are spread about an ofrenda, or public offering table that is displayed in a prominent place. In 1998, Day of the Dead commemorations were held in New Brunswick and, as depicted here, in Perth Amboy. Courtesy, Middlesex County Cultural and Heritage Commission

Upon its completion, the Ferry project was celebrated by thousands of people from the City of Perth Amboy. Mayor Joseph Vas was joined by state and federal dignitaries for an outdoor ceremony that was held at the foot of Smith Street, in the shadow of the ferry berth. Courtesy, City of Perth Amboy, Office of the Mayor

Los Pleneros de la 21 performed bomba and plena, music from the coastal regions of Puerto Rico, before an audience of more than 800 people in Perth Amboy. Their name derives from a well-known bus stop in their homeland. Courtesy, Perth Amboy Association of Cultural Arts

to a myriad of ethnic establishments in the downtown business district, a preponderance of ethnic restaurants, and places of worship reflective of the cultural mix.

South Amboy

South Amboy, situated at the juncture of the Raritan River and the Raritan Bay, has great potential for development of water transit, both passenger and commercial. Here city planners are hoping to build a 300 slip marina and restaurant complex that will be in addition to its 11 existing parks. With visions of South Amboy as a transportation center, the city will be accessible by New Jersey Transit Bus service, New Jersey Coast Line trains and a proposed ferry to Staten Island. Easy access to the Garden State Parkway, Routes #9 and #35 encourage the formation of an intermodal hub between New York and Central Jersey.

Today, South Amboy is 1.5-square miles in size with approximately 8,000 residents. In the 1800s, however, it encompassed nearly 60-square miles. Political squabbling, strong local identity and social issues during the late 19th century caused two villages to secede from South Amboy.

Old Bridge/Madison

Madison was the first to separate from South Amboy. In 1869, residents in a 40-square mile section of town, along the southern rim of Middlesex County, rebelled and incorporated as Madison Township. The community proceeded to hum with activity during the late 19th and early 20th centuries, with paper mills, bustling shipyards and pottery manufacturers. Situated over rich deposits of fine clay, Madison's pottery production was highly desirable and easily shipped throughout the country via its proximity to accessible waterways. But, Madison Township was often confused with Madison Borough, which is found in Morris County. The constant confusion precipitated a name change from Madison to Old Bridge Township, in 1975.

Old Bridge is the largest of the county's municipalities, and today is a mix of rural areas and suburban neighborhoods. Cheesequake State Park with more than 1,200 acres is located here, as is the Laurence Harbor beachfront recreational area. Cheesequake offers bird watching, excellent fishing at the Hooks Creek Lake and workshops and lectures in its Nature Center. Old Bridge recently invested $1.8 million in the development of Geick Park off Route #516, upgrading and installing state-of-the-art park facilities that are accessible to persons with disabilities. Most recently, Old Bridge entered into a landmark agreement, leasing 1.3 miles of superb waterfront to the County of Middlesex. Here the County will create a network of bicycle paths and pedestrian walkways.

Famed musician, ethnomusicologist and music historian Mick Moloney is seen on the PBS broadcast "Out of Ireland," where he discusses the societal and cultural context of his beloved Irish music. In 1999, President Bill Clinton conferred upon him the honor of National Heritage Award winner. Mick has also been delighting audiences in Old Bridge Township and Woodbridge with Irish folk and regional songs in a March concert each year. Courtesy, Mick Moloney

Among the most spectacular redevelopment projects is the expansion and upgrade of the Perth Amboy marina. Brick walkways, lighting, benches, fishing piers and gardens have been combined to create an inviting bayside park. Courtesy, City of Perth Amboy, Office of the Mayor

Lastly, County government acquired approximately 1,728 acres of undeveloped property and has designated the area as the John A. Phillips Open Space Preserve. The largest contiguous holding in the County's extensive park system, the area includes 1,051 acres of wetlands, 677 acres of uplands, and incorporates heavily forested parcels that are an extension of the New Jersey Pine Barrens. The preservation of this open tract has far reaching benefits, protecting not only groundwater supplies, but the rare plant and animal specimens within its boundaries, including the Pine Barrens Tree Frog and the Bog Turtle.

The history of Old Bridge and Madison Township are preserved by the Thomas Warne Historical Museum and Library, housed in a building that was once the Cedar Grove School, constructed in 1885.

Sayreville

Sayreville was the second municipality carved from the township of South Amboy. It undertook legal measures to separate in 1876. The borough takes its name from the Sayre and Fisher Brick Works, once a key national supplier of fine quality, clay brick.

The occasion of a new pumper fire truck was celebrated in Sayreville with an open house to the public. Young and old alike found much to explore. Throughout Middlesex County, the station houses of local fire departments serve as centers of the community and often sponsor fairs, pancake breakfasts and special events. Courtesy, Greater Media Newspapers

When the community was founded, it was agricultural and wooded, with its 100 families relying upon the farm market for their livelihood. Today, however, its agricultural base has been overtaken by large scale industrial and residential development. Bounded by the South River, Raritan Bay and Raritan River, Sayreville's present-day infrastructure is commercially driven, with such companies as DuPont, Hercules and other industrial giants calling it home.

Sayreville garnered national attention in 1995 due to a deposit of amber located there. Identified as part of the topographical tract that scientists have named the Sayreville Clay Member of the Raritan Formation, it is one of the oldest amber-bearing regions in the world. Exciting scientists even more than the amber bed was its content—gnat-like insects trapped millions of years ago when the amber was still the sticky sap substance of trees. The bug specimens were ants, in both a primitive and more advanced stages of evolution—three worker ants and four male ants, captured 92 million years ago in the fossilized resin. Since 1991, when the fossil-rich nature of the amber bed first became known, scientists have made extraordinary discoveries. The tract extending from Sayreville into East Brunswick has yielded a 90 million year-old mushroom, a 65 million year-old stingless honey-bee and flower blooms dating back 90 million years. All were the oldest ever found anywhere in the world.

"Succeed in Sayreville," is a phrase repeated often in the neighborhoods and downtown sections of this municipality. Here, in the spring of 1998, the State of New Jersey sanctioned the Sayreville Economic and Re-Development Agency—yet another tool of change. It is charged with the responsibility of attracting new businesses to the area, and to improving the existing conditions for industrial and commercial enterprises.

Recent grants have allowed the commu-

The bucolic setting and sparkling waters of the lake in Kennedy Park in Sayreville present an inviting picture. Courtesy, Greater Media Newspapers

Following the extraordinary success of the Providence, the people of Perth Amboy hosted the H.M.S. Rose in May of 1998. A stunning replica of a ship that served in the French and Indian War and the American Revolution, the Rose has three masts and 17 sails. During her stay in port, public programs and a "classroom under sail" were sponsored by the City, the Perth Amboy Board of Education, the Perth Amboy Public Library, CoreStates Bank and Middlesex County Cultural and Heritage Commission. Courtesy, Middlesex County Cultural and Heritage Commission

nity to build bikeways and paths from Park Village to President Park. A shared effort by the County of Middlesex, the borough of Sayreville and the municipality of South Amboy to redevelop the waterfront has created the Raritan Bay Waterfront Park. The award-winning design of the park is replete with ball fields, a nature preserve, a bandstand and a magnificent view. Selected by the New Jersey Recreation and Park Association, the County of Middlesex was recognized for aesthetics, usability, accessibility and safety. For the 1998 commemoration of the park, a date was selected in August, reminiscent of the August salt hay festivals, held on this very waterfront in the 1800s.

South County

In 1985, Middlesex County was 26 percent agricultural, with extensive farmlands in the southern end of the county. Today that is changing, with ever-encroaching commercial, industrial and residential developments. In an effort to slow the loss of rich and environmentally desirable farm acreage, the Middlesex county Board of Chosen Free-

Visitors to the sloop Providence *were trained by the crew who discussed and demonstrated 18th century seamanship and permitted the public to climb the riggings and hoist the sails. Courtesy, Middlesex County Cultural and Heritage Commission*

holders, in 1985, established the Agricultural Development Board. Their main function is the administration of the Farmland Preservation Program. Based on state-enabling legislation, this initiative provides financial incentives to farmers, to maintain their lands in an inventory of agriculturally designated parcels. At its core, is the "purchase" of an easement by the County of Middlesex, in the form of a deed restriction prohibiting non-farm development. This assures that the acreage will, in perpetuity, remain as open space while allowing the tract to continue as an active farm. Both the landowner and the public clearly benefit from this forward-thinking land use management.

The County and local municipalities partner in cooperative ventures to preserve undeveloped land, as well. Through a voter approved special tax of one cent per $100 of assessed property value, a fund has been created for the sole purpose of acquiring and preserving open spaces called the Middlesex County Open Space Trust Fund Program. Potential acquisitions are determined by a committee of local leaders and professionals.

South Brunswick

South Brunswick benefited from such a purchase in the fall of 1998, when 85 acres of wetlands and woodlands were acquired. Known as Heathcote Brook Park Extension, located off Route #27, the property forms a connector between other park land and conservation areas in the southern portions of the county. This was good news to the residents of South Brunswick, as they celebrated their bicentennial year.

South Brunswick's 200th birthday in 1998 was an opportunity for change, as it adopted a council-manager form of government, whereby the voters elect a mayor of their choosing. Previously, council members selected the mayor from their ranks.

The semi-rural nature of South Brunswick enables the villages that make up the township to retain their ambiance and character. These include Kingston, Rhode Hall and Dayton (formerly Cross Roads), all settlements that grew around tavern stops, and the villages of Kendall Park, Fresh Ponds, Deans and Monmouth Junction.

Kingston, located on the Millstone River, bustled with activity in the 1800s, as its inns and taverns were popular overnight stops for travelers making the land journey between New York and Philadelphia. An oral tradition tells of a single day when the inns and taverns of Kingston served 400 who came on horseback and the passengers from no less than 49 stage coaches.

Dayton is so named in honor of William L. Dayton, a 19th century attorney for the Freehold/Jamesburg Agricultural Railroad,

who is credited with justly settling the bitter disputes that erupted from the location of the railroad right-of-way. He later rose to national prominence and served as a U.S. Senator, vice presidential candidate and Minister to France.

In 1980, South Brunswick had only 18,000 people. By the year 2000, the population is estimated to reach 35,000, an extraordinary rate of growth.

Jamesburg

Within the southern tier of the county is Jamesburg, the "little town that could." Incorporated in 1887, Jamesburg separated from Monroe Township, apparently over a dispute regarding increases to the tax levy, in order to pay for the paving of roads. Among the historic properties in Jamesburg is Lakeview, a 23-room edifice, parts of which were constructed in the 1600s. Built by a Scottish settler, Lakeview was subsequently purchased by James Buckelew. His deeds and influence were recognized by local leaders when the town was ultimately named for him. Lakeview, now called Buckelew Mansion, houses the famed Lincoln Coach that transported Abraham Lincoln on his journey to the New Jersey State House in Trenton, part of the trip to his inaugural ceremonies.

Only nine tenths of a square mile in area, Jamesburg is nearly 90% built, and has just over 5,000 residents. Despite its tiny size, Jamesburg has four parks, with Thompson Park the best known among them. Shared with Monroe Township, but owned and administered by the County of Middlesex, this park preserves wide expanses of naturally wooded lands and is a haven for migratory birds and small woodland creatures. The main street of Jamesburg is called Railroad Avenue. A quaint boulevard, the avenue is divided in half by ground level railroad tracks, used not for passenger service but for multi-car freight trains.

Crossroads Theater on Livingston Avenue in New Brunswick, is the 1999 Tony award winner, as the best regional theater in America. Begun more than 20 years ago under a CETA federal project grant, in part with help from Middlesex County Cultural and Heritage Commission, the theater presents cutting-edge original works, which explore the black experience. A recent production of Blues for an Alabama Sky, *by Pearl Cleage was highly acclaimed, with actors Gwendolyn Mularnba and Scott Whitehurst in lead roles. Photo by Ron Wyatt. Courtesy, Crossroads Theater*

Monroe

In contrast to Jamesburg is Monroe, a township that, as the millennium approaches, encompasses the most undeveloped land anywhere in the county. Originally settled in the 1600s, Monroe and its 43 square miles is rural—corn and vegetable farms, horse breeders, strawberry and pumpkin patches. It is not uncommon to see a road sign cautioning the automobile driver to a crossing for farm machinery.

In recent years the township has swelled to more than 24,000 residents, a modest number of persons but unique nonetheless, as more than half of this population is senior citizens. A trip to the grocer or local bank in Monroe bespeaks of this fact, as commercial establishments have been designed barrier free and offer amenities that accommodate senior populations. Still more unusual to

Although many of the Dutch, English and other European settlers were seeking religious freedom, economic opportunity and political independence, they did not believe the Lenape were entitled to the same. The Lenape tried to live cooperatively but the settlers were intolerant of the Indian way of life and of their values. Ultimately, the Lenape retreated to Oklahoma, Wisconsin and Canada, where many descendants still live. Courtesy, Herbert C. Kraft

New Jersey is that the majority of the seniors reside in one of the six private, residential, gated communities of Monroe Township. A considerable political force, the seniors have fought development proposals which they believed infringed upon the tranquility of Monroe and the surrounding areas.

Plainsboro

Plainsboro is one of the two most southern townships in Middlesex County. Here, important archaeological findings were unearthed in 1982 during a dig conducted in anticipation of highway expansion. The project documented prehistoric habitation as early as 1700 B.C., by an organized society which used knives, hammers, fishing spears and other tools, and who created large, oval, community structures. Recorded history tells us that the area was inhabited by the Unami, a tribe of the Lenape and part of the Delaware Indians. Evidence is insufficient to determine whether the prehistoric archaeological discoveries relate to the forebears of the Lenape. In the 1600s, the English and the Dutch from New Amsterdam began to arrive. The Lenape fell victim to diseases carried by the new settlers and survivors retreated from this region.

Situated on the Millstone River, Plainsboro has some of the most fertile land in the state. For nearly 100 years, it was the home of the Walker-Gordon Laboratory Company, which grew to be the largest, certified dairy in the world, stretching over more than 2,400-acres and supporting a milking heard of 1,650 cows.

The state-owned Carnegie Lake in Plainsboro is manmade, a creation that resulted from the flooding of an area once known as Aqueduct, so named because of the conduit that enabled the Millstone River to flow under the Delaware and Raritan Canal. It also was commonly referred to as Scudders Mills, as this was the site of three active mills, a wheelwright shop, blacksmith shop and general store.

Until 1919, Plainsboro was not an independent township. Rather, the lands north of Plainsboro Road were part of South Brunswick while properties to the south were part of Cranbury Township. A controversy over education encouraged local residents to partition the State of New Jersey for the establishment of their own community. In 1955, the Wicoff House, originally home to John V.V. Wicoff who argued before the state for the formation of Plainsboro, became the headquarters for the Plainsboro Historical Society.

Today Plainsboro is among the more diverse communities in the county and it has built one of the most highly regarded school systems. It has encouraged the growth of both residential neighborhoods and corporate parks that boast some of the most influential corporations in the nation. Sadly, some of the most historic structures have given way for this development.

Cranbury

The second most southern of the 25 municipalities that comprise Middlesex County is Cranbury. Although formally established in 1872, the township traces its origins to the late 1600s. Its downtown, surrounded by stately homes and tilled fields, is old fashioned, with the charm and quiet elegance of a bygone era. Many of Cranbury's architecturally splendid properties were built in the 18th and 19th centuries and today are in a remarkable state of preservation. In 1980 the town of Cranbury had the distinction of being placed on the State and National Registers of Historic Places. Clearly one of the treasures of the county, this community is serious about preservation. Its citizens value history and are committed to the restoration of the community's historic fabric.

The Gristmiller's House, dating to 1860, was acquired by the township for use as the Cranbury Police Station, over 30 years ago. When the squad outgrew the structure, the building was abandoned and fell victim to the elements. The Cranbury Historical and

Preservation Society, in an effort to preserve the property, leased the structure from the township and obtained a grant from the New Jersey Historic Trust in 1993, for its repair and restoration. The work now completed, the Gristmiller's House has been re-dedicated as the Cranbury History Center and is open to the public for research. Additionally, a circa 1834 construction site serves as the Cranbury Museum.

Development, however, is not unknown to the outskirting areas of Cranbury. Equidistant from New York City and Philadelphia, and prime real estate, Cranbury is active in the Farmland Preservation Program of the County of Middlesex, conferring designations of open space to offset the recent spate of development. On the eve of the millennium, Cranbury has formed an Arts Council that is engaging the community in arts, education and cultural pursuits.

Mid County

Helmetta

In 1880, George Washington Helme, a major general in the Confederate army, selected a site for his mill in East Brunswick, and began producing snuff, a tobacco derivative that was very popular among the working and gentry classes in the 19th century. Helme created a "company town." He owned the general store and his company constructed and owned the cottages in which the workers lived. By 1888, doing business and living under the rule of East Brunswick was no longer tolerable to him, so George Helme led a secession effort that separated 1.1 square miles. The new town, for which he took credit, was named Helmetta, combining George's given name and his daughter Antoinette's nickname, "Etta."

By 1915, the population of Helmetta was 663. Of this number, as stated in an industrial directory listing non-English speaking people, 200 were Polish immigrants, 50 were Hungarian, 50 were Jewish, having escaped from a tumultuous Russian homeland and 25 were Italian, all exemplifying the rich cultural diversity of the people of Middlesex County.

In the ensuing years, the Helme Snuff Mill flourished, so much so, that at its peak of production, the mill compound consisted of 117 buildings. Today, the mill and remaining company buildings are recognized for their role during the Industrial Revolution, and have been placed on the State and National Registers of Historic Places.

In 1993, the Snuff Mill closed, a harbinger of changes to come, as Helmetta shifted from a company town to a residential community. Subsequently, the mill was marketed to potential buyers for age-restricted housing,

to be augmented by commercial space. Condominiums and single family homes have been constructed nearby.

Helmetta, with only 1,500 residents, has the distinction of being the smallest municipality, not only in Middlesex County, but in the entire State of New Jersey.

The Jazz Institute of New Jersey was founded by Leslie Ford (seated front) and is dedicated to the promotion of jazz education. Since 1989, the group has been working with young people from ages eight to 18, providing instruction by master musicians and offering performance opportunities for which it has received numerous awards. Most recently, the youth ensemble was honored with a Louis Armstrong Fellowship grant. Courtesy, Jazz Institute of New Jersey

Milltown

The State Department of Environmental Protection (D.E.P.) annually rates places that permit public fishing. By far, the best fishing in Middlesex County, according to D.E.P., is found in the waters of Mill Pond and Farrington Lake (extending also to North Brunswick and East Brunswick). A community small in size—1.6 miles— Milltown's 7,000 residents are large in spirit. In fact, many of the borough's citizens descend from the founding fathers, having chosen to continue a family heritage and tradition of residency in Milltown.

Milltown was originally named Bergen's Mill, after Jacob I. Bergen, who brought commerce to the area by constructing a gristmill. Later, the town became the site of the Meyer Rubber Company, among the first rubber production facilities in America. Meyer Rubber was purchased in the early 1900s by Michelin Tire Company of France, which continued to expand the business and ultimately the town's population. Although Milltown has since lost its industrial base, its hometown quality and viable downtown have not suffered.

Each year the Middlesex County fair attracts crafters and needleworkers who display their talents and handiwork. In 1997, this quilt which was designed by several residents of Milltown, and garnered several blue ribbons for its makers. Courtesy, Greater Media Newspapers

Spotswood

James Johnston arrived in Middlesex County from Spottswoode, Scotland, in 1685. He was pleased to find a bounty of walnuts, peaches and venison, and documented these resources in letters he wrote to those he left behind. His good fortune extended to his relationships with the Lenape, who helped him make his way in his adopted home. Today, the community Johnston founded is called Spotswood. It is located at the juncture of two waterways, Matchaponix Creek and Manalapan Creek, names reminiscent of the indigenous people who once flourished there.

During the Revolutionary War, Spotswood assumed key wartime functions. It produced charcoal for manufacturing and was a center of bog-iron smelting. Tradition holds that notes of the Continental Army were printed on paper milled in Spotswood. It is not surprising, therefore, that Spotswood was the target of British troops, and in particular, Colonel Nelson, who raided the town.

After the War, Spotswood continued to play a significant role in the industrial development of Middlesex County. Snuff producers, iron factories, shoe manufacturing businesses and paper mills contributed to the community's thriving economy. In the early 1900s, Spotswood became a refuge for the wealthy, who arrived to partake of hydrotherapy, exercise and nutritional instruction at a vacation health camp situated on Spotswood Lake. The camp prospered for more than two decades.

For a period, Spotswood was part of Monroe and later part of East Brunswick, until such time as the borough incorporated independently, in 1908. Today, Spotswood residents are concerned with the preservation of their older structures. Interestingly, the borough remains a producer of paper products, with a manufacturing and office facility that employs approximately 500 persons.

The pleasant weather and picturesque scenery are a perfect setting for local anglers who gathered at DeVoe Lake in Spotswood, hoping to catch the "big one." The fishing derby was sponsored by the Spotswood Recreation Department. Courtesy, Greater Media Newspapers

In a 1993 ceremony to dedicate the Veterans Memorial Walkway in Spotswood, Color Guards from the Spotswood American Legion and the Veterans of Foreign Wars fired a volley over the park's reflection pool. Constructed as a permanent reminder of Spotswood's involvement in all conflicts from the Revolutionary War to Desert Storm, the walkway represents the efforts and determination of students from the Spotswood High School History Club, who worked tirelessly on the project. Photo by Frank Yusko. Courtesy, Spotswood High School History Club

The 1999 Raritan River Festival celebrated the rejuvenation of the river and the redesign and redevelopment of Boyd Park where it is held. Festivities included a cardboard canoe race, music under the tent, crafts, food and merriment. Courtesy, City of New Brunswick, Division of Recreation

East Brunswick

One of the county's fastest growing residential communities is East Brunswick, which calls itself the "heart of Middlesex County." English, Scottish, Dutch and German settlers were attracted to the rich farm land and water resources of the South River and Farrington Lake. Today, in such a mobile society, persons are attracted to the township by the stellar school system and its location along a major transportation corridor. The latter has also been a magnet for businesses, suburban shopping districts and—traffic.

East Brunswick is a hybrid, formed in 1860 by combining a portion of Monroe Township with part of North Brunswick. The Weston Mills section is so named because of the active gristmill that once existed here during the 1700s, and which accounted for the financial prosperity of the village. The Old Bridge section of East Brunswick (not to be confused with Old Bridge Township) derives its name from an old bridge that spanned the South River. It has the distinction of being the first, federally designated, historic district in Middlesex County.

One of the oldest Chinese American schools on the East Coast holds classes in the township, teaching young people the language and traditions of their elders. East Brunswick has welcomed emigres from many

parts of the world, as evidenced by the community's diverse religious centers, among them: Chinese-Mission, Korean-Methodist, Mormon, Baptist, Jewish, Catholic, Lutheran, Russian Orthodox, Byzantine Catholic, Presbyterian, Hindu and Unitarian.

Highland Park

Highland Park is similarly a community rich in diversity. It has a thriving central business district, unusual in this day of sprawling malls and mega-stores. Many of the professionals who work at Rutgers, The State University and in the corporate complexes of New Brunswick live here, in this primarily residential community. Highland Park, settled in 1667, was so named because of its location, situated on high ground above the Raritan River and its park-like, wooded appearance.

Highland Park has given rise to five orthodox congregations of Jewish families, among which is the only Sephardic synagogue in the county. Founded in 1926 by a group who emanated from Salonika, Greece, the congregation further welcomed Sephardic emigres from the Balkans, following the collapse of the Ottoman Empire. Highland Park, together with the neighboring southern portion of Edison Township, is completely enclosed by an *Eruv.* Here are located two Yeshiva day schools and a Yeshiva high school. Within the *Eruv,* are a glatt kosher butcher, two kosher bakeries, pizza and Middle Eastern restaurants, a Chinese restaurant, a donut shop, ice cream store and bagel store—all under the supervision of the *Vaad HaRabbanim* of Raritan Valley.

Edison

Edison is a sprawling township with a land mass of more than 30-square miles and a population of 88,680. Edison is among the most dense communities in the county, having sustained the highest growth rate of any town in the state of New Jersey. From 1960 to 1990, the last census, Edison experienced a 97 percent rise in population, while the county grew at only 13 percent and the state at 5 percent. Township officials estimate that at the turn of the new century, the number of residents will equal 95,900, in part from a recent influx of Latino and Chinese Americans. Edison has the highest concentration of Asian Indian residents anywhere in the U.S., and was selected as the site for a spectacular, international Indian festival, one of only three ever held outside the borders of India.

Edison was settled by the English and Dutch, part of a tract deeded by the Dutch King to Augustine Hermanns. Originally under the jurisdictions of Woodbridge and Piscataway Townships, the first families of Edison were the Dunhams, Martins, Bonhams, Hulls and FitzRandolphs, who had received land grants to settle the area. The township was incorporated in 1870, under the name of Raritan Township, but includes several sections or villages.

The earliest known habitation, dating to

the Stone Age, was uncovered through archaeological investigation, in the Piscatawaytown section. Evidence of the Lenape was found in the Dismal Swamp area and most believe that the Bonhamtown region was the site of an old Lenape village. Bonhamtown later served as campground for the Continental Army and as a battleground during the Revolutionary War. This neighborhood's landmark church, St. James Episcopal located on Woodbridge Avenue in Edison, had been pressed into service as a hospital for British troops injured during the skirmishes of the Revolution. However, the edifice now standing was built in the 1830s, after a tornado destroyed the original.

In the 19th century, Thomas Alva Edison selected the Menlo Park section as the home for his laboratories. The township received worldwide recognition when it became the focal point for the most innovative and far reaching technologies man had ever known. Here, in the "invention factory" as Edison called it, his ideas garnered more than 400 patents for the man who came to be known as the "Wizard of Menlo Park." These

The lake at Roosevelt Park in Edison was encircled with 4,500 linear feet of pathways and 500 feet of boardwalk that included handicapped accessible fishing areas. Courtesy, Middlesex County Department of Parks and Recreation

Every year thousands of people from throughout the state travel to the North Brunswick Heritage Days. A unique combination of dance, music, puppetry, song, crafts, games and food, the celebration focuses on the diverse cultures found in central New Jersey. Among the best loved of all the performers are the American Thunderbird Dancers who perform traditional dance. Courtesy, Greater Media Newspapers

North Brunswick

North Brunswick was founded in 1761, when Dutch and French settlers purchased land from the Lenape, who by that time were already retreating further south along the Delaware and to points farther west. North Brunswick's name has always been a conundrum, since its actually south of New Brunswick and west of East Brunswick (although it is north of South Brunswick).

North Brunswick has a population of approximately 33,000, the majority of whom are Italian, Irish or German, although most recently Latino and Asian families have settled here. Vigorous growth has brought mostly economic and land use changes to the area. The New Jersey Economic Development Authority, for instance, constructed a 21st century research laboratory at the Technology Center of New Jersey, a facility designed to foster businesses in the fields of telecommunications, biotechnology and pharmaceuticals.

Two of the oldest, continuously held festivals are in North Brunswick. The first, Festival

inventions included the phonograph, the incandescent bulb and the electric railway. In 1954, Raritan Township changed its name to Edison Township, in honor of the man that altered the course of human history.

Edison Township was home to two military installations: Camp Kilmer and Raritan Arsenal. Today, the Sutton Industrial Campus and the Livingston Campus of Rutgers, The State University are located on the former Camp Kilmer. The Raritan Arsenal similarly found an educational purpose, when part of this massive encampment was reused for the campus of Middlesex County College. The balance of the arsenal property was taken over by Raritan Center, which today is the largest industrial park east of the Mississippi River, with 2,500 acres. Here more than 350 businesses are located. During the workday, the population of Raritan Center equals that of a small city, 45,000 in total, more people than many municipalities in the state.

The smith was an integral part of everyday life in the community, forging tools, hinges and utilitarian objects for households of Raritan Landing. Museum sites such as East Jersey Olde Towne maintain the richness of such practices through hands-on demonstrations. Courtesy, Middlesex County Cultural and Heritage Commission and New Jersey Designer Craftsmen

A cooper's bench and barrels are part of a permanent display featured in the Runyon House at East Jersey Olde Towne Village. Coopers played an important role in Colonial commerce, as barrel makers supplying local vineyards and merchants. Courtesy: Middlesex County Cultural and Heritage Commission.

Italiano, reflects the large, ethnic enclave of Italian Americans residing in this community. The second is North Brunswick Heritage Days which celebrates the diversity of central New Jersey.

Metuchen

Metuchen was first settled in the 1680s, named for Delaware Chief, Matouchin. By 1701, sufficient numbers of homes and businesses existed that an overseer of roads was appointed for the district, which was called Metuching, by the end of the 18th century. The borough was officially incorporated in 1900 with the name now used.

Metuchen has been known as the "brainy borough" since the early part of this century when university professors, members of the financial community and the literati, who worked in New York and New Brunswick, selected this locale in which to live and raise their children. Feminist leader Hester M. Poole and author Mary Wilkins Freeman resided in Metuchen. Henry James Alden, a direct descendent of John Alden and the

editor of *Harper's Magazine* lived here and entertained such prominent figures as Mark Twain and poet Joyce Kilmer.

Where other localities have changed dramatically, Metuchen has remained fairly stable. It has avoided industrial development, instead nurturing small and family-owned businesses. With a hometown atmosphere, Metuchen is known for its excellent neighborhood schools, local galleries and regional theater, and for a viable downtown that attracts shoppers from outside the borough.

Piscataway

The families which founded Piscataway in 1666 once lived along the Piscataqua River in New Hampshire. It is believed they conferred the present name in honor of their New England homeland. The township is comprised of small villages and neighborhoods, such as New Market, Possumtown (so named because of the opossums once common here) and Quibbletown, with the areas of North Stelton, Randolphville, Fieldville and New Durham named after local prominent families.

In 1912, followers of the Spanish martyr and anarchist Francisco Ferrer, exploring the concept of experimental living, established the Fellowship Farm Cooperative. Intended as a utopian community, members supported themselves through truck and poultry farming and espoused socialist and Marxist philosophies of life. The Cooperative lasted until the mid-1940s when World War II discouraged such undertakings.

At the time the Cooperative was failing, the U.S. government acquired an enormous tract of land in Piscataway for U.S. Army Camp Kilmer and used it as an embarkation point for troops going overseas (portions also extended into Edison Township). It remained as federal land until 1963. Rutgers, The State University established college campuses in Piscataway—Bush and Livingston—as did the University of Medicine and Dentistry of New Jersey.

The County of Middlesex/Cultural and Heritage Commission owns one of the most important historic sites in the state, the Cornelius Low House, located high on the River Road bluff in Piscataway. Developed as the Middlesex County Museum, it has received coveted state and national honors for its educational programs. In 1997, a restoration of this circa 1741 manor house was completed, at a cost of $1 million, funded in part by the New Jersey Historic Trust.

On the river, lowland side of River Road, is East Jersey Olde Towne. Begun in 1971 by Dr. Joseph Kler and a group of volunteers, the site includes 12 structures from the 18th and 19th century, that have been relocated, reconstructed or replicated here. Middlesex

County/Cultural and Heritage Commission acquired the Village in 1980, in order to stabilize the site and create an interpretive museum. To that end, the Commission completed a 1.2 million restoration in 1997, and offers exhibits, programs and storytelling on a year-round basis.

Skirting the Raritan River is Johnson Park, one of the largest county-owned parklands. Portions sit atop the Raritan Landing archaeological site, a treasure trove of colonial and early 19th century history, that has been mapped by ground-penetrating radar but remains primarily unexcavated.

Today, Piscataway is highly diverse; 17 percent of its population is African American, with some families tracing their history over 150 years; 15 percent of the residents are Asian Indian and 5 percent are Latino.

North County
South Plainfield
Despite its name, South Plainfield is in the northern end of the county. Found here are:

Monument Square is a popular gathering place for visitors and residents of New Brunswick. Here one will find four-star restaurants, concerts and special events by the cool spray of the fountains. In December, the monument area boasts the City's holiday tree lighting and Dickens display. Courtesy, New Brunswick City Market

In May a celebration of the City of New Brunswick is sponsored by the special improvement district known as City Market. With the support and effort of the staff, local merchants and businesses, the event brings hundreds of people into the downtown area to enjoy food, music and the ambiance of the city. Courtesy, New Brunswick City Market

Spring Lake Park, a superior location for fishing and outdoor activity; the Highland Avenue Woods Environmental Education Preserve; and Dismal Swamp. New Jersey's Watchable Wildlife Program, a project of the New Jersey Division of Fish, Game and Wildlife, has cited the South Plainfield nature preserve as one of the best locations for bird watching and viewing of wildlife. It is not uncommon to see cardinals, finches and bluejays along with migratory birds such as catbirds, downy woodpeckers, sharp-shinned hawks, ruby-crowned kinglets and cedar waxwings.

Dunellen, Cartaret, Middlesex Boro

The northern section of the county also includes Dunellen, Carteret and Middlesex Borough. Although once home to a tannery, dye factory, curtain manufacturer and brick-yards, Dunellen is a residential borough of only one square mile. Little has changed in the last 100 years. Instead, many homes along its wide boulevards date from the late 19th and early 20th century, and display Victorian architecture and charming wrap-around porches.

Carteret is industrial, and has been for nearly 200 years. Manufacturing giants have at times been part of the landscape: Chrome Steel, Bethlehem Steel, and the Williams Company, which erected the world's largest mahogany saw and veneer mill. Today, Carteret supports enterprises such as metal refining, trucking, fish processing, chemical distribution and petroleum-based companies, attracted by the proximity to major waterways and overland transportation.

Middlesex Borough, nestled in the northern portion of the county, is bordered by Union and Somerset counties. Once known for its extensive greenhouses and the cultivation of flowers, it is struggling against encroachment from industrial development and the effects from loss of open space.

183

Woodbridge

Woodbridge, at the northern tip of the county, is the fifth largest municipality in New Jersey, with a population nearing 100,000. Chartered in 1669, it is the oldest original township in the state. James Parker established the first permanent printing press in the Colonies here, and the first anti-slavery meeting was held, seven years after the Declaration of Independence. In the late 1880s, Woodbridge was known for its production of fire brick, that at its zenith fabricated more than 80 million bricks annually.

Comprised of 10 communities with decidedly distinctive characteristics, Woodbridge is 26-square miles in area. By the 1990 census, Woodbridge was larger in population than either Trenton or Elizabeth. It encompasses 42 major and vest pocket parks and has 24 public schools under the jurisdiction of its board of education. Woodbridge is the only township in the county that finances and provides fulltime staff for a cultural

Woodbridge Township residents enjoy the programs, exhibits, concerts and poetry readings offered at the Barron Arts Center on Rahway Avenue. Administered by the township and the Woodbridge Cultural Arts Commission, the Center recently presented Alan Brown, an outstanding printmaker, who conducted a workshop for the public. Photo by Susan J. Meyer. Courtesy, Woodbridge Township Cultural Arts Commission

facility—the Barron Arts Center, located in a Romanesque Revival stone structure that has been accepted for the State and National Registers of Historic Places.

Once a much larger township, Woodbridge thrice gave up portions of its land mass: in the formation of Edison Township, in 1860 by act of the State Legislature which transferred the Lower Rahway and Rahway sections to Union County, and at the creation in 1906 of the Borough of Roosevelt, now known as Carteret. The communities that remained and collectively form the township are: Colonia, Avenel, Fords, Hopelawn, Iselin, Keasby, Menlo Park Terrace, Port Reading, Sewaren and Woodbridge proper.

Woodbridge has announced major plans to revitalize its Sewaren waterfront. Park development and recreational facilities are anticipated, revitalizing a once-proud heritage when the Sewaren peninsula was a fashionable, resort community. Sewaren lies across the Arthur Kill waterway from the City of New York. Alleging that waste from a New York landfill was escaping, floating across the Arthur Kill, and washing ashore at Sewaren, the township and the city have had a contentious relationship.

Conclusion

Middlesex County, in 1999, is 11 percent park, wetlands and forested lands. Yet it ranks number one in the state in the establishment of new capital ventures. It is second in retail sales and in the volume of housing units. As the county enters into the 21st century, it supports 24 public libraries and over 250 places of worship. Twenty-two thousand acres of land are devoted to agribusiness, to producing fruits and vegetables for sale at roadside farmers' markets, and to hay, soybean, wheat and nursery stock grown for wholesale distribution.

Following in the footsteps of Thomas Alva Edison, the major research facilities in Middlesex County are considered to be on

No city or municipality in Middlesex County has undergone more change in the last 15 years than New Brunswick.

Top: *Nine Livingston Avenue was known for years as the New Brunswick Y, complete with swimming pool, lockers and a gymnasium. When it had outlived its usefulness, the Y was not torn down, but rather the subject of a massive adaptive reuse project.*

Bottom: *The structure seen above has been given a new purpose and today functions as the George Street Playhouse. Here it is not uncommon to attend national or New Jersey premieres of outstanding works, such as Collected Stories by David Margulies, with Uta Hagen (tight) as an author named Ruth and Lorca Simon (left) playing her protege Lisa. Photo by Miguel Pagliere. Courtesy, George Street Playhouse*

the cutting-edge. Spearheading research related to fisheries and aquaculture for the State of New Jersey, scientists at Rutgers, The State University are attempting to identify and isolate organisms with disease-fighting properties, and thus improve marine and fishery development.

Research efforts are a logical outgrowth of the extensive university and educational systems that have been created within the county borders. Rutgers, The State University which grew from humble beginnings in 1766, today encompasses 11 undergraduate colleges and nine graduate colleges on the New Brunswick/Piscataway campuses. In total, there are 175 public schools in Middlesex, 5 vocational schools and in the fall of 1999, a new Arts High School of the Performing Arts situated within the East Brunswick Vocational Technical School Campus. Middlesex County College offers more diverse and unique programs—over 550 degree courses and more than 300 non-credit courses-than any other county college in the state. Situated on 220 acres in Edison Township, it has expanded to include outreach centers in New Brunswick and Perth Amboy. Robert Wood Johnson Medical School and the University of Medicine and Dentistry of New Jersey, graduate more than 600 top-level students each year and have twice the national average of under-represented minorities admitted to their programs.

Middlesex County is recognized as a cultural hub. It is considered the nation's center of pharmaceutical research and a region where medical advancements and outstanding facilities provide excellent health care.

The chambers of commerce in Middlesex County project more than 35,000 more jobs in the fields of health and business, by the year 2005. Careful planning, visionary management and good government will assure that the county sustains this rate of expansion while retaining its dignity, character and diversity in the new millennium.

At the time of this 1896 photo, the population of New Brunswick was 5,000 and the well-to-do lived on Burnet Street and on nearby Albany Street. Trade along the main avenue was largely wholesale, with dry goods being sold on the section of Burnet Street below Hiram. As many as forty to fifty wagons of grain arrived in New Brunswick daily to be shipped to New York. Courtesy, Special Collections and Archives, Rutgers University Libraries

CHAPTER EIGHT

CHRONICLES OF LEADERSHIP

Middlesex County businesses are as interconnected and interdependent as pieces in a puzzle. Major corporations provide the foundation. Service industries respond to the needs of large corporations and their employees. Encouraged by the healthy economic climate, new businesses enter the county while existing ones expand their operations. The area's outstanding educational, health care, and recreational facilities add to its desirability for commercial and residential real estate development.

Middlesex County has evolved from a stopping place for stagecoach travelers between Philadelphia and New York to the distribution crossroads of the Northeast, offering access to major traffic arteries, an extensive freight network, and deep-water shipping facilities.

The area's importance as a distribution center dates back to the opening of the Raritan Canal in 1834 and the railway system that eventually replaced it. The county's consistent population growth and economic development continue to create a need for warehouse-distribution facilities to accommodate both the consumer and commercial marketplace.

Although the "Sunbelt of New Jersey" is the state's leader in industrial growth, service businesses such as data processing are emerging in importance. Reflecting this trend are the new data-processing businesses sprouting up along the Route 1 corridor, forming one of New Jersey's greatest volume areas of high-technology employment.

These rapidly developing service businesses have fueled one of the largest commercial and office building booms in central New Jersey. Newly constructed office buildings and corporate parks along major highways throughout the county have created thousands of new jobs.

Corporate giants have made Middlesex County a leader in research and development. The spirit of that leadership is rooted in achievements such as Thomas Edison's invention of the first incandescent light bulb in 1879 and Nobel prize winner Selman A. Waksman's discovery of streptomycin at Rutgers.

The county's overall business outlook is one of continued growth and diversity in manufacturing, wholesale and retail trade, government, and services. Middlesex County, and New Brunswick in particular, are blossoming after having weathered the difficult years of the 1960s and 1970s. The faith and commitment of the business community—major corporations such as Johnson & Johnson, second- and third-generation family businesses, young entrepreneurs—has made the revitalization of New Brunswick a reality.

The organizations whose stories are detailed on the following pages have chosen to support this important literary and civic project. They illustrate the variety of ways in which individuals and their businesses have contributed to the area's growth and development. The civic involvement of Middlesex County's businesses, institutions of learning, and local government, in cooperation with its citizens, has made the area an excellent place to live and work.

ALPINE AROMATICS INTERNATIONAL INC.

In 1956, Raoul Pantaleoni established Alpine Aromatics in the small borough of Metuchen, NJ. Occupying an abandoned old firehouse with a partner and a secretary, he decided to devote his time and talent to making the world smell better. He was born in Italy's Appenine mountains into a family that traced its lineage far enough to include nobility and Pope Urban VI. He came to the United States with his parents during World War II and stayed. After receiving a B.S. in Chemical Engineering from the City College of New York, he eventually headed the aromatic laboratories of DuPont. He sharpened his skills

Home of the original Eagle Hook and Ladder Company of the Metuchen fire department—the building was occupied by Alpine Aromatics thereafter in May, 1956, known as 398 Main Street, Metuchen, NJ.

at two more companies before starting out on his own.

At first, the odors emanating from Alpine's building competed with those from a neighboring Chinese restaurant, and the rapidly-expanding business soon outgrew the space. Alpine Aromatics moved to the Edison Industrial Center where it became a strong influence in the fragrance industry. Milestones included the masking of strong odors in the Raritan River with fragrances developed at Alpine, as well as the production of the fragrances for the movie *Scent of Mystery*. The film, produced by Michael Todd, Jr. "in glorious SMELL-O-VISION" in 1959, was made less than four years after the company was established.

This endeavor involved the creation and production of over 14 fragrances and aromas including the: "happy odor of baking bread," "nicotinous smoky character of pipe tobacco," "strong, juicy greenness of clover and grass," "a strong perfume (cheap!)," and a "final, wonderful and beautiful fragrance of Scent of Mystery." Alpine especially created the uncommon odors synchronized with the movie so that certain odors were wafted into the theater at the moment specific objects or scenes appeared on the screen.

Alpine Aromatics continued to grow, supplying fragrances for cleaning materials such as soaps, detergents and industrial cleaners, as well as

Alpine Aromatics founder, Raoul Pantaleoni.

for personal care products including creams, lotions, shampoos, and fine perfumes and colognes. Its clients included Dorothy Gray, Lever Brothers, and S.C. Johnson. During this time the already national company expanded its reach outside the borders of the United States to eventually establish contacts in over 110 countries. Alpine's international scope also applies to its workforce, with many members—from production to creation to administration—either foreign-born or at least bilingual.

But, on September 11, 1978, tragedy enveloped the company and its family. A deranged former employee returned and shot to death Raoul Pantaleoni and two production foremen before turning the gun on himself. This event shook everyone in the community where the Pantaleoni's were a well-loved and respected family, much involved in civic and charitable endeavors. He was mourned deeply.

To many enterprises, this would have been a terminal event.

However, through the strength of Raoul's wife Heath Evans Pantaleoni and the bonds among the extended family of Alpine's employees, the business managed not only to survive, but to grow. After an interval of about two years, John Yorey assumed the presidency of Alpine Aromatics International. Building on his experience in heading sales at Alpine and the company's growing reputation in the industry, he soon expanded its customer base and volume of products and moved Alpine to new, greatly-expanded quarters in Piscataway, NJ. In the process, the company became the largest supplier of candle fragrances.

Throughout Alpine's history, family, leadership, and community were extremely important. Raoul Pantaleoni's daughters Flavia Blechinger and Nina Weil assumed chairmanship of the company's board of directors after their mother's passing. Many of the employees' sons and daughters began their careers at Alpine. Many of the marriages and births are celebrated company-wide, and no event goes unnoticed. Alpine has been held by the same family for three generations.

President John Yorey.

Starting with Raoul Pantaleoni, many of the company's perfumers became president of the American Society of Perfumers, some after they had been trained at Alpine and had moved on to other endeavors. Leadership is also encouraged in community affairs, where positions on school boards, on the boards of Muhlenberg and JFK hospitals, and the Piscataway Chamber of Commerce are held by persons associated with Alpine. In addition, Alpine supports numerous activities for children and the elderly, such as local high school activities, Little League teams,

health centers and support groups for women and veterans.

One of the most gratifying social projects in which Alpine Aromatics is involved is the New Jersey Sanitary Supply Association's Operation Clean Sweep. Starting in 1993 as a purely regional effort, this industry group organized its membership to assist non-profit, charitable community organizations in maintaining their facilities in a clean and sanitary manner. It involves cleaning the facility top to bottom with donated supplies and its members' labor, all in one day. Targets of the efforts included a homeless shelter, a child care center, an orphanage and a soup kitchen. This operation was copied by other national associations, and went international in 1997.

All of this, as well as Alpine's credo of providing quality fragrances and conscientious customer service, have made the company what it is today and what it hopes to continue to be in the future.

Alpine Aromatics International's present headquarters.

AMERCHOL CORP.

Amerchol was founded as American Cholesterol Products by Lester I. Conrad, in concert with his uncles, George and Julius Garfield, in 1938. He began operations in Milltown, NJ, trying to extract cholesterol from lanolin for use in cosmetics. He was never really successful in finding a process for this extraction, but did succeed in fractionating lanolin into its alcohol and fatty acid components and forming derivatives of these fractions, as well as whole lanolin.

The business grew, and in 1956 the American Cholesterol staff consisted of 11 people, and the number of products and sales increased to a point where the Milltown building was no longer adequate for the company's needs. Construction was started on a new building and the company moved to its present location at 136 Talmadge Road in Edison, in 1957. American Cholesterol Products, now well-established in the United States, began worldwide export operations. Due to the greatly increased demand for its products, Amerchol was rapidly outgrowing its new manufacturing and office facilities. Construction began to expand the Edison location in 1964; the expanded facilities were completed and became operational in 1966, with two buildings side by side at the Edison site.

Up to this point, Amerchol's ethoxylated lanolin derivatives had been ethoxylated by outside manufacturers. The increased sales volume and the company's wish to have greater control over the manufacture of these products necessitated the construction of its own ethoxylation facility at Edison. The alkoxylation plant, also on the Talmadge Road site, was completed and became operational in

Lester Conrad.

1968. The plant was now recognized as a model facility.

The business remained owned and operated by the family until 1970, when it merged with CPC International, Inc. and became a unit of its Industrial Division. The company name changed to Amerchol, a trademark of one of the lanolin derivative product lines. At this point there were approximately 100 employees.

In 1974, continuing its program for product line diversification, Amerchol executed extensive research on the manufacture of glucose derivatives for use as cosmetic ingredients. New products based on this research were introduced to the market in the mid-1970s. Sales growth in Europe for the lanolin-based products spurred on new construction. A European manufacturing facility located in Vilvoorde, Belgium, near Brussels, was completed and dedicated as Amerchol Europe in 1976.

In 1977, American Cholesterol Products' founder Lester Conrad retired, and was honored

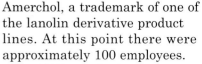

Quality Control at Amerchol.

with the title of President Emeritus. Amerchol was incorporated and became a subsidiary of CPC International, Inc. Under CPC, Amerchol Corporation continued to develop the glucoside derivative product line using the strength of CPC's glucose chemistry.

In 1980, Amerchol acquired the Robinson Wagner Company, operating out of Mamaroneck, New York. The acquisition, named Amerchol Manufacturing, Inc., a subsidiary of Amerchol Corporation, was made to enhance the product portfolio with some additional lanolin derivatives and basic purified lanolin, as well as some esters and emulsifiers. It also gave Amerchol the technology for another fractionation of lanolin, i.e., lanolin oil and lanolin wax.

1980 also marked a tragic event. Lester Conrad was lost at sea while enroute in his yacht from the Bahamas to Florida.

Amerchol Edison facility.

Despite an extensive search by the Coast Guard, no trace of Lester *or* his boat was ever found. Several awards have been created in his memory by the International Federation of Cosmetic Chemists and member countries, in recognition of Mr. Conrad's international contributions to cosmetic science.

In 1986, the Union Carbide Corporation acquired the Amerchol Corporation. Under Union Carbide, Amerchol has diversified its product portfolio again to now include a wide range of water-soluble polymers and resins as well as hyaluronic acid and alkoxylated butyl ethers. The business brings skin care and hair care products to the personal care market as raw materials. Amerchol supplies more than 100 specialty ingredients to manufacturers of hair and skin care products that are sold worldwide. In fact, when you take a bath or shower, or apply make-up, there is a good chance a product sold by Amerchol and produced at its Edison facility may have been involved.

Amerchol is now a worldwide organization with more than 150 employees and manufacturing plants in the U.S., Europe and China. More than 90 Amerchol employees work in Edison, and many either live in the Edison area or have family nearby. Amerchol's top priority is to have a safe operation for its people, community and environment. Amerchol works closely with the Edison Fire Department, the Middlesex Local Emergency Planning Committee, and the State Department of Environmental Protection and is committed to the safe, reliable operation of its facility.

Today, Amerchol is a worldwide supermarketer of performance chemicals to the personal care industry, and is recognized as a leader in product innovation, manufacturing quality, sales and customer service. Its worldwide marketplace includes North America, Europe, Asia, Australia and South America, and proudly calls as its clients some of the finest companies in the world, including Procter & Gamble, Revlon, Estee Lauder, Clairol, L'Oreal, Shiseido, Wella and Unilever, to name a few. Amerchol now has four manufacturing locations, in Edison, NJ; Greensburg, Louisiana; Vilvoorde, Belgium; and Xiaolan, China. In addition, it utilizes the corporate research facilities of Union Carbide, Amerchol's parent company.

Amerchol has been in business for over 60 years, more than 50 of which have been spent at its Edison facility. Its founder, Lester Conrad, was an entrepreneur who saw a future in supplying specialty ingredients for use in the personal care market. His original vision is still alive within Amerchol today.

BESSEMER TRUST COMPANY

Bessemer Trust Company was founded in 1907 by Henry Phipps, a partner of Andrew Carnegie in the Carnegie Steel Company. Bessemer Trust Company was originally located in Jersey City, later Newark, and since 1986 in Woodbridge, is part of The Bessemer Group, Incorporated, a bank holding company (also located in Woodbridge). The Company provides investment, trust, and other financial services to high net worth individuals and families and select institutions.

Founded originally to serve as trustee of trusts for Mr. Phipps' five children and to serve as their "family office," Bessemer continues to be privately owned by the descendants of Henry Phipps. However, since it began to take on non-shareholder clients in the mid-1970s, The Bessemer Group's assets under supervision have grown to in excess of $25 billion and it now serves approximately 1,000 clients. Offices of the various subsidiary trust companies include New York; Washington, D.C.; Palm Beach; Miami; Naples; Chicago; Los Angeles; San Francisco; Atlanta; London; and the Cayman Islands. Bessemer's clients include over 75 current or retired chief executive officers of Fortune 1,000 companies, the retired heads of several top-tier investment banking firms, athletes, and entertainers. Increasingly, its client base includes first-generation wealth created in recent years in such areas as technology, healthcare, entertainment, and the media.

Several factors distinguish Bessemer from its competitors:
• Bessemer has achieved consistently superior investment results over a 20-year period in U.S. equities, fixed income, and balanced portfolios.
• Bessemer offers a unique

Henry Phipps

combination of investment management and financial and fiduciary services—including tax and financial planning, executor and trustee services, and personal banking—not readily available at other financial institutions.
• Bessemer is engaged exclusively in the investment and trust business, so is able to commit all of its resources toward success in this area.
• Bessemer develops innovative tax, estate and investment solutions addressing the complexities associated with the ownership

Offices of Bessemer Trust company in Woodbridge, NJ.

of significant assets.

• Each client's account is managed by a senior officer who is thoroughly familiar with all aspects of the client's situation and relationship with the firm.

• Bessemer's staff-to-client ratio (370 personnel/1,081 clients) is one of the highest in the industry, enabling it to provide services on a highly personalized basis.

• All Bessemer clients, as well as its shareholder clients and employees, share in the investment results Bessemer achieves.

• Bessemer's 92-year history of private ownership has given it a unique level of organizational stability.

Bessemer investment management starts and ends with each client's individual investment objectives. First, it helps each client define and clarify his or her objectives. Then, it works toward meeting these objectives with innovative strategies across a broad range of investment classes – including domestic and international equities, fixed income and private investments.

Four factors are key to Bessemer's investment philosophy:

• We believe it is possible to achieve consistently superior investment returns through all market environments if a disciplined and opportunistic style of investing is coupled with a global perspective.

• Our emphasis is on real, after-tax total return over the long-term. Accordingly, we are biased towards investments expected to achieve long-term capital appreciation.

• The most important investment decision is *how* a client's assets should be allocated among different asset classes.

• Once the allocation decision has been made, rigorous fundamental analysis is the key to individual stock selection.

Bessemer Trust Company has served New Jersey clients for 92 years and is committed to continuing that tradition into the next century. As New Jersey in general, and Middlesex County specifically, are expected to experience excellent growth and be home to a large number of high net worth individuals and families, Bessemer will maintain its substantial commitment to this area.

EXPRESSWAY USA FREIGHTLINES, INC.

It seemed almost like a dream come true as Steve Fleischer ran his hand over the bright new shiny fender of the Peterbuilt truck. Well, it wasn't exactly new, but it was new to him. Driving a truck must have been in his blood. After all, his maternal grandfather had delighted him with stories of his father's prowess with a truck, hauling sugar from the southern states to northern vantages. It was those wonderful stories, coupled with the hit TV program *BJ & The Bear:* a story about a young truck driver taking in the adventures of the highways of America, that prompted Steve to talk a longtime close friend into purchasing a truck with him. The life of long haul trucking seemed to be an adventurous one, an exciting one where he would be able to meet new people and experience new places.

It was a very different lifestyle than he had been used to growing up on Queens and Long Island

Our new, modern office facility.

There is 24-hour security for the large truck yard.

with his parents and his younger brother Phil. He had pursued various crafts from jewelry salesman to electrician, but none sparked his interest as much as trucking did. With the purchase of the truck and the acquisition of a partner, he enjoyed the long distances that he traveled, taking in the scenery as well as all the new experiences presented to him. Alas, it was not meant to be a

long partnership. He had found an ad that promised contract trucking and suggested his partner check out that employment possibility while he made a road trip. In his absence, his partner took the position for himself, and offered to buy Steve out. Steve bade farewell to both the truck and the partner, and headed out on his own.

Using a loan from his parents, he purchased his own truck and managed to stay on the road for about a year and a half. On one particularly cold winter night near the Canadian border he began to realize that his home life meant more to him than the adventure of the open road. He finished his run, turned the truck around, and went back to Long Island. It was relatively easy finding jobs running the long hauls, but staying in local territory was quite a different matter. He knew he needed his own accounts if he were to stay in business for himself. He set up an office in his parent's home, and had brochures printed. He continued to drive the truck, but knew

he wouldn't be able to do that and sell his business, too, for very long. He hired a local man to drive his truck while he began his career as a salesman. He had his mother painstakingly go through the phone book page by page, sending brochures to any business she thought might use his trucking services.

In the meantime, Phil had begun his own vending machine business and used a local merchant as his supplier. It dawned on Steve that somebody was trucking that soda to the supplier, so, why couldn't it be him?

Unlimited warehousing capabilities and the latest equipment, provides a full range of comprehensive import/export services.

The soda account became his first steady customer. At around the same time, one of his mother's mailings got into the hands of the traffic manager of a prestigious customhouse brokerage. Steve was asked to attend a meeting to discuss future business ventures. This same brokerage remains one of their clients to this day. Little by little, business began to pick up, and Phil became more and more interested in the business, as he occasionally lent a helping hand. After Phil passed his CDL test, Steve bought another truck and Phil took on a run that kept him moving from NY to Florida. He, too, became enamored with the industry and the thrill of the open road.

Two trucks parked on a Long Island street became a hindrance. Tickets became an everyday occurrence, and something had to be done. A small office was found in Maspeth, Queens with a very restricted yard. They made do in this tiny space for about a year, but they all knew it couldn't last as the rate of business grew. They became acutely aware of their need for some type of warehouse space, if only for short-term storage purposes. Steve began to search in New Jersey for something that was closer to the piers, with a small warehouse. He found such a place in Jersey City. Phil had long since come into the office and had become the company's dispatcher. Steve still managed to do all the

Company truck leaving the rail-side-equipped facility.

been flourishing, but not enough to fill the warehouse. They began looking into the possibility of bidding for a position as a container freight station. There were not many at the time, only five or six, and since they alone were located in the Perth Amboy district, they qualified for Customs on premises. They searched for the right personnel. As this was new territory for the company, they needed people knowledgeable enough to handle the intricate paperwork necessary to comply with all of Custom's rules and regulations. They worked diligently, always learning something new and always trying to improve their line of services. They now had long-term storage, along with segregation, distribution and across-dock services. They were awarded their first container freight station/Custom exam site contract in February 1989. They had finally realized one of their dreams. Customs on the premises held much prestige, and finally the ability to strip containers, which had been

Partial view of experienced workforce.

outside sales, as well as the day-to-day business at the office. Their mother accompanied them to their new location several times a week, but new office personnel was hired along with a full-time warehouse man.

In time, Phil became more of the in-house salesman and soon a new dispatcher was hired as Phil took over more of the day-to-day duties and Steve spent more time on outside sales. They began to compliment each other as a team; whereas one was aggressive, the other tended to be more conservative. It was the perfect business duo, with each working off the other. Steve was always dressed in a suit, organized and always businesslike to perfection. Phil dressed casually, employed his own work methods, and exercised a more easygoing profile. They were the consummate pair. They both met and married their spouses while in the Jersey City location. Steve was married to Karin in 1986, and Phil was married to Nora in 1988. As business picked

up, additional drivers, equipment and office personnel were added. In 1987, it became apparent that the Jersey City locale had become too small for their operation and Steve started looking for something larger. Their warehouse business had grown them right out of Jersey City and into Port Reading.

It was there that they segregated the two businesses. Their warehousing business had indeed

Partial view of their large, dependable fleet of company-owned, serviced trucks and trailers.

prohibited by the 50-mile rule for so long, was allowed.

With the additional and different capabilities afforded by becoming a container freight station and Custom exam site, new accounts had to be found. Steve and Phil spent long hours on the phone and visiting prospective clients. As the two brothers complimented each other, so did the two businesses. The increased warehousing enterprise required appended trucking services. Yet more additional trucks and equipment were added to the Expressway fleet. Three children were born to the brothers during their Port Reading stay, a son named Dustin and a daughter named Meaghan to Phil, and a daughter, Alexis Karin, to Steve.

Again it was time for a move to a bigger facility. In 1995 they found their new location in Carteret. It was almost 200,000 square-feet, with office space and a huge yard to hold all the equipment and containers. Although they had increased the number of services offered in Port Reading, they were finally ready to 'pull out

all stops' as they settled into the bigger facility. Exporting had always figured in their operation, but now with a larger location that business could be generously augmented. Pick and pack and distribution services grew along with the increased space. Needless to say, the trucking business grew right along with the warehousing trade. A son, Chad Joseph, was born to Steve in 1997.

Today, Lin Warehouse offers a complete array of services. They are a bonded warehouse, still with Customs on premises, and they provide long and short term storage, export containerization, and an entire line of computerized pick and pack and distribution services. Their original trucking dream has become a reality, as well. They offer import and export bonded trucking services with 48-state authority. Over-dimensional size loads, loose freight, full containers and distribution services can all be provided. During a typical day, it is not unusual for hundreds of pieces of equipment to be routed through the dispatch office.

With the onslaught of the computer, the future is surely bright with prospective new projects. Steve is working diligently toward completing a new Expressway USA web site. Phil still continues his in-house sales and manages general operations. To sum up, they are most proud of their ability to survive in an industry that has seen so many businesses fail, including some quite large and prestigious. It is important to them to treat their personnel with as much respect and professionalism as they treat their clients. They truly personify their company slogan, "The Company You Can Depend On— Service You Can Trust." They trusted their dreams, and most of them have come true.

We would like to thank Carol Kelly, our long-term committed employee for her contribution in writing this story.

AMERISOURCE

AmeriSOURCE is a prime example of the kind of entrepreneurial effort that led to Middlesex County's economic renaissance in the last decade of the 20th century. Silicon Valley (CA), Technology Highway (MA) and the Research Triangle Park (NC) might flaunt their I.T. manufacturing muscle, but no place on earth can boast such a rich accumulation of I.T. consulting talent packed tightly into such a limited geographical area as Middlesex County. Dubbed by *The Star Ledger* as the "Guru Corridor," Middlesex County is indeed replete with companies employing software gurus, making it one of the more venerable sources of I.T. professional services in the country.

AmeriSOURCE was incorporated in 1996 with a global vision —to build a multinational I.T. company that transcended political borders, to bring worldwide resources together, to craft and deploy solutions internationally— and a mission that not only catered to the fulfillment of clients' needs but to the attainment of their employees' dreams as well.

A dynamic management team is central to the AmeriSOURCE vision of success.

Probal Das Gupta says, "at AmeriSOURCE a promise means nothing until our consultants deliver."

"We don't just want to be a well-known company, we want to be endorsed by our employees, too," says CEO Probal DasGupta.

The official AmeriSOURCE credo is unabashedly individualistic: "We choose not to be just another company It is our right to be uncommon—if we can." BIG dreams, passion for work and relentless persistence are just some of the values the company believes in. Calling the nine-to-five business hours a relic of the past, the company touts itself as a "24-hour company for a 24-hour marketplace." The official credo says: "While others dream of success, we stay awake and work hard at it."

Starting with a 30'x20' office and a $9,616 payroll in the first month, AmeriSOURCE grew exponentially in the first three years, each year more than doubling its revenues. An aggressive, market-driven technology company whose quintessential drive is growth, AmeriSOURCE today—in its fourth year—is a $15 million company with branches in Boston, Philadelphia, Nashville and Atlanta; affiliates in 12 different countries including the U.K., Germany, India, Scandinavia, Singapore, Trinidad and Indonesia; and 150+ consultants scattered in 17 states nationwide. Through its conglomeration of global affiliates, it harnesses a pool of over 1,200 I.T. professionals worldwide.

Not only does AmeriSOURCE provide I.T. solutions for its clients, the company also builds state-of-the-art systems for its own internal use. Believing that excellence lies in a constant quest for change and betterment, AmeriSOURCE is quick to seize the latest ideas and technologies for its own use. In 1999, for instance, the company totally restructured its marketing methodology using CRM techniques, and quickly developed new software to accommodate this paradigm shift, when the rest of the world was just waking up to something called "Customer Relationship Management."

A firm believer in community values, AmeriSOURCE is involved in giving Edison Township a Kiosk Network to act as an information system for the township and its citizens—a project completely funded by the company. AmeriSOURCE is also working with the state government towards holding free computer training for unemployed citizens.

AmeriSOURCE is a textbook example of what can be achieved by a dedicated team driven by a common vision. It is also proof that the American Dream is alive and well in Middlesex County.

FIRST SAVINGS BANK

In 1901, five businessmen in Perth Amboy got together to form an association to provide mortgages to homebuyers in that thriving city. They called it the Modern Building and Loan Association. The institution's facilities were very modest, and business initially was conducted for just two hours on Monday evenings. However, it grew steadily, and by the early 1930s, assets were approaching $1 million. Over the years, many distinguished citizens served as officers and directors of the Association, including the Mayor of Perth Amboy, Frank Dorsey.

The Modern Building and Loan Association survived the Great Depression, and by the end of World War II it was obvious that a wider range of services were needed for the post-war boom. In July 1945 the local press announced that the Modern Building and Loan Association would become the First Savings and Loan Association of Perth Amboy, "to afford residents the means to construct their own homes and to enable small investors to incorporate their savings in a sound investment program." The new thrift, the only federally-insured institution of its kind in the city, would accept accounts up to $5,000.

As the suburbs outside Perth Amboy grew, First Savings expanded, opening its first branch office in Woodbridge in 1959 and another branch in nearby Edison in 1961. The computer age came to First Savings in 1967, when the Association contracted with a service bureau to process customer transactions on-line. Unfortunately, the system debuted just before the great East Coast Blackout, causing bank employees to wonder for a moment just how powerful their new system was.

During the 1970s and '80s the bank continued to expand, build-

The Bank has its new corporate headquarters at 1000 Woodbridge Center Drive, in Woodbridge.

ing new branches and purchasing branches from other institutions. By 1990 there were thriving branch offices in Hopelawn, Iselin, Fords, Old Bridge and in multiple locations in Edison and Woodbridge. The bank also had its own mainframe computer by then, to administer the many new products being offered, including checking accounts, money market accounts, automobile loans, home equity loans and credit lines, automated teller services and credit cards.

The 1990s were the most dynamic years for the institution, which had a new name—First Savings Bank—to reflect its broadened line of products, services and delivery systems. Eight branches were acquired from other financial institutions, and the Bank converted to a public stockholder-owned institution. In addition, the Bank moved its headquarters to Woodbridge and acquired Pulse Savings Bank, a $500 million savings institution with six offices. When the acquisition was completed, First Savings Bank had $1.8 billion in assets and 23 full-service retail banking offices in Middlesex, Monmouth, Union and Mercer Counties.

First Savings Bank is committed to being a good neighbor in the communities its serves and manifests that commitment with support for many charities, civic organizations and youth groups. The Bank's officers serve on the boards of various non-profit

organizations, including hospitals, chambers of commerce, community development organizations and social service providers. Annually, the employees conduct a toy drive for underprivileged children, and participate in numerous charitable fundraisers to benefit organizations such as the March of Dimes, American Cancer Society and Habitat for Humanity.

First Savings Bank is committed to assisting all segments of the community with affordable banking services, and especially to helping low-to-moderate income households and first-time homebuyers achieve homeownership. The Bank has special reduced-rate mortgages for low-to-moderate income buyers and conducts home-buyer education classes for first-time buyers, a benefit which thousands of individuals have taken advantage of over the years.

Although First Savings has come a long way from its founding 98 years ago, in some ways it has not changed much at all. Generations of customers have come to this local institution for friendly, efficient service, safety and security for their deposits and assistance when they need a loan— and they have not been disappointed. First Savings has always put its customers' needs first and will continue to do so into the new millennium and beyond.

GREENBAUM, ROWE, SMITH, RAVIN, DAVIS & HIMMEL LLP

As one of the largest law firms in New Jersey, Greenbaum, Rowe, Smith, Ravin, Davis & Himmel LLP has had a substantial impact on the economic life of Middlesex County and the state of New Jersey, as well as on those of its many individual clients.

William L. Greenbaum founded the firm in Newark in 1914. His emphasis was on real estate law, and by the late 1940s the firm had a statewide reputation in that area. His sons Robert and Arthur joined the practice in 1949 and 1950, respectively. Paul Rowe joined in 1964 and Wendell Smith in 1968.

Rowe developed the firm's real estate litigation practice which in the 1970s and '80s extended to business, matrimonial and criminal cases.

The firm moved to the Woodbridge area of Middlesex County in 1971. Its practice had become statewide, and the area had a good workforce and ready accessibility. The Garden State Parkway, NJ Turnpike and railroad lines converged there, making it easy to maintain contact with clients throughout the state, particularly

Members of the firm include (seated) Wendell A. Smith, partner; and (standing, from left) Alan S. Naar, partner; and David L. Bruck, partner and chair, Banking and Creditors' Rights Department. Photo by A.J. Sundstrom Photography

The GRSRD&H Management Committee includes (seated) Paul A. Rowe, managing partner and chair, Litigation Department; and (standing from left) Arthur M. Greenbaum, partner; Michael B. Himmel, partner and chair of the White Collar Criminal Defense Group; and Alan E. Davis, partner and chair of the Corporate Department. Photo by A.J. Sundstrom Photography

its many residential developer clients building in Middlesex, Monmouth and Ocean Counties.

When Michael Himmel joined the firm in 1982, it had 23 attorneys. In 1984, Greenbaum merged with Ravin, Davis & Sweet, an 18-lawyer firm founded 10 years earlier in Edison. Their respective expertise in real estate, commercial litigation, and corporate law proved a perfect fit.

Greenbaum, Rowe, Smith, Ravin & Davis started with approximately 48 lawyers. It was the largest such merger in the state up to that time and proved one of the most successful. Himmel became a name partner in 1996.

By 1999, Greenbaum, Rowe had more than 90 attorneys and 20 paralegals and had become noted for its expert litigation and corporate transactions as well as real estate work. It regularly represented clients in the New Jersey and New York federal and state courts and throughout the country. Nearly half of the attorneys were involved in general commercial litigation with

the balance split evenly among the real estate and corporate, tax and estate planning areas.

Today, the firm's clients range from Fortune 500 to medium-sized companies in many industries. It also represents several municipalities and public agencies throughout the state.

It consists of five major departments: litigation; real estate; corporate; banking and creditors' rights; and tax, trusts and estates. It also has several collaborative practice groups which draw on the expertise of the departments. Among these are white collar criminal defense, environmental law, special improvement districts, computer and technology law, and labor and employment law.

Its attorneys have national reputations. Alan Davis and the recently deceased Allen Ravin were the principal draftsmen of the New Jersey Franchise Practices Act, which became the model throughout the country. Other partners drafted New Jersey statutes regulating fiduciary obligations of executors and trustees, municipal redevelopment, and utility deregulation.

Rowe is the coauthor of the standard reference book for chancery litigation in New Jersey. Arthur Greenbaum frequently lectures on land development and financing. Smith is the author of numerous articles on condominium law. Himmel regularly writes and lectures on white collar criminal defense topics.

Greenbaum, Rowe has a diverse practice focused on its areas of proven expertise and interest, providing timely, top-quality service, emphasizing client loyalty and the dedicated protection of its clients' rights.

HATCO CORPORATION

Hatco Corporation is a worldwide leading producer of synthetic lubricant basestocks for technically demanding and precise specification applications, including aviation turbine oils and lubricants for CFC-free refrigeration compressors. In addition to synthetic lubricants, the company produces a biodegradable surfactant for use in household detergents, and specialty esters for the automotive, medical, cosmetic and personal care markets. Hatco sells its products to chemical, petrochemical and consumer products companies as well as government agencies worldwide. Hatco is based in Fords, New Jersey.

In 1959, Hatco was acquired by

Hatco was started in 1950 in Kearny, NJ and moved to its present location in Fords, NJ, shown here, in 1953.

W. R. Grace and Co. At that time, there were about 20 salaried employees and approximately 45 hourly employees. The company operated as a division of W. R. Grace and Co. until 1978, when it was purchased by Alex Kaufman, previously an executive vice-president and board member of W. R. Grace. Today, the 180-employee company has plants and offices in Fords and East Hanover, New Jersey, Aspen, Colorado and The Netherlands. Hatco products are sold to companies in more than 35 countries.

The company has received numerous accolades for its role in civic and state affairs and projects. Hatco played a key role in bringing together nine other companies to form the Woodbridge Township Community Advisory Panel

(CAP). The CAP facilitates emergency response activities and builds trust. Hatco supported numerous educational causes including: sponsoring local teachers to the Teacher's Industry and the Environment Workshop; sponsoring local students to Chemical Careers Conference at various NJ colleges; and donating to the Woodbridge School District Science Department for support of Lynn Crest School's Nature Trail. The company supports many charities and local causes including: the Raritan Bay Medical Center; Woodbridge Community Playground; Woodbridge Township Children's Olympics; Salvation Army Holiday Food Collection in Perth Amboy; Boy Scouts of America; and the Mayors Council on Physical Fitness & Sports.

HIGH GRADE BEVERAGE

High Grade Beverage was originally founded in 1940 by Nicholas DeMarco and Harry "Butch" Levine. They began by distributing Rupperts Knickerbocker beer to taverns and retailers in both Middlesex and Somerset counties. This operation was located on Redmond Street in New Brunswick and consisted of only eight people—Nicholas DeMarco, Harry "Butch" Levine and three delivery men, two salesmen and one secretary. That secretary, Marion Skriloff, still works for High Grade Beverage 59 years later! In 1941 they started distribution for Anheuser-Busch Products and eventually expanded their territory into Hunterdon and Warren counties.

In 1951, after their sales had increased dramatically, they created A & D Express, Inc., an interstate trucking firm, headed by Albert DeMarco. Today, A&D has over 30 trucks and 100 trailers serving several distributors in New Jersey, New York, Delaware and Pennsylvania.

A second distributorship was opened in 1956, in Kenvil, New Jersey. However, in order to keep up with this ever-expanding business they then moved to a larger facility in Mine Hill, New Jersey in 1963. The De Marco's moved from Mine Hill in 1983 and opened yet a larger distribution center located in Randolph, New Jersey. This is operated by George Policastro and is modeled after the South Brunswick facility.

Joseph DeMarco, son of founder Nicholas DeMarco, joined the firm as sales manager in 1956 and became president and chief executive officer in 1961. Upon his father's death in 1971, Joe DeMarco became the sole owner of High Grade Beverage. In 1971 he purchased Rutgers Distributors, another Anheuser-Busch Distributorship, in Staten Island, New

Joseph DeMarco, circa 1970s.

York. In 1977 he bought White Sales and Service (a White Truck Dealership) from his father-in-law Anthony Policastro. A few years later, in 1981, Volvo purchased the assets of White Motor Corp., and in 1995 Joe DeMarco obtained the franchise for GMC trucks—creating what is now known as Volvo & GMC Truck Center.

In the early 1950s, High Grade Beverage also developed a relationship with Briar's Birch Beer. In fact, they became the first company to distribute this product. Briar's continued to prosper and added another flavor—Sarsaparilla—and in 1986 the DeMarco family bought 51 percent of Briar's, adding to the "mini" conglomerate. In 1995 they purchased the remainder of the business, which was the manufacturing and bottling of the product. The product line has since expanded to include seven other flavors: Root Beer, Diet Birch Beer, Diet Sarsaparilla, Orange Cream, Golden Ginger Ale, Lemon Swirl, and Raspberry Fizz. Briar's soft beverages are currently available in 10 states.

To contend with the expanding business in 1976, Joseph DeMarco decided to move to a larger facility. Thus, the advent of High Grade Beverage's South Brunswick facility, located on Georges Road. The latest "state of the art" equipment was purchased and installed—from electric forklifts to computerized climate-controlled warehousing and refrigeration, which can store up to 7,000 half kegs of beer. The new warehouse was designed with a large main aisle to stage and load product, allowing the truck fleet to be loaded quickly and efficiently to better service customers. Today, High Grade Beverage serves Middlesex, Somerset, Union, Hunterdon, Warren, Morris, Sussex and parts of Passaic counties.

High Grade is committed to superior service and quality. In 1981, 1982 and 1983 they won Silver Awards for outstanding performances from Anheuser-Busch. Subsequently, in 1984 they earned the Golden "Ambassador" Award, the highest accolade given by Anheuser-Busch to any distributor in the United States. This award met Anheuser-Busch's standards of sales, inventory, management and warehousing. High Grade Beverage also distributes Heineken USA, LaBatt's USA, and Yuengling beers, which adds substantially to their business.

Joseph DeMarco was born in Philadelphia, Pennsylvania in 1935. He graduated from the University of Florida in 1956. He also served in the Army, Army Reserves and the New Jersey National Guard from 1957-1963. He married Elizabeth (nee Policastro) in 1957. Elizabeth works side-by-side with her husband, and though semi-retired she still holds a seat on the board of directors as the corporate secretary/treasurer. They have three children, Diana Battaglia, Anthony DeMarco and Denise DeMarco. They also have four grandchildren, Michael, Maria, Anthony and Joseph Battaglia.

The DeMarco family is very close-knit; many family members have worked and are still active at High Grade. One might consider the board of directors a "family affair," which includes: Joseph DeMarco, president; Elizabeth DeMarco, corporate secretary/ treasurer; son Anthony DeMarco, corporate senior vice president; brother-in-law George Policastro, corporate executive vice president; son-in-law Guy Battaglia, corporate vice president; daughter Diana Battaglia, corporate assistant secretary/treasurer; and cousin Richard Policastro, corporate vice president. Also on the board are Herb Schloss, corporate financial vice president; Joseph Lawler, corporate marketing director; and Jeffrey Epstein, corporate controller.

Diana Battaglia had been the assistant personnel manager until she left to raise a family in 1983. Anthony DeMarco has worked closely with his father since he was a youngster. Anthony worked during the summers in the warehouse and as a helper on the delivery trucks. Anthony has worked his way up from labor coordinator to the corporate senior vice president, effective in 1993. He graduated from San Diego State University with a B.A. in Business Administration, while also earning his M.B.A. in Marketing from Drexel University. Anthony had been named successor-manager for High Grade Beverage in 1992 and most recently became the equity manager, making him the chief executive officer and the third generation to manage the business.

High Grade Beverage and Joe

High Grade Beverage, circa late 1950s.

DeMarco are very involved with their community. Locally, Mr. DeMarco has served on the board of directors of Brunswick Bank & Trust since 1976; St. Peter's Foundation Board since 1981; and was a board member for St. Peter's Medical Center from 1981 to 1988. He has been a member of the New Brunswick Elks since 1960; crusade chairman for the American Cancer Society, Middlesex County 1986-1987 and board chairman, 1988-1990; board member of the Middlesex County Regional Chamber of Commerce since 1985; Knights of Columbus Council No. 6572, New Brunswick; board members George Street Playhouse from 1991-1993; chairman of Monsignor Francis J. Crupi 40th Anniversary dinner in 1992; Board of Governors-Forsgate Country Club since 1993; and chaired the First Annual American Heart Walk, Middlesex County in 1992.

Other credits to his name include: president of the State Beverage Beer Distributors, 1964-1966; member of the National Anheuser-Busch Wholesaler Panel, 1970-1973, to which he was appointed chairman in 1972; member of the National Ecology Panel, 1970-1973; member of The New York Beer Wholesaler's Association, 1971-1993 and the New

Jersey Beer Wholesaler's Association from 1956 to present; chairman of the Italian Earthquake Relief Fund, 1980-1981; member of the Governor's Council on Physical Fitness, NJ, 1985-1991; board member of the Bishop's Fund, 1986 to present; and chairman of St. Mary's Forward in Faith Campaign, 1984.

Mr. DeMarco has received many honors, including: Unico Man of the Year 1984; induction into the Knights of Malta in 1985; Regina Nostra Award-Diocese of Metuchen, 1986; presentation of the Israel Peace Medal by Banking-Industry-Labor Committee and Middlesex County Committee of State Israel Bonds, 1987; The McCarrick Award presented by St. Peter's Hospital, 1990; Humanitarian Award of the National Conference of Christians and Jews-Central New Jersey Chapter, 1993; Humanitarian of the Year Award-Diocese of Metuchen, 1996; and the Middlesex County Regional Chamber of Commerce-Leadership of Distinction, 1998. Clearly, Joseph DeMarco and High Grade Beverage are committed to serving the community and have done a great deal for Middlesex County over the years.

JFK MEDICAL CENTER AND SOLARIS HEALTH SYSTEM

Founded in 1967, the 535-bed JFK Medical Center is noted for its innovative healthcare management and quality patient care. Today, JFK Medical Center annually records approximately 20,000 admissions, nearly 2,000 births, and more than 40,000 emergency room visits. JFK consists of the 441-bed Anthony M. Yelencsics Community Hospital, the adjacent 94-bed JFK Johnson Rehabilitation Institute, and the New Jersey Neuroscience Institute. The medical center provides a complete array of acute care services, from emergency medicine and specialized surgery to maternity and pediatrics.

The Dream Begins: JFK Medical Center began in the 1960s as little more than a dream and an idea in response to the increasing demand for healthcare services created by rapid population growth in Edison Township and its surrounding communities. The late Edison Mayor Anthony M. Yelencsics, for whom the original community hospital was named, led a grassroots effort to open a hospital to meet this demand. Initially, he convinced Edison officials to

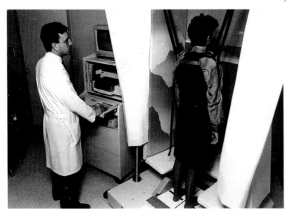

Martin Gizzi, M.D., Ph.D., Director of Neurology for the New Jersey Neuroscience Institute of New Jersey at JFK Medical Center, examines a patient. The Institute's opening in 1992 helped give JFK Medical Center a national presence in the field of neuroscience.

donate nearly 40-acres of township land for the hospital. He then lobbied with congressional leaders, including Middlesex County's own Rep. Edward J. Patten to win $1.1 million in Hill-Burton Funds, which at the time represented the largest single grant awarded in New Jersey under that program. Following a tireless fundraising campaign pioneered by trustees, physicians, auxilians and community residents, the original 205-bed hospital opened its doors and admitted its first patient in 1967. Nearly one year later, the first baby was born at JFK.

JFK-Johnson Rehabilitation Institute Leads Growth: The 1970s represented a period of significant growth for JFK. One of the most important highlights in its history was the opening of The JFK Johnson Rehabilitation Institute in 1974, following a merger with Middlesex Rehabilitation Hospital. Since that time, The Johnson Rehabilitation Institute has forged a reputation for excellence in patient care and has become a national leader in physical rehabilitation medicine. The JFK Johnson Rehabilitation Institute and its satellite facilities compose one of

An aerial view of the original 205-bed JFK Community Hospital which opened in 1967.

the first rehabilitation centers in the nation to recognize that individuals with acquired traumatic brain injury require a specialized treatment environment. With its unprecedented, comprehensive approach to care, the Institute's Center for Head Injuries is regarded as pioneering in head trauma evaluation and treatment. In addition, the Institute's Pediatric Rehabilitation Department provides children with the adaptive and coping skills they need to achieve success in everyday life— through such special disciplines as physical therapy and occupational therapy. The Institute also offers inpatient and day rehabilitation, outpatient therapies, and prosthetics and orthotics. JFK also unveiled its Radiation Therapy Center and its Family Practice Center during this decade.

Long-Term Care Added to Scope of Services: During the 1980s JFK expanded its scope of services by entering the long-term care arena. The health system now boasts three JFK Hartwyck Nursing, Convalescent & Rehabilitation Centers, which provide a wide range of special services for long-term and residential care. The first, JFK Hartwyck at Cedar

Brook, joined in 1984, with the Hartwyck at Oak Tree facility opening in 1987. All offer skilled nursing services and respite care in pleasant, comfortable surroundings. In addition, each facility is complemented by the medical and rehabilitation services offered by JFK Medical Center and Johnson Rehabilitation Institute. In 1990, New Jersey's first Huntington's Disease Unit opened at JFK Hartwyck at Cedar Brook. The system witnessed further growth with the addition of the Hartwyck at Edison Estates facility in 1993.

National Reputation Expands: New Jersey Neuroscience Institute Opens at JFK: The medical center reached a significant milestone in 1992, when it opened the New Jersey Neuroscience Institute at

New Jersey Governor Christine Tood Whitman was an honored guest during JFK Medical Center's 30th birthday celebration in 1997. During the celebration, the center unveiled one of its most ambitious expansion projects - the new five-story Patient Tower. Shown with Governor Whitman are: (left to right) vice president of education-Solaris, vice president of long-term care human resources, Mary Jane Meehan; past JFK Medical-Dental staff president Michael Kleiman, DMD; senior vice president J. Scott Gebhard; executive vice president & COO Lou Amato, past JFK Medical Center board chairman Dr. Earle N. Peterson and past JFK president and CEO and current Solaris Health System CEO John P. McGee.

JFK Medical Center. Now, only seven years later, The New Jersey Neuroscience Institute is a nationally recognized comprehensive center for the diagnosis, treatment and study of neurological disease. The Institute continues to attract top neuroscience experts from across the United States and works to promote investigative efforts in basic and clinical research.

Patient Tower Opens: JFK completed its most recent major expansion when the new, five-story Patient Tower opened its doors in 1997. The expansion project included:

• eight new operating rooms featuring state-of-the-art equipment and a flexible design to accommodate future needs;

• the Family Suite maternity unit;

• larger recovery areas to allow for easier monitoring of patients;

• an expansion of the JFK Johnson Rehabilitation Institute to include Independence Square and a new Day Hospital;

• a centralized location for the New Jersey Neuroscience Institute at JFK; and

• a new medical/surgical wing for orthopedics.

Other significant additions made during the past three decades include: JFK's Cancer Center featuring state-of-

A view of JFK Medical Center as it appears today. The medical center witnessed significant growth during the 1970s, 1980s, and 1990s with the addition of the JFK Johnson Rehabilitation Institute, the JFK Hartwyck long-term care facilities, and the New Jersey Neuroscience Institute.

the-art cancer diagnosis and treatment capabilities, hospice care and participation in nationwide cancer research networks; JFK's outpatient Mediplex Surgery Center providing same-day procedures including laser, endoscopic and arthoscopic surgery. Also, the JFK Imaging Center and its Breast Center both offer a full-range of diagnostic examinations, including CAT (computerized axial tomography) scan and MRI (magnetic imaging resonance) services.

JFK Enters New Millenium as Solaris Health System: Responding to the changing market demands that gripped New Jersey's healthcare industry in the 1990s, JFK Medical Center and Plainfield's Muhlenberg Regional Medical Center merged in 1997 to form Solaris Health System. This community-owned, not-for-profit health system serves the residents of Central New Jersey. Combined, the two hospitals have approximately 5,600 employees, 850 affiliated physicians and 1,575 beds. The new system enhanced both facilities' ability to provide a full spectrum of high-quality, cost-efficient services to the residents of central New Jersey.

ROBERT WOOD JOHNSON UNIVERSITY HOSPITAL

Robert Wood Johnson University Hospital captures the latest advances in medicine and brings these innovations immediately to New Jersey residents. In some cases, Robert Wood Johnson University Hospital physicians pioneer clinical trials that provide new medical science to the nation and the world. From its humble beginnings in 1884 as a small community hospital, Robert Wood Johnson University Hospital has evolved into one of the leading academic health centers in the nation.

In 1884, under the leadership of Grace Tileston Wells, a group of women began to meet and raise money for the purpose of starting up a hospital in the city of New Brunswick. By March 1885, a small cottage was rented on the corner of Commercial Avenue and Seaman Street to serve as a hospital. The hospital opened its doors on April 1, 1885 and the first patient, a victim of a railroad accident, was admitted on April 7.

Due to the overwhelming need for the hospital, and through a generous donation by Mrs. Wells, a new hospital (with a bed capacity of 15) was built in 1889 and named the John Wells Memorial Hospital in honor of Mrs. Wells' late husband. In 1899, an additional wing was added to the hospital, increasing the bed capacity to 20.

By 1916 it became clear that an additional building was needed. Construction soon began on the Middlesex Pavilion, which is the oldest building still standing on the Robert Wood Johnson University Hospital campus. The Middlesex Pavilion increased the bed capacity to 40 and the hospital was renamed Middlesex General Hospital.

Middlesex General Hospital had seen extensive growth and

The Brown Street Building.

progression between 1916 and 1958. The Brown Street Building was completed; a nurses residence and School of Nursing Building was erected; the Boiler House and Laundry were constructed; the hospital Auxiliary was founded and a volunteer program was initiated; a recovery room and orthopedic clinic were opened; the Central Supply system was started; and an intern program, radioisotope program, and Speech and Hearing Clinic were introduced. By the time the "1958 Building" was opened and dedicated in 1958, the bed capacity at Middlesex General Hospital had grown to 237.

Middlesex General Hospital continued to grow through the late 1950s, beginning with X-ray technician training. The School of

Nursing building was converted to administration offices, and still exists today. During the 1960s, the EKG laboratory opened, a new operating suite was dedicated, the Inhalation Therapy Department was instituted, the first Intensive Care Unit was open, the very first Service Awards Dinner was held and a wing known as "4Private" was opened, bringing the bed capacity to 278. The hospital ended the decade with the establishment of the Nuclear Medicine Department in 1970.

Middlesex General Hospital continued to expand in the 1970s. In 1972, the opening of the Robert Wood Johnson Memorial Tower provided central New Jersey with a new state-of-the-art hospital and health care facility, offering extended services and additional bed space. In 1977, an affiliation agreement between Middlesex General Hospital and the College of Medicine & Dentistry of New Jersey was signed, designating Middlesex General Hospital as the "primary" teaching hospital for the medical school. Middlesex General Hospital became the first

Robert Wood Johnson University Hospital Campus.

The Children's Hospital at Robert Wood Johnson University Hospital.

hospital in central New Jersey to be equipped with a CT Scan. It continued to grow with the addition of a new Medical Education building, Acute Services and Ambulatory Care buildings, the "South Building," a power plant, garage and the Courtyard, renamed and dedicated in 1999 as the "Arline and Henry Schwartzman Courtyard."

By 1982 the bed capacity was up to 416 and the hospital was now known as Middlesex General University Hospital. It was not until 1986 that the medical school changed its name to UMDNJ-Robert Wood Johnson Medical School and the hospital was renamed Robert Wood Johnson University Hospital.

The 1990s brought more dynamic changes for Robert Wood Johnson University Hospital. The dedication of the CORE Pavilion in 1993 allowed the hospital to expand its services to the communities it serves. Robert Wood Johnson University Hospital, a founding partner of The Cancer Institute of New Jersey offers oncology patients the opportunity to seek treatment here in New Jersey, eliminating the need to travel to New York and Pennsylvania. The hospital's designation

as a Level I Trauma Center for adult and pediatric has resulted in the development of life-saving techniques and therapies. In 1994, Robert Wood Johnson University Hospital opened the 110-bed Heart Center of New Jersey. It also opened a Bone Marrow Transplantation Program and the Pediatric Hernatology/Oncology Unit, in partnership with The Cancer Institute of New Jersey. The Vascular Center of New Jersey and the Center for Alternative and Complementary Medicine add new dimensions to medical therapies.

Robert Wood Johnson University Hospital is committed to a fourfold mission of the highest standard of

patient care, researching the cures for disease, educating the health care professionals of tomorrow and outreach to the communities it serves.

As Robert Wood Johnson University Hospital enters the next century, the hospital will continue as a national leader in the development of new and advanced protocols to save lives and to improve the quality of life. Key centers of excellence include: The Heart Center of New Jersey; The Vascular Center of New Jersey; The Center for Heart and Kidney Transplantation; The Children's Hospital; The Cancer Institute of New Jersey; Women's Wellness and Healthcare Connection; Level I Trauma Center; The Center for Digestive Disease; and The Clinical Neurosciences Center. Working closely with community physicians and faculty medical school physicians, the hospital continues to build on its international reputation for combining world-class research with innovative treatments.

Dr. Barton A. Kamen with several of his young patients.

THE LANDIS GROUP

Real estate developer Alan Landis, 57, has turned his dreams into a multimillion-dollar success story by following his instincts, anticipating market trends, and understanding his customers' needs.

Landis received his bachelor's degree in accounting from New York University in 1965 and worked in his father's accounting firm for two years. Not satisfied as an accountant and after a stint in the military service, Landis decided at age 24 to make a career move into real estate.

He was initially involved in land sales and appraisals. During the late 1960s and early 1970s Landis built several small office buildings, a hotel, and a racquetball club. His first major project was Loehmann's Plaza, a multistore shopping center along Route 18 in East Brunswick.

Landis built Loehmann's Plaza after borrowing $1.152 million from the National State Bank of Elizabeth, a debt that would require 11 years to repay. Despite the fact that the general contractor of the job went bankrupt, Landis personally completed the project and, serving as contractor, chief financial officer, and director of marketing, repaid the entire debt. Eventually, he sold the shopping center and other Route 18 office buildings. "Many people had told me to just walk away from the project," says Landis. "But I couldn't because I had made a commitment."

During the late 1970s Landis realized that the Princeton market was on the verge of a building boom. Market surveys conducted by his company confirmed his instincts. In 1979 he persuaded five business partners to buy a 54-acre land parcel on Route 1 in West Windsor. He then engaged a team of experts led by The Stubbins Associates, Inc., a well-known

Alan Landis, chairman of The Landis Group.

architectural firm from Cambridge, Massachusetts, to create an initial $75-million development plan that included four office buildings and a hotel.

After his initial investment, Landis received substantial financial support from Chemical Bank. Tenant commitments from the Hyatt Regency Hotel and Summit Bank, which built its headquarters facility there, persuaded Chemical to invest further. Eventually, that 54-acre land parcel blossomed into one of the largest projects in New Jersey—Carnegie Center—which now totals more than 550 acres.

Carnegie Center has since evolved into an office/commercial/hotel/residential development worth $1 billion. Office and commercial space alone will total almost five million square feet. Today its occupants include corporate giants such as Prudential Securities, RCN, Summit Bank, Covance, Raytheon, and Paine-Webber.

Seventeen buildings have been constructed to date, with final

construction expected to be complete in the early 21st century. According to Landis, "I never imagined that buying that one piece of land would develop into this. It's been a dream."

Tower Center, located 18 miles north of Carnegie Center, is another testament to Landis' real estate instincts. Landis had believed for years that the site, at the crossroads of Route 1 and 18 and the New Jersey Turnpike, Exit 9, was one of the best locations in the state. He eventually acquired five adjoining parcels of land there, part of which included an old Ramada Inn.

The complex is located opposite Landis' original project, Loehmann's Plaza, and is a $200-million, 1.1 million- square-foot office/hotel complex that includes two 23-story office buildings, a 405-room Hilton Hotel/conference center, and a major park-and-ride

facility. The Stubbins Associates worked on the project, in conjunction with a local architectural firm, Rothe-Johnson Associates of Edison.

At present, the first of the two office towers is occupied by the communication division of AT&T. AT&T Resource Management was a partner in the 25-acre project. The second of two towers is home to PNC Bank, The Copeland Companies and Prudential Bache, to name a few.

As principal investor in Tower Center, Landis spent more than $4 million on engineering and preliminary roadwork to lessen potential traffic problems. He also invested a total of $11-12 million in off-site and road improvements as the project progressed.

Landis believes the private sector must join forces with the state Department of Transportation to combat traffic congestion.

"Routes 1 and 18 needed upgrading and it had to happen immediately. I'd like to see the entire corridor improved. I'd also like to see the private sector, including developers, jump in and lessen the funding gap. We all need these two highways to survive," he says.

Landis fares well in a competitive office real estate market by keeping leasing rates comparable with those in the area and by providing outstanding tenant service. He believes it's essential to monitor the market and tailor products to market needs. One example of the approach is a nine-month survey contracted to the University of Pennsylvania's Department of Anthropology to determine customer priorities in selecting corporate sites. Both locations have been awarded numerous industry accolades. The most notable honor is the

Urban Land Institute's Award for Excellence for large scale-industrial office park development.

The staff of Landis' business divides their effort between offices at Carnegie Center and Tower Center. Both offices retain a close-knit atmosphere. Landis was born in New Brunswick and grew up in North Brunswick and Highland Park. He attended school in Highland Park and Princeton. Although currently living in New York, Landis remains firmly committed to the area where he was raised and worked for more than three decades. "I'm interested in focusing on people's needs in this area," he states. "I like to see people smiling."

Tower Center presently consists of two 24-story office buildings and a 405-room Hilton Hotel.

A. J. JERSEY, INC.

In 1970, A. J. Jersey was incorporated in the State of New Jersey with the sole purpose of providing material handling equipment to end users of all "types in order to solve their material handling problems. Material handling is an $80 billion industry nationally, and the Middlesex County area is one of the most competitive in the country.

Initially, this company existed in New York as a partnership and was called Astorlyn Corporation. Mr. Patrick Rizzo and his partner were from Brooklyn and Astoria, New York. Hence, they founded the company name from a combination of the two boroughs. Astorlyn Corporation existed as a Crown Lift Truck dealer until 1970, when Patrick Rizzo decided to open his own branch for Crown, in New Jersey.

Business demanded hands on, local representation of the Crown product. Therefore, in 1989, the company moved its headquarters to So. Plainfield in Middlesex County. This entirely new company was now a corporation on its own and called Astorlyn Jersey Corporation. Over time it was shortened for simplicity purposes and called A. J. Jersey, Inc. A. J. Jersey is currently the authorized dealer for Crown and Daewoo Lift Trucks in Central New Jersey (Union, Hudson, Middlesex, Somerset, Hunterdon, Essex, and Monmouth counties).

A. J. Jersey, a leader in the sales and service of lift trucks, maintains its focus on developing solutions for companies large and small, in the area of material handling. Its goal is to stay on top through the implementation of state-of-the-art communication, selling only quality and superior products with a good track record and standing behind everything it sells with excellent service.

A. J. Jersey headquarters, South Plainfield, NJ.

No matter what business you are in, if you have a product to move, it must be handled by something A. J. Jersey sells. A.J. Jersey deals with Fortune 500 Companies as well as companies with as few as five employees, providing them with storage and handling solutions.

A. J. Jersey currently exceeds $18 million in annual sales and remains a profitable company year after year. It maintains this level through the hard work of all of its employees, managers, and owners. A. J. Jersey employs over 70 people and remains a leader in the material handling sales and service industry. The owners feel that being in and identified with Middlesex County provides excellent logistics and is critical to the success of the company.

A. J. Jersey remains a family-owned and operated business with the second generation Rizzo family in key management roles. Steven and David Rizzo are both vice presidents and Patrick is still president and entering his third decade of ownership. The com-pany will be celebrating its 30th year of operation in January 2000, and in those 30 years has taken on many materials handling lines. Electric lift trucks used to be its mainstay, however, over the years allied equipment such as pallet racking, shelving, conveyor systems, dock equipment and gas powered forklifts have been added to complete the level of service provided to A. J. Jersey's customers. As the company grows and becomes even more of a presence in Middlesex County, its owners plan to keep the original headquarters in South Plainfield and expand to additional sites within the county.

LEVINSON AXELROD

Jacob Levinson.

On September 1, 1939, a partnership was formed, with two partners assisted by a single associate. That associate was Jacob Levinson, who in 1945 was left in charge to run the firm on his own.

Jacob's practice flourished, and the growth of the firm began in earnest with the addition of his nephew Alfred Levinson in 1951. In 1956 Jacob's son, Richard, joined the firm after graduating from Columbia Law School. At that time the firm had only five attorneys, two secretaries, a part-time bookkeeper and a part-time high school girl.

In the 1960s the firm, seeking the best legal talent available, began to grow beyond Levinson family members, as David Wheaton and Bob Axelrod came aboard. The 1980s saw the addition of Ron Grayzel, and the 1990s witnessed a further increase, adding partners Pat Caulfield, Jim Dunn, Rich Marcolus, John Schwarz

and Mark Kuminski. In 1980, Levinson Axelrod moved from its old home in the little house on Hobart Street in Perth Amboy to its present quarters in the imposing Levinson Building in Edison. In addition, the firm now has offices in Flemington, Somerville, Howell and Belford, and continues to welcome new additions to the staff each year.

The firm has had only one aim since its inception: to provide effective service for injured people. The firm's verdicts and settlements have consistently been among the highest in the state. The case load per lawyer has always been carefully regulated to ensure maximum client service. The firm continues to handle thousands of automobile, fall-down and accident cases for New Jersey residents each year, forming strong relationships with clients who, in turn recommend Levinson Axelrod to their relatives and neighbors.

Levinson Axelrod has participated in some of the most important cases of the last decades. The firm was deeply involved with the hemophiliac victims of AIDS, when the entire U.S. supply of anti-hemophiliac factor blood plasma was infected with the HIV virus. It represented 200 victims of the Durham Woods gas explosion disaster, which occurred less than a mile from Levinson Axelrod's Edison office. It also represented hundreds of women with faulty silicone breast implants, assigning an entire unit within the firm to pursue their claims. And it has pressed hundreds of claims on behalf of victims of asbestosis.

Levinson Axelrod has also taken action against job discrimination. Age and sex discrimination are extremely widespread, but discrimination can also be

based on race, religion, or color.

Today, one of Levinson Axelrod's most important areas is the condition of nursing homes, where elderly people should be safe in their declining years. But that peace of mind can often be an

Levinson Axelrod's headquarters in Edison, NJ.

illusion. When an accident occurs, it may be the fault of a nursing home employee who didn't provide assistance, or some other form of negligence.

In the past several years, Levinson Axelrod expanded its practice to cover Social Security Disability and professional and medical malpractice, as well as cases arising from the difficulties of managed care. The firm stays current on all the new laws, and teaches and attends seminars. The lawyers are actively involved in continuing education and often write important articles on aspects of the law.

The law is a challenging and dynamic field. Levinson Axelrod does everything possible to guarantee its clients the best possible representation.

MAGYAR SAVINGS BANK

Built on Immigrant Dreams. By the early 1900s, the City of New Brunswick was a thriving town located on the banks of the Raritan River. Waves of new immigrants, including Hungarians from the country of Magyarorszag (or Hungary in the English language), became city residents.

These new immigrants usually had one dream—homeownership. While acknowledged for their thrift and industrious work habits, the Hungarian immigrants nonetheless had to face the bias prevalent in those days. Home-ownership was usually limited to those who could accumulate the funds for a cash purchase; mortgage loans were not generally available to immigrants.

Spurned by mainstream banking, local Hungarian businessmen decided to create a 'Building and Loan' association. B&Ls were cooperative ventures which members joined for the purpose of pooling funds and lending it to other members.

Thus, in August 1922, the Magyar Building and Loan Association was established. Early board meeting minutes are hand-written in the Hungarian language—and reflect the association's commitment to providing homeownership opportunities for its membership.

New, rebuilt full-service location in South Brunswick, NJ.

Within the first few years, the association was financing construction of one and two family homes throughout the city's fifth and sixth wards. In this manner, Magyar played a significant role in the city's expansion into what had been a sparsely populated sector, but which presently provides much of the off-campus housing for Rutgers University's New Brunswick campus. Having no home office at first, Magyar eventually established an office on the French Street section of State Highway 27 in the City of New Brunswick—which by then housed a vibrant mix of Hungarian-owned retail shops.

The B&L successfully survived the Depression years. In September 1954, Magyar received approval for federal insurance of deposits and converted to a Savings and Loan Association. Financing home-ownership opportunities for all groups of people remained the association's primary purpose. Magyar again changed its charter in December 1993 to a state savings bank, thus solidifying its identity as a community bank.

In 1965, Magyar opened a new headquarters office at 101 French Street. A small second office, also on Route 27, opened in 1969 in South Brunswick Township. By this time Magyar was serving the second and third generations of its original membership, many of whom had moved out of New Brunswick to the surrounding suburbs. Magyar's focus on home financing continued to attract new immigrants moving into the area. The second office was so successful, that in 1997—Magyar's 75th anniversary—plans were finalized to replace it with a larger facility, which opened in September 1998.

Today, Magyar Savings Bank customers represent the diversity of the central New Jersey communities served by the bank. A variety of languages is spoken in the bank's lobbies. No longer tied to its original customer base, the name 'MAGYAR' has been retained for two reasons—to reflect the bank's proud 'grassroots' heritage, and to proclaim the bank's continued commitment to providing quality financial services to *all* residents of central New Jersey!

Office headquarters, 101 French Street, New Brunswick, 1965.

METUCHEN SAVINGS BANK

Rooted in the past—Committed to the future: For more than a century, Metuchen Savings Bank can claim continuous service to the community of Metuchen and the surrounding areas. It was chartered as The Metuchen Building and Loan Association in 1897 for the purpose of developing the then new Woodwild Park area of Metuchen. The Association had limited hours and services and grew steadily with the town. From its founding through 1960, income share certificates and installment shares were the only two accounts offered as a source of funds to provide mortgage loans to its members.

Through conservative management and expansion of services, Metuchen Savings Bank has survived two world wars, the Great Depression and numerous economic recessions, helping thousands of people realize their dreams of home ownership, while keeping pace with financial services.

Upon receiving approval for insurance of accounts in 1960, the Bank moved to Main Street and changed its name to The Metuchen Savings and Loan Association.

Mortgage Division, 50 Pearl Street, Metuchen.

Main Office, 429 Main Street, Metuchen.

With the change came passbook savings. Interest was paid semi-annually, and rates were increased over the years. Interest-bearing club accounts were added, as well as student loans and five-year certificates of deposit.

The Bank's first computers were installed in the early '70s, permitting interest to be compounded daily and paid quarterly. Tax deferred Keogh and IRA accounts allowed people to save for their retirement. Direct deposit and short-term certificates were available. FHA, VA mortgages were offered, as well as home improvement and auto loans. The hours were expanded with the addition of a walk-up window.

The '80s saw interest-bearing checking accounts, as well as the popular six month certificates and money market checking. Computer equipment and programs were upgraded. Saturday hours were added. Fixed and revolving equity loans were offered, as well as commercial mortgage products.

Metuchen Savings' First Time Home Buyer Mortgage and Down Payment Club were introduced in the 1990s. An ATM was installed in the walk-up window. The name was changed to Metuchen Savings Bank in 1993, in response to the business community's request for additional services.

Commercial checking accounts were offered and a night deposit was installed. Construction of the mortgage division and drive-up window was completed in 1994. With improved technology, automated and home banking products were added.

Throughout the Bank's history active membership in the Metuchen Area Chamber of Commerce has been an integral part of the business. A long history with the Metuchen Edison YMCA can be traced back to its beginnings, as Charles S. Edgar was one of the original founders.

Metuchen Savings Bank is proud to play an active role in the community and to provide services that have helped make Metuchen the special place that it is.

MIDDLESEX COUNTY COLLEGE

In 1963, the Middlesex County Board of Chosen Freeholders heard the community voice calling for a county-based institution for higher education that would be open to every resident who could benefit from it. The following year, the county acquired a 200-acre portion of the former Raritan Arsenal from the Federal government, and the dream began to take shape.

Middlesex County College opened its doors in 1966 with 728 full-time and 800 part-time students taking courses leading to associate degrees in eight areas, and taught by 45 faculty members. Under the inspiration of its first president, Dr. Frank M. Chambers, and corporate leader Paige D. L'Hommedieu (first chairman of the Board of Trustees), the College sought to meet complex demands. Among these were the first two years of a four-year college degree, direct career preparation, additional training to keep pace with jobs and local industry's need for skilled employees.

As the county has grown, so has Middlesex County College. At the close of the century, more than 500 full and part-time faculty members are teaching nearly 11,000 students during day, evening and weekend classes. Thousands more are taking continuing education classes on the main campus in Edison, at outreach centers and at selected educational and business sites throughout the county, as well as on the Internet.

Outreach to all segments of the population has always been important to the College, and centers in Perth Amboy and New Brunswick were opened in 1978 and 1980, respectively. Today those centers occupy spacious quarters, serving thousands of local residents with academic

Hotel, Restaurant and Institution Management is one of the outstanding career preparation programs offered at Middlesex.

courses, job and basic skills training, after-school and enrichment programs and childcare.

"Middlesex County College has always taken pride in its responsiveness to the educational needs of the citizens of the county. As those needs change and evolve, the College must correspondingly adapt its programs and services."

Spoken by Dr. John Bakum, fifth president of the College, the above statement underscores the commitment that Middlesex has made and the impact it has had on the lives of all residents of the county. Middlesex is continually meeting the challenge of educating, training and re-training a diverse population, while continuing to contribute to the area's economic growth.

"Perhaps the greatest challenge facing the College today," Dr. Bakum continued, "is keeping up with the demands of rapidly-changing technology and the

demands on tomorrow's graduate. It is essential that the academic programs remain current, both in terms of technology taught and the technology employed in the teaching and learning processes."

Recognized as a leader in engineering technology education by the National Science Foundation, the College received $5 million in grant support to develop the New Jersey Center for Advanced Technological Education. This program has developed new methodologies for the teaching of engineering technology and telemedia communications that will ultimately be adopted in community colleges throughout the United States.

Construction on campus keeps pace with growing technology. The Technical Services Center, completed in 1991, continues to be the state-of-the-art facility for the engineering technology departments. The Learning Resources Complex, dedicated in 1998, contains hi-tech classrooms with

The Technical Services Center, which houses The New Jersey Center for Advanced Technological Education (NJCATE).

An interactive television distance learning facility is part of the new Instructional Resource Center, the centerpiece of the Learning Resources Complex.

built-in computer/video projection systems, computer laboratories connected to the Internet, an interactive television distance-learning facility and a legal studies resource room. And, as of 2000, select high school students will be attending the new Academy for Mathematics, Science and Engineering Technologies operated by the Middlesex County Vocational and Technical Schools, constructed on the College's Edison campus, and supported by the faculty and administrators.

Through an agreement forged in 1988 with New Jersey Institute of Technology (NJIT), New Jersey's public comprehensive technological university, Middlesex students are guaranteed admission to NJIT with no further admissions review when certain criteria are maintained.

In 1991, Rutgers University initiated a dual admissions program with Middlesex County College that reflected many years of successful transfer by Middlesex

students to the state university. The purpose, then and now, was to streamline this process so that more qualified community college students will transfer to, and graduate from, Rutgers. This innovative program was so successful that Rutgers subsequently implemented similar ones with

The fine arts are represented in both the liberal arts curriculum and on-campus performances.

each of the 18 other public community colleges in New Jersey. From the beginning Middlesex was, and continues to be, the largest provider of transfer students to all branches of Rutgers University.

In 1986, the College established the Institute for Management and Technical Development, a college/ employer partnership designed to improve the skills of the local workforce and boost economic development. Large corporations, individuals and non-profit agencies alike turn to the Institute for customized competency-based training programs, problem solving, upgrading of employee skills, professional education, networking opportunities, and small business and entrepreneurial development. Among the 200 companies that have collaborated with the Institute over the past 13 years are Bristol Myers-Squibb, Johnson & Johnson, Ford Motor Company and the Superior Court of New Jersey. The Institute also works with the New Jersey Department of Labor in assisting companies and individuals.

In addition to its academic programs, the College offers learning and enrichment programs outside the classroom in such forms as sports activities, a school newspaper and literary magazine, performing arts and special interest clubs. Theater productions, films, lectures, trips and summer camp programs are widely attended by the community-at-large. Students speaking 45 different native languages are enrolled in one of the most comprehensive ESL (English as a Second Language) programs in the state. A certified Child Care Center operates year round, providing day care, pre-school and camp experiences for the children of students, staff and the community.

THE MIDDLESEX COUNTY UTILITIES AUTHORITY

SERVING THE COMMUNITY SINCE 1950: Preserving and protecting central New Jersey's environmental resources has always been at the heart of the Middlesex County Utilities Authority's mission. The Middlesex County Utilities Authority (MCUA) is a public organization that provides essential waste management services to over 750,000 residents of central New Jersey. The members of the Authority's Board of Commissioners and the MCUA staff fulfill an important civic responsibility by providing cost-effective, environmentally-responsible services to the communities in which they live and work.

The MCUA's Wastewater Division has been central New Jersey's primary treatment facility since its inception in the 1950s. The MCUA's wastewater treatment services and facilities have expanded to accommodate the growth of central New Jersey during the last five decades. Its operation has become increasingly sophisticated, creating efficiencies in the wastewater treatment process that were not thought possible a few decades ago. In the late 1980s the MCUA was also given the responsibility of managing Middlesex County's solid waste and currently operates the sole landfill in Middlesex County.

Landfill workface activities.

MCUA Treatment Plant facilities in 1976.

HISTORY: As the population of Middlesex County grew in the early 1900s, discharges of raw wastewater into the South and Raritan Rivers increased tremendously. By 1930 the pollution began wreaking havoc on the rivers, endangering many species of fish and the local economy. Several local wastewater treatment facilities were constructed to address the problem and prevent the death of these two river systems and subsequent economic hardship throughout the area. Due to the post World War II baby-boom and rise in the suburban populace, by the late 1940s the amount of wastewater generated was more than the small plants could handle.

The Middlesex County Utilities Authority (originally named the Middlesex County Sewerage Authority) was created in 1950 with the mission of treating wastewater and cleaning up the rivers. The MCUA has evolved and its mandate expanded over the years; in its present form it consists of two divisions: the Wastewater Division, which collects, treats, and pumps wastewater, and the Solid Waste Division, which operates the Middlesex County Landfill where county generated trash is deposited.

THE WASTEWATER DIVISION: Building First-Class Wastewater Treatment Facilities. In the 1950s, the MCUA designed and built a large regional wastewater treatment system in Sayreville. By 1958 the primary treatment plant was processing 52-million gallons of wastewater per day, serving 17 municipalities and 10 directly connected industrial participants. Many of the inappropriate sewer discharges into the Raritan River had been replaced by the properly cleaned wastewater treatment effluent that flowed in the Raritan Bay.

In 1966 the MCUA began pilot programs to develop a secondary treatment facility design. The new facility was needed to meet changing regulations from the New Jersey Department of Health regarding higher-level wastewater treatment standards. The designs were completed for a new micro-biological treatment plant in 1972. Also that year, several key sewer main pipelines in Sayreville, Bound Brook, and South River were planned for expansion, along with a new pump station in Greenbrook and expansion of the largest pump station in Sayreville. The secondary treatment facility broke ground in 1974 and was put into operation in 1978, with a capacity to treat 120-million gallons of wastewater per day. Concurrent with the treatment plant construction were expansions of the pump stations and sewer mains that conveyed sewage from within the service area to the treatment plant.

In the late 1980s the remaining primary wastewater treatment plants in Perth Amboy, Woodbridge, Carteret, South Amboy, Old Bridge, and other areas of Sayreville connected to the MCUA system. Today, five pumping

Aerial view of Middlesex County Landfill in East Brunswick, New Jersey.

Settling tanks in wastewater treatment plant.

stations and nearly 140-miles of sewer lines deliver more than 110-million gallons of wastewater per day to the treatment plant which now has a capacity of 147 MGD.

The Wastewater Division has also been an innovator in utilizing the formerly useless sludge generated from the treatment process. In 1991, when regulations changed regarding disposal of sludge, the MCUA constructed a facility to treat and recycle the residual now termed "Biosolids." The resulting product, called MeadowLife,â is licensed as a fertilizer, liming agent and marketed by the MCUA. The product is managed by the Wastewater Division, and has won several awards for environmental achievement.

THE SOLID WASTE DIVISION: Responsible

Solid Waste Management. In 1998, the Middlesex County Board of Chosen Freeholders voted to put the MCUA in charge of operations at the Edgeboro Landfill, which was previously a privately-owned facility. The MCUA restricted the Landfill's use to waste generated only by Middlesex County residents. Concurrent with the Edgeboro Landfill operation, the MCUA initiated planning for the construction of a new facility, known as the Middlesex County Landfill.

The Edgeboro Landfill is an older facility that is closed and capped. Groundwater protection is accomplished with a subsurface low permeability cut-off wall that encompasses the site and joined with the naturally occurring clay deposits beneath the Landfill. The landfill encompasses 315 acres, and has 46 groundwater monitoring wells located outside of its cut-off wall. The new Middlesex County Landfill (MCLF) is located within the cut-off wall as well and state-of-the-art technology is used to maintain the double liner system, leachate and methane gas collection systems, and daily and intermediate covers. These systems are essential to maintain a modern environmentally-sound sanitary landfill.

The MCLF opened on February 5, 1992, after six months of intensive construction. Each day 210 trucks transport approximately 1,300 tons of garbage to the landfill, amounting to 400,000 tons per year. It is anticipated that the MCLF will be able to accept 20-million cubic yards of solid waste. The landfill will remain open for an estimated 25 years, depending on the degree to which residents of the county are able to reduce and recycle the amount of solid waste they generate.

TOWNSHIP OF MONROE

Monroe Township, Middlesex County's largest, was incorporated on February 23, 1838. Named after President James Monroe, it extends 43.8 square-miles across the heartland of New Jersey. Monroe Township was a parcel of the vast tract of land belonging to the South Ward of Perth Amboy. In 1685, the Township of South Amboy was established and Monroe Township became part of that area. Inhabitants of South Amboy petitioned the Council and General Assembly of New Jersey to separate the two, in 1838. Historians presume that the separation of South Amboy and Monroe Township was a result of the economic differences between the two. Monroe Township was primarily agricultural, whereas South Amboy was industrial and commercial. Their needs were clearly different.

Rhode Hall School House in 1894, located at Route 522 and Cranbury Road, was shared by Monroe Township and South Brunswick. The teacher was Sara Clayton.

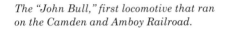
"hn Bull," First Locomotive to Run on Camden and Amboy

The "John Bull," first locomotive that ran on the Camden and Amboy Railroad.

With the completion of the Amboy Bordentown Road in 1684, Monroe Township had become a prime location for immigrants. The road meant freedom and profit for immigrants. The East Jersey Proprietors offered 50-acres of land to each head of household, as well as 25-acres for each additional person—prompting households to import numbers of indentured servants. Monroe Township's plush farmlands and dense forests lured settlers from Scotland, England, and Denmark in search of religious and political freedom. The first white settler came from Scotland in 1685. James Johnstone found the land bountiful and sent news to others abroad. Large numbers of settlers from Europe arrived and chose to live along the banks of the Manalapan Brook and Matchaponix River.

With the opening of the Camden and Amboy Railroad in 1832 came social and economic change. Passengers were able to travel 34 miles from Bordentown to South Amboy in approximately three hours in railroad cars drawn by horses. In 1833, steam engines replaced horse-drawn cars. The "John Bull," constructed in England, was the first locomotive to run on the Camden and Amboy Railroad. Although farmers were unaccustomed to the railroad because of the noise, pollution, and uncertainty, they grew to accept the opportunities that it brought to the area. Lodges and literary societies were forming to meet the needs of the diverse groups that were entering Monroe Township. Prior to the railroad, socialization occurred in church, at a barn or

house raising or a hog-killing. By 1838, the population grew to 2,435. Monroe Township had eight stores, four gristmills, 18 sawmills, and one paper mill, an academy and eight schools. Farming and lumbering were the primary ways of earning a living for the settlers. Close proximity to New Brunswick and Perth Amboy allowed for easy product outlets to New York from the South River as well as the railroad lines to Perth Amboy and Freehold.

Rapid progress brought about the need for governmental structure. The first town meeting was held at Jacob Vancleaf's house on the second Monday of April 1838. Any legal voter defined as male, white, over 21 years of age and residing in the Township for six months before the meeting date could attend. Nominations for Township officials were made from the floor and elected by a show of hands. Among the first elected were John A. Davison, town clerk, James Buckelew, collector and George A. McDowell, assessor. Business generally pertained to the construction of new roads, schools, sheep damage, entertainment fees and relief for the poor, and was accomplished in an atmosphere of good fellowship and orderly conduct.

Sundays were special in Monroe Township. It was a day of reconciliation, a time for all to meet and share the week's experiences. Meetings occurred in church, and Monroe Township had several churches in its Cranbury, Jamesburg and Spotswood sections. In the early 1800s Sunday schools became increasingly popular. During the sessions, many religious and educational topics were approached, thus becoming a forum for discussing policy and administration as well.

DEDICATION
First Monroe Township Police Headquarters
Middlesex County, N. J.
August 8th 1936

Police Headquarters, dedicated August 8, 1936 was originally a one-room schoolhouse.

The Civil War abruptly disrupted the serene lifestyle of Monroe Township's residents. A call to arms by President Lincoln between August and September 1862 was seemingly unheard by the inhabitants; thus, a $200 bonus was offered to any individual who volunteered to enlist. But Monroe Township still failed to meet its quota. Bonuses rose to $600 during the course of the war, and peace was most welcomed, if only to end the drive for recruitment. Sixty-five veterans are laid to rest in local cemeteries.

Despite war efforts, mail was still delivered. The general store at Prospect Plains was home to the Post Office. Storeowner Derrick G. Davison was the first postmaster and remained so for 19 years. In 1888, a Post Office opened on Applegarth Road, through the efforts of United States Senator John R. McPherson and A.S. Applegate, Esquire. Still, on March 31, 1891, the Prospect Plains Post Office closed and mail processing transferred to the Hightstown facility. Rural free delivery began in 1901. It took two men eight hours to deliver the mail by horse and wagon.

In addition to a storeowner doubling as a postmaster, in 1856 a police officer would collect back taxes as well as perform his

regular tasks. Better known as a constable, this person would primarily serve legal documents. Misdeeds were uncommon in Monroe Township until 1896, when crop thieving and cow theft became prevalent. In 1936, a police headquarters was established in a one-room schoolhouse.

While travelling through Monroe Township today, one may witness splendid reminders of days gone by. Tree-lined roads honor the names of original settlers. Soft green meadows whisper a weather report while preparing for harvest. Fields of corn, soybean and wheat glimmer after a fresh rain. The Monroe Oak, a 300 year-old majestic figure is reminiscent of strength and perseverance. Open space dominates. The Township's first Post Office since 1891 opens in October 1999, almost 110 years later. The millennium will unite past and present in a barn raising and an historical village that will house artifacts that have been gently tucked away for centuries. The one-room schoolhouse will be resurrected to greet children's laughter once more. Monroe Township recognizes that its future depends on embracing the past.

NEW BRUNSWICK THEOLOGICAL SEMINARY

Mission: New Brunswick Theological Seminary is a teaching institution of the Reformed Church in America, called by God to be a servant of the whole church of Jesus Christ. The Seminary's mission is to continue the ministry of Jesus in our time and place by enabling persons to translate their calling and gifts into faithful Christian ministry.

History: New Brunswick Theological Seminary has been in Middlesex County since 1810. Its history, however, begins much earlier. It was founded in New York City in 1784, the first theological seminary in the United States. Its original purpose was to provide graduate theological education for candidates for the ministry of the Reformed Protestant Dutch Church in North America—now the Reformed Church in America. The first faculty consisted of two persons, the Rev. Dr. John Henry Livingston (1746-1825) and the Rev. Dr. Hermanus Meyer (1733-1791). There was but one person in the first graduating class in 1786, John Martin Van Harlingen (1761-1813), who was himself

Students take a break from evening classes.

View of the Seminary campus, circa 1885.

appointed to the faculty of the Seminary in 1812, but died before he could serve.

For three years, during the 1790s, the Seminary was moved to Brooklyn, in an effort to reduce the cost of ministerial preparation. It was returned to Manhattan in 1799 and remained there until the General Synod of 1809 determined that for the good of both its institutions of higher education, Queens College (later renamed Rutgers) and the Seminary, should be combined in New Brunswick. For 45 years, from 1811 to 1856, Rutgers College and New Brunswick Seminary both carried out their academic programs together, in the building that is now known as Old Queens Hall.

The Seminary moved to its own campus, just one block away, in 1856. Ms. Ann Hertzog (1786-1866) funded the construction of the Seminary's first building in memory of her husband. The Peter Hertzog Theological Hall, reminiscent in design to Old Queens Hall, provided dormitory space, a dining hall, chapel and library for the Seminary. Large faculty residences were constructed during the 1860s. Dedicated in 1873, James Suydam Hall provided a new chapel, four large classrooms, a gymnasium, and museum. The Gardner A. Sage Library was

completed in 1875. By 1885, the Seminary's campus and facilities were arguably the most outstanding among American seminaries.

In this century the Library has been greatly enlarged, totally renovated, and equipped for the evolving era of electronic information and communication. Additional housing units have been constructed for faculty, administration, and students. In 1966, Hertzog Hall and Suydam Hall were razed to allow for the construction of a new academic center, the Samuel Zwemer Hall. This flexible facility has allowed the Seminary's program to expand significantly over the course of the past two decades.

Program: The Seminary is accredited by the Association of Theological Schools in the United States and Canada, and licensed by the State of New Jersey to offer three professional degree programs, all at the graduate level. The Master of Divinity (M.Div.) is the normative degree to prepare persons for ordained Christian ministry. The Master of Arts in Theological Studies (M.A.T.S.) provides a basic level of understanding theological discipline

Studying in Sage Library.

for further graduate study. The Doctor of Ministry (D.Min.) in Metro-urban Ministry is offered in cooperation with the Edward J. Bloustein School of Planning and Public Policy, Rutgers University. This program enhances the practice of ministry for those who hold the M.Div. degree and have engaged in ministerial leadership. Since 1986, the Seminary's M.Div. and M.A.T.S. programs have also been offered on the campus of St. John's University, Jamaica, Queens, New York.

For most of the Seminary's history it had a student body of about 50 students— almost entirely male, Caucasian, enrolled in what in now the M.Div. program, and members of the Reformed Church in America. Since the 1980s, the student body has grown in numbers and diversity. The typical enrollment now is over 200 persons. About half of the students are women. More than 60 percent of the students come from ethnic minorities—African American, Asian and Asian American, and Hispanic American. Members of the Reformed Church in America still comprise the largest block within the student body, but the Presbyterian, United Methodist, African Methodist Episcopal, and Baptist denominations each have large numbers of candidates within the student body. In all, over 30 different denominations and Christian traditions are represented. Most of the students are answering God's call to ministry in mid-life. These students come to seminary from various careers and bring with them a richness of experience in faith and life. The Seminary's innovative curriculum seeks to provide a context in which all this diversity of ethnicity, culture, denominations, and experience can be expressed in a common conversation—and an educational process that values each person's calling and gifts. The result is an unparalleled educational opportunity for the women and men who will lead the Christian church in this era of increasing complexity and pluralism.

Resources: In addition to the campus resources listed above, New Brunswick Seminary is blessed with an outstanding residential faculty of nine full-time and three part-time persons. More than 30 adjunct faculty persons contribute to the Seminary's rich course offering. In addition to the faculty, the Seminary is served by an outstanding administration and staff of 24 persons. The Gardner A. Sage Library houses a book collection of over 150,000 volumes; receives more than 300 professional journals and periodicals; and offers personal, professional, and technological access to resources in theological research. The Seminary operates on an annual budget of about $2,800,000. In 1999, the permanent and quasi-endowments total $10,600,000.

Samuel Zwemer Hall—the main administrative and classroom building—and the Seminary Chapel.

OLD BRIDGE MUNICIPAL UTILITIES AUTHORITY

The Old Bridge Municipal Utilities Authority (OBMUA) was created in 1985 when the governing body voted to consolidate the Old Bridge Township Sewerage Authority and the Old Bridge Municipal Utilities Authority into one agency. The original Madison Township Municipal Utilities Authority was the Water Company, established in 1960 and changed to OBMUA in 1975 with a change in Township name. The Madison Township Sewer Authority was established in 1953.

Old Bridge Township, a 42 square mile suburban community 30 miles from New York City is anticipating growth in the 21st century to reach a population in excess of 100,000 people, while maintaining expansive open space and parklands from its rural interiors to the Raritan Bay, "Gateway to the New Jersey Shore."

The Old Bridge Municipal Utilities Authority is responsible for water treatment and distribution, as well as for wastewater treatment and collection. Combining these entities and integrating their operation has resulted in improved efficiency and cost-effectiveness for both operations. The Authority currently supplies in excess of 2.5 billion gallons of water annually.

The Authority is composed of five regular members appointed by the Township Council to staggered five-year terms and two alternates who may vote in the absence of regular members. The current commissioners are: Rocco Donatelli, Michael Hegarty, Thomas Galante, Joseph B. Murray, Edna Gordon, and Charles Searlaski.

The Authority is administered by an executive director appointed by the commissioners and directly responsible to them. The current executive director, Arthur M. Haney, assumed the position on May 4, 1998. Mr. Haney is a former Old Bridge councilman, 1984-1987; mayor, 1988-1991; and Middlesex County Freeholder, 1992-1994.

The administrators of the Authority reporting to the executive director are comptroller

Seated commissioners, left to right: Charles Searlaski; Joseph B. Murray; Thomas Galante; Rocco Donatelli, chairman; Edna Gordon; and Michael Hegarty. Standing management, left to right: John E. Murphy III; Henry Penley; Stephen A. Florek II; Arthur M. Haney, executive director; Michael Roy; and Ike Welcome.

Water and Engineering Divisions—Throckmorton Lane.

Stephen A. Florek II; staff engineer Michael Roy; sewer division superintendent Ike Welcome; sewer division deputy superintendent Henry Penley; water division superintendent John Murphy III, and deputy water division superintendent Guy Donatelli.

The OBMUA provides water and sewer service to residential, commercial and industrial customers within Old Bridge Township, whose population is approximately 60,000. In total, the Authority provides service to 23,635 water customers and 23,015 sewer customers, which services 95 percent of the population.

The Authority interacts with water and sewer customers, the general public, potential property developers and governmental agencies in the day-to-day operation of the water and sewer systems.

As the municipality moves into the 21st century, the Authority is expanding its facilities to allow for the development of the southwest area of the Township. The Authority is constructing a water distribution system infrastructure to support the buildup of this area, which is largely undeveloped. When completed, the water infrastructure will service existing residents and approximately 2,500 proposed residential units, with availability for an additional 1,000 units.

The Authority's sewer system includes 25 sewerage-pumping stations and approximately 400 miles of sewer lines. The Authority also maintains an interceptor pumping station at Cliffwood Beach that pumps all wastewater collected by the Authority to the treatment facilities of the Middlesex County Utilities Authority. The Authority conducts an ongoing maintenance program in the sewer system, including inspections, testing, flushing, repairs and replacement.

In conjunction with bringing water to the southwest area of the Township, the Authority will construct sewer mains to service existing residents who live in close proximity to the new residential developments.

The Authority has purchased land next to the Municipal Complex, which is the future site of the OBMUA Administrative Offices.

The OBMUA's goal is to provide two vital services—a continuous supply of high-quality drinking water that not only meets, but also exceeds, State and Federal drinking water standards and matches the customers' expectations for safety and reliability, and the efficient removal of sanitary sewage wastewater.

The OBMUA's dedication to service is clearly reflected in its commitment to its customers and its emphasis on maintaining its plants and equipment ensuring quality service for its customers into the 21st century.

Administration & Sewer Division personnel at Cleffwood Beach.

MIDDLESEX COUNTY VOCATIONAL & TECHNICAL SCHOOLS

At a regular meeting of the Middlesex County School Board Association, held in Perth Amboy on January 31, 1914, a resolution was passed to appoint a committee to investigate the necessity for the establishment and maintenance of County Vocational Schools.

The committee organized on April 15, 1914 and discussed the following: the drop-out rate at Middlesex County elementary schools; the number and types of industries in the County likely to employ County Vocational School graduates; the effect that County vocational schools might have on apprenticeships and the trades; the probable cost of equipment for the schools; and the most suitable locations for the schools.

The committee conducted extensive research and found that the true aim of vocational schools was to train boys and girls to enter the industry of the community with preparation for earning their living. In view of the favorable endorsement of vocational schools by National and State School Authorities the committee unanimously concluded that there was a need for County Vocational Schools, as provided by law, and that they should be established and maintained in Middlesex County.

On October 26, 1914, Judge Peter F. Daly issued an order establishing a Board of Education for Vocational Schools in the county of Middlesex and appointed five members, including the Middlesex County Superintendent of Schools. With this act the school system became the first County Vocational School system in the United States.

On September 20, 1915, the first full-time all-day vocational school known as Middlesex County Vocational School No. 1 was opened

On September 20, 1915, the first all-day vocational school known as Middlesex County Vocational School No. 1 opened in a rented building on Guilden Street in New Brunswick, NJ.

in a rented building on Guilden Street in New Brunswick. Fifty-one boys enrolled in woodworking, mechanical drawing and the related subjects.

During the school year 1915-16, a one-story building was built on Bertrand Avenue in Perth Amboy to be known as Middlesex County Vocational School No. 2. It opened on October 1, 1916 with an enrollment of 45 students.

In October 1919 the boys' vocational departments at the Guilden Street School were moved to the present building on Easton Avenue in New Brunswick.

In September 1927 the faculty and pupils of the Middlesex County Vocational School No. 2 moved to the present building located on New Brunswick Avenue in Perth Amboy.

In 1938 the Board of Education accepted a grant from the Federal government to build a girl's vocational school. On property given by Mr. and Mrs. Hampton Cutter, the present school in Woodbridge opened in September 1939 with an enrollment of 194.

As demand for skilled workers grew, a fourth Middlesex County Vocational and Technical High School opened in East Brunswick

in September 1970. The school offered 18 trades and doubled the capacity of the schools.

In 1972, with a grant from the Division of Vocational Education of the Department of Education, the Middlesex County Vocational and Technical High Schools initiated a Special Needs Program for classified handicapped students and in 1975 adopted a Cooperative Industrial Education program enabling students to work in the trade trained, while completing the 12th grade.

The demand for vocational-technical education in the county continued to grow, and a fifth school, located at the site of the former Camp Kilmer in Piscataway Township, opened in 1977.

Throughout the 85-year history of the Middlesex County Vocational and Technical School, thousands of residents have been served. Most recently, during the 1998-99 school year, the five schools served 4,273 individuals in day programs and 3,936 adult students in evening schools, for a total of 8,209 individuals.

Technology and computers significantly influenced the schools during the latter part of the 20th century. Individual computer laboratories were added to each of the five schools and interactive TV studios to the East Brunswick and Piscataway campuses. The district's goal is to have computers in all classrooms over the next three years.

The district currently offers an excellent high school and adult program with training in 60 career majors. From the humble beginnings in 1914, the Middlesex County Vocational & Technical Schools and their services to the people, businesses and industry of Middlesex County, have grown significantly.

THE FRANCIS E. PARKER MEMORIAL HOME

The Francis E. Parker Memorial Home was founded on November 23, 1907, by Mrs. Francis E. Parker, in memory of her husband who died in 1905. During Mr. Parker's illness, he required constant care and often spoke sympathetically of sick people who were unable to afford nursing care.

The Home, situated on about four acres of land adjacent to Buccleuch Park in New Brunswick, was built on part of the land surrounding Mr. Parker's own home. The Home was designed to supply convalescent and long-term nursing care in "home-like" surroundings, including three solariums for its residents.

On November 30, 1908, a board of managers was organized to oversee the operations of the Home, and initiated a short course in "nursing." At that time, a bed in the ward, with board and nursing care was $5.00 per month. In 1908, the nurses earned $15.00-18.00 per week.

When Mrs. Parker died in 1931, her daughters carried on her tradition of personal interest in the Parker Home. During the early years, the Home was supported by its residents, donations of food and money from caring citizens, and the time and talent given freely by volunteers.

In 1954, the Parker Home was granted its first license by the New Jersey State Department of

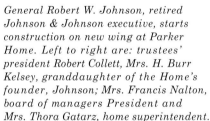

General Robert W. Johnson, retired Johnson & Johnson executive, starts construction on new wing at Parker Home. Left to right are: trustees' president Robert Collett, Mrs. H. Burr Kelsey, granddaughter of the Home's founder, Johnson; Mrs. Francis Nalton, board of managers President and Mrs. Thora Gatarz, home superintendent.

Institutions and Agencies, as a non-profit nursing home. Over the years the Home was fortunate to have an active Board of Managers and a dedicated Board of Trustees. These individuals and the many loyal employees contributed greatly as the Home's reputation for excellent care continued to grow. At that time there was a staff of about 30 running the home, including five registered nurses. In 1957, a bed on the ward with 24-hour registered nursing care, fine meals, laundry and other services cost approximately $5.00 per day.

During the mid-1960s, General Robert Wood Johnson's interest in the Home culminated in a substantial gift. General Johnson's philanthropy considerably eased the financial burden on the residents and permitted two expansions to take place: the first in 1969 and

the second in 1978. Both of these expansions added resident rooms and improved the physical environment of the Home, increasing capacity from nine to the current 51 residents.

In 1980, the Board of Trustees, recognizing the need for further expansion, purchased property in Piscataway and developed plans for a 60-bed long-term care facility, which opened in June 1983. In 1995, under the auspices of Mr. Robert Piegari, president of the Home from 1979 to 1998, the Piscataway facility opened a non-denominational chapel accommodating 100 people, in memory of Stanley C. Anderson, who served on the board from 1964-1994.

The reputation of the Home for providing quality care has continued to expand and flourish. Today the Home, under current president Mr. Roberto Mufiiz, is focusing on a specialized Dementia Care Unit and an Assisted Living facility, and has embraced the Eden Alternative™ philosophy of care.

PARKER, REMSEN & SULLIVAN, INC.

It was 1884. Grover Cleveland was President of the United States. George T. Werts was Governor of New Jersey. It was before the automobile, the airplane or the radio. The telephone and typewriter were in use, but on a very limited basis. Travel was primarily by rail and boat. Fire engines were hand-pulled or horse-drawn. Insurance policies, the specifics handwritten in quill pen, usually with exquisite penmanship, were delivered on horseback.

In 1893-94, the New Jersey Association of Insurance Agents was organized and founded, the fourth state to so organize. One of the 88 original members was Neilson T. Parker, whose insurance business was ultimately to be known as the Neilson T. Parker Co.

The Parker, Remsen & Sullivan, Inc. agency's roots date back to 1884 when Mr. Parker founded the agency which bore his name for over 80 years. The firm was initially located in a storefront on George Street in New Brunswick near Church and Albany Streets. Business developed and grew under Mr. Parker's guidance in an

Detroit.—A view of the fire which destroyed this brick and steel manufacturing plant.

This photo proves that a seemingly fire-proof building may be totally destroyed and the necessity for adequate Fire and Business Interruption Insurance.

era when fire insurance was the basic coverage offered and when most of the forms of insurance as we know them today did not even exist. Auto policies were not written until after the turn of the century and the initial policies offered were only fire, theft, and collision insurance.

Following Mr. Parker, ownership and management was turned over to one of his longtime employees, Mr. William Van Nuis, Jr., whose grandfather was mayor of the City of New Brunswick during the Civil War era. In 1929, the Neilson T. Parker Co. acquired one of its New Brunswick competitors, the J. Bayard Kirkpatrick Agency, which was founded in 1871 and was also one of the original 88 member agencies in the New Jersey Association of Insurance Agents.

Mr. Van Nuis was active in local and community affairs and in 1935 was one of the organizers and founders (and subsequently second president) of the Middlesex County Board of Insurance Agencies. He retained the name of the Neilson T. Parker Co. and operated the agency well past the middle of the 20th century.

Ownership was ultimately transferred to Dennis Sullivan, who currently is president of the agency and who has been with the firm for over 30 years. In 1969, the name of the firm was changed from the Neilson T. Parker Co. to the Parker-Sullivan Agency.

The Parker-Sullivan Agency continued its growth pattern by acquiring numerous established central Jersey agencies, including the Highland Park agencies bearing the names of Harold R. Fick, George T. Gilbert and John B. Herbert. Other acquisitions included the New Brunswick firms of Morris Bros., Ralph S. Faulkingham and Peter Biro, and the South River businesses of Ralph Gonier and Edward Alexander. Subsequently, the Frank Regnault firm in Milltown, the Joseph J. Rea Agency in Piscataway and the Fred Sbrilli business in Edison were incorporated into the growing agency.

In 1977, Remsen-Wilmot Co., a New Brunswick agency established in 1923, was merged into

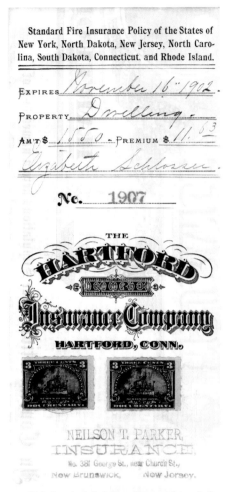

the Parker-Sullivan Agency with the resulting entity known as Parker, Remsen & Sullivan, Inc.

Parker, Remsen & Sullivan, Inc. purchased the Salisbury & Salisbury agency in December 1986 and with this acquisition came Larry Robinson, previously the owner of the Deutsch and Robinson Agency, and William Burton (Tripp) Salisbury III. Tripp is a third-generation insurance man; his grandfather had been active in the insurance business in New Brunswick since 1924, ultimately becoming a partner in the firm of O'Connell & Salisbury. His father operated Salisbury & Salisbury prior to its acquisition by Parker, Remsen & Sullivan, Inc.

In 1988 the firm, after 104 years on either George Street or Paterson Street in New Brunswick, moved across the Raritan River to neighboring Highland Park to occupy the top floor of a new office building.

Three generations of Salisburys and two of Sullivans have continued a tradition of activity and involvement in church, community, civic and alumni affairs. Tripp Salisbury's grandfather was president of the Middlesex General Hospital Board of Trustees (now Robert Wood Johnson University Hospital) in the World War II era.

Dennis Sullivan was a councilman in Bound Brook for three years and has been involved in numerous church and community activities, including a six-year term on the Board of Trustees of Rutgers, the State University of New Jersey.

Today, the agency is a full-service agency offering a broad range of commercial and personal insurance coverages, including group life and accident and health products. Policies provide coverage in many states in the United States and Canada, and in the Caribbean, Bahamas, Europe, and Asia.

Dennis Sullivan remains as president, and employees include third-generation Tripp Salisbury and second-generation Michael Sullivan.

The agency looks forward to continued growth and success in the 21st century.

Left to right: William B. Salisbury, III, Dennis Sullivan, and Michael Sullivan.

PUBLIC SERVICE ENTERPRISE GROUP

Public Service Enterprise Group (PSEG) is the parent company of Public Service Electric and Gas Company (PSE&G), a regulated gas and electric utility. Unregulated subsidiaries include: PSEG Power, which runs fossil and nuclear generating stations; PSEG Global, which is building and operating electric generation and distribution systems throughout the world; PSEG Resources, which invests in assets that provide for future growth; and PSEG Energy Technologies, which markets energy services on the Eastern seaboard.

PSE&G, which has the most immediate impact on Middlesex County, was founded in 1903 and is the largest utility in New Jersey. It is one of the largest combination electric and gas utilities in the United States, serving approximately 5.5 million people, nearly three-quarters of the state's population,

Bob Engler, service specialist for Summit District, working on a gas furnace.

including more than 265,000 customer accounts in Middlesex.

The Company's service area, covering some 2,600 square miles, runs diagonally across the state's industrial and commercial corridor from the New York State border in the north to Camden in the south. This diversified and heavily-populated area includes six major cities as well as nearly 300 suburban and rural communities. PSE&G, an investor-owned electric and gas utility formed through the merger of predecessor companies, serves a major portion of Middlesex County.

The Company is actively involved in encouraging business development throughout the state. This includes the Princeton-Route 1 Corridor stretching from South Brunswick to Lawrence Township, which is rapidly becoming the nation's newest high-technology belt.

A prime example of PSE&G's development efforts is the Raritan River Steel Company in Perth Amboy. Raritan River Steel found

its way to Perth Amboy with assistance from PSE&G's area development department. Since its opening in 1980, Raritan Steel has become one of the Company's largest electric customers.

A 1996 survey of PSE&G's impact on various New Jersey counties indicated that Middlesex County was home to 1,147 employees and more than 7,250 shareholders (NSE: PEG). In addition, PSE&G spent more than $33 million with nearly 600 different Middlesex County vendors and paid more than $50 million in taxes to Middlesex communities.

PSE&G's Middlesex County facilities include a 30,000 square-foot Maintenance Training Center located in Sayreville. The facility houses shops, electric laboratories, conference rooms, and a 60-megawatt steam turbine generator that serves as a maintenance training tool. The center is used to train employees in the operation of PSE&G's various electric and gas production plants.

ROTHE-JOHNSON-FANTACONE ARCHITECTS

Twenty-five years ago in a Metuchen basement, architects Edward N. Rothe, FAIA, and Allan R. Johnson, AIA, combined their strong design skill with business talent and vision and established Rothe-Johnson Architects/Planners. Today, with long-time associate and new Partner Thomas A. Fantacone, AIA, the multi-disciplined, 40-person firm is Middlesex County's largest architectural firm. Rothe-Johnson-Fantacone thrives as a company with an excellent reputation in the design of corporate, health-care, governmental, college and university facilities, and as an acknowledged leader in the area of designer-led design/build project delivery services.

Rothe-Johnson-Fantacone's design excellence was recognized by the NJ/American Institute of Architects for its award winning design of Brookwood Corporate Plaza I in Piscataway. More than two dozen other AIA and industry awards have been received by the firm.

Rothe-Johnson-Fantacone expanded throughout the booming 1980s designing office buildings for real estate and corporate clients throughout the central and northern regions of New Jersey, including the office and hotel complex of Edison Square, where its offices are located. Throughout Middlesex County, the distinct architectural style of Rothe-Johnson-Fantacone is evident in buildings such as the 24-story office buildings at Tower Center on Route 18 in East Brunswick, HIP Headquarters on Route 1 in North Brunswick, and Wick Corporate Center in Woodbridge. The firm has also designed award-winning interiors for Middlesex County-based corporations including Sunshine Biscuits, Inc. and the law firm of Wilentz Goldman & Spitzer.

In the late 1980s, with the real estate market dropping, Rothe-Johnson-Fantacone adapted and survived by turning its attention to governmental and higher educational facilities, including the Middlesex County Adult Correctional Facility, the Middlesex County Shelter Alternative School for Youth, and the Electrical Engineering Building at Rutgers University. Rothe-Johnson-Fantacone's presence in the higher education arena is most noted at the Middlesex County College campus in

Edison. The firm designed the Technical Services Center, the Instructional Resource Center, the Public Safety & Welcoming Center, and the Campus Bookstore; the latter two are currently under construction.

With the completion of Civic Square II, a two-building, $35 million government complex designed to house county and city agencies, and the ground-breaking of the $110 million Cancer Hospital of New Jersey at Robert Wood Johnson University Hospital, the firm continues its major role in the downtown revitalization process of Middlesex County's largest city— New Brunswick. Previous projects in New Brunswick include the "cornerstone" building at 410 George Street (Golden Triangle Plaza), the University of Medicine & Dentistry of NJ's award-winning Clinical Academic Building, Robert

Wood Johnson's CORE Pavilion, and the Parking Authority's award-winning Patterson Street Deck.

The firm has achieved its success by striving for a single goal– effective architecture–with a combination of excellence in design and solid, economic value. Rothe-Johnson-Fantacone built a strong reputation based on this goal and has won numerous design awards for the aesthetic strength of its projects.

Middlesex County College: Instructional Resource Center.

By expanding its service capabilities and more importantly, maintaining its focus on quality control and design value, the firm broadened its success.

Now in 1999, celebrating its Silver Anniversary, Rothe-Johnson-Fantacone has once again prospered, this time as a more diverse firm with a more diverse clientele base.

410 George Street, New Brunswick.

S.S. WHITE TECHNOLOGIES, INC.

Just off Rt. 287 on Old New Brunswick Road in Piscataway is a brick building owned and occupied by S.S. White Technologies, a manufacturer of, amongst other products, flexible shafts. Flexible shafts are used to transmit rotary motion around obstacles and through bends. S.S. White sells it products mainly to other manufacturers, so although most people have not heard of them, many have used their products.

In the '60s amd '70s, S.S. White Technologies supplied speedometer cables to almost every car manufacturer in the United States. In today's automobiles, every power seat uses four or five flexible shafts to make it move. More than half of the automotive power seats built in this country use flexible shafts made in the Piscataway plant.

Middlesex County is home to some of the largest companies in the world. S.S. White Technologies is a small company, employing 180 people in an 88,000 square-foot building. Few people in the county know that this is one of the oldest companies in the country, with a rich and a wonderful history.

Dr. Adam Black, the world's foremost authority on flexible shaft technology.

Rahul Shukla, president/CEO at their newest Electro Synchronous Machine for flexible shaft winding.

It all started in 1844 when a practicing dentist, Dr. Samuel Stockton White, needed some special products for his trade and decided to begin making them himself. He initially began by making porcelain teeth in his uncle's attic. Soon it became apparent that Samuel Stockton White was destined to be a manufacturer. He founded S.S. White Company in 1844 in Philadelphia. His display of teeth at the 1851 World's Fair in London won him highest honors, launching him into new fields of dental manufacturing.

The company rapidly became a pioneer in the field of dentistry with the introduction of high-speed flexible shaft dental drills. Flexible shafts were designed as a component of these drills. In 1881, two years after Dr. White's death, his estate merged the company with Johnston Brothers Company, a dental manufacturing company in Staten Island, New York. The two merged companies retained the S.S. White name and manufactured their products from a 15-acre facility in Staten Island.

In 1919, while still a leader in the dental instrument market,

S.S. White found additional uses for flexible shafts. One of the first applications was to replace the chain links used in the Ford Model T automobile to transmit the motion of the transmission axle to the speedometer dial. It soon became apparent that there were many industrial uses for flexible shafts. A separate division named S.S. White Industrial was formed within the Dental Company. Soon flexible shafts found their way into hand tools, garden equipment, marine and aircraft applications. In 1931, the company published the industry's first flexible shaft handbook that quickly became "the source" for all engineers interested in rotary motion.

In 1941, during World War II, there were two major manufacturers of flexible shafts in the country. The U.S. Military asked one of them to make parts for Marine Applications and they asked S.S. White to supply complex drive assemblies for U.S. fighter planes. It was this assignment that fostered the expertise of designing complex flexible shaft assemblies of exacting quality. By 1950, S.S. White, known for its progressive management, became the largest employer in Staten Island, employing more than 1,200 people. In 1968 the company was acquired by Pennwalt Corporation, a Philadelphia-based Fortune 200 company.

The Industrial and Dental divisions were physically separated when, in 1972, Pennwalt moved S.S. White Dental Manufacturing to Holmdel, NJ and S.S. White Industrial Division to its current location in Piscataway, NJ. Many Staten Island employees made the move to Middlesex County and the location started with 125 employees.

The following year, a young engineer, Rahul Shukla, joined the company as an inspector in the second shift but was quickly moved to the engineering department. There, to his great surprise, Shukla found out that flexible shafts, a century-old product,

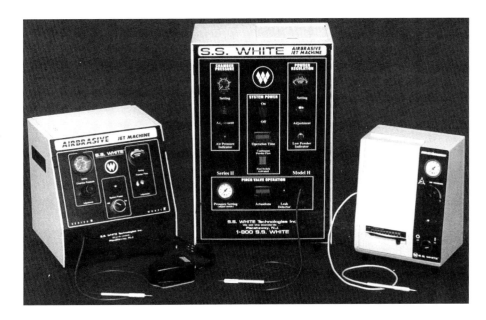

were designed by trial and error. He ran to his boss and said with incredulity, "Boss, we don't have scientific formulas to design flexible shafts."

"Neither do our competitors," said his boss. "We all do it by trial and error. It's not a problem." But it was a problem for Shukla that created a life-long obsession. A decade of

Air abrasion units by S.S. White Technologies.

S.S. White's plant at the corner of Old New Brunswick Road and South Randolphville Road in Piscataway.

long days, nights and weekends of experiments and research studies followed. "I don't want to die before I unlock the mysteries of flexible shafts," Shukla would say to his boss William Bogan. A turning point came when Adam Black III joined the R&D department in 1984. He used spring theories to predict the characteristics of flexible shaft. While employed at S.S. White, Adam Black joined Stevens Institute of Technology as a Doctoral student. After five years of exhaustive work, a Doctoral degree was awarded to him for his breakthrough discoveries on designing flexible shafts. Shukla's dream had come true. The company soon took all of Dr. Black's formulas and created a design software called Perflexion®. Today, Dr. Black is the only person in the world with a Ph.D. in the design of flexible shafts and is considered the world authority. S.S. White Technologies is the only company in the world that uses scientific formulas to design flexible shafts. All others still use trial and error.

There was another turn of events in store for this historical company. In 1987, Pennwalt, the parent corporation, decided to sell off the division. Strange people walked through the plant and there was an uncertain hush in the building. Everyone was nervous. Shukla gathered some of his friends and suggested they buy the company themselves. His friends laughed. Tom Sarnoski, Shukla's friend and co-worker for over 15 years asked "Why would they sell the company to us?"

"Tom, why do beautiful women marry ugly men!?!" said Shukla. His point, "If you try, you may succeed." It took 12 months to arrange the financing for a management buyout.

"Our knowledge of flexible

shafts was unparalleled, our machinery was not." says Shukla. "In the prior years, the management was not keen on investing in new machinery for this century-old product. Flexible shaft winding machines are not the kind that you can place an order for with a company and have them delivered to your plant."

In 1994, the company hired 12 additional engineers and gave them a mission to design and manufacture the most modern winding machines in the world. Four years later the first 55 foot-long, computer-controlled ESM winding machine started making flexible shaft. This new Electro Synchronous winding machine makes all the layers of a flexible shaft in one pass. An on-board computer continuously synchronizes the speed of all the motors giving precise wire gap controls not available to any other manufacturers in the world.

This old company has a very young attitude, thanks to its spirited top management team which includes president Rahul Shukla and vice presidents Brian

Parlato, Tom Sarnoski, Carolyn Ketcham and Bernie Marx. Today the company operates three divisions specializing in abrasive jet machining, instrumentation for trucks and heavy duty vehicles and flexible shaft assemblies. The Piscataway building also houses two separate, wholly-owned companies: Oz Dental Products, a manufacturer of Air Abrasion equipment for dentists and S.S. White Medical Products Inc, a company that makes orthopedic surgical instruments.

S.S. White is currently a $15 million company that has grown from 130 people in 1988 to 180 people today. Much of the work done in the company's plant requires specialized skills, and the company has been fortunate to benefit from the availability of bright and motivated workers.

That is the history. Now, Dr. Samuel Stockton White's dream continues on, into the next millenium.

S.S. White Technologies' primary product, flexible shaft, being wound.

SUMMIT ASSOCIATES INC.

Developers of Quality Business Environments: Summit Associates Inc. is one of New Jersey's premier real estate developers. It has built, owns and manages more than 4.5 million square-feet of office, high-tech and distribution space throughout the state.

Summit Associates was founded by current Chairman of the Board Vincent Visceglia. His sons, Diego R. Visceglia, president and John B. Visceglia, executive vice president, are currently running the company.

As a major developer of Raritan Center in Edison, the Visceglias' vision stretches beyond the next century and calls for the continued development of the 2,300+ acre business park in Edison. One of the largest sites east of the Mississippi, Raritan Center stands ready to meet the changing needs of the times. With over 35 years of professional development already behind it, the 2,300-acre, former Raritan Arsenal has now evolved into one of the largest and most prestigious business parks in the northeast with a daily work force in excess of 15,000.

Combine its vast and diversified inventory, superior accessibility to New Jersey's major highways and the extensive and talented labor pool within close proximity, and it is easy to see why Raritan Center continues to be a thriving business hub and home to some of the nations most prestigious corporations.

Raritan Center's largest office structure is Summit Associates' Raritan Plaza I, a Class A, 262,500 square-foot office building attached to the new 284-room Sheraton Edison Hotel.

Summit Associates believes that there are several key factors to its success. Property management, an area that deals directly with tenants on a daily basis, is

Raritan Plaza I, the nine-story 262,500 square-foot class A office building located at the entrance to Raritan Center.

handled internally. The management team is made up of Summit employees dedicated to satisfying their customers.

An on-site maintenance staff of Summit employees is available at all times, and is quite aware of the vital role that they play in a business based upon customer service. Also providing years of professional experience is Summit's in-house legal and leasing staff.

In over 35 years of operating experience, Summit Associates has acquired an in-depth knowledge of the real estate business and marketplace. Summit has the pride and the professional expertise to provide businesses large and small with the highest standard of service available.

Summit's business enterprises and expertise extend beyond Raritan Center. Summit properties are situated in choice loca-

tions throughout the Garden State—from Somerset County to Monmouth County, and west to Hunterdon County. Each reflects the Summit commitment to customer service and excellence.

Moreover, Summit prides itself on its ability to adapt to, and thereby accommodate, the complex needs of a changing business world. Summit realizes that serving clients is more than dedication and expertise—it is applying hands-on, innovative and creative solutions that satisfy its clients' needs.

As Summit looks to the future, it intends to continue the trademark quality of service its customers enjoy. It envisions the continued development of Raritan Center and its other properties. And, because the firm knows that it is not merely a member of the business sector but part of the larger community as well, Summit is dedicated to maintaining an active commitment to worthy charitable, educational and cultural causes and organizations.

A TIMELINE OF MIDDLESEX COUNTY'S HISTORY

1609 Henry Hudson discovers Raritan River.

1615 Six Dutch settlers sail up the Rarachons River (Lenape word from which we derive Raritan) and establish a community at New Brunswick.

1682 Middlesex County is given a name and its boundaries are defined.

1683 Middlesex County officially incorporates.

1686 Government of East Jersey moves to Perth Amboy.

1688 The first of several changes to the County's boundaries is approved.

1692 Woodbridge, Perth Amboy and Piscataway Townships are formed.

1698 Aaron Louzada, the first

known Jewish settler, arrives in Middlesex County (in a portion of the County now part of Bound Brook).

1713 County Board of Chosen Freeholders is created.

1734 First boat and stage line begins shipping freight from New York across New Jersey, on a scheduled basis.

1751 First printing press in New Jersey is established in Woodbridge by James Parker (Parker Press).

1753 Joseph Bloomfield is born in Woodbridge, later to become Governor of the State.

1758 Parker Press publishes the first magazine ever printed in New Jersey.

1760 William Dunlap, author, playwright and painter is born in Perth Amboy.

1762 William Franklin is appointed Royal Governor of the Province of New Jersey by the British crown and resides at the governor's mansion in Perth Amboy.

1766 Charter granted for Queens College (now Rutgers, The State University).

1766 The world's first Medical Society is founded in New Brunswick.

1771 First classes are held at Queens College.

1774 New Jersey Provincial Congress holds its first meeting in New Brunswick.

1776 Alexander Hamilton's artillery battery defends New Brunswick.

Broadway in South Amboy was electrified in 1896 but was traversed more by horse drawn carriage than by automobile. Courtesy, Middlesex County Cultural and Heritage Commission

1777 British officer Wayne, nick-named "Mad Anthony" occupies New Brunswick for the second time.

1778 The County Court system is moved to New Brunswick.

1778 George Washington and his troops celebrate the second anniversary of the Declaration of Independence along the banks of the Raritan River.

1779 British Lieutenant Colonel John Simcoe, notorious for burning sites in the Raritan Valley, is thwarted in his attack on East Brunswick and South Amboy.

1781 Captain Adam Huyler from New Brunswick and his whaleboat "navy" raid British vessels in the Raritan Bay and at Sandy Hook.

1789 George Washington stays at Cross Keys Tavern in Woodbridge.

1789 The *Home News* now the *Home News Tribune* was founded.

1790 Population of Middlesex County is 5,000.

1796 Three pounds and 15 shillings were paid for a Seal of the County of Middlesex but no record of its design survives.

1798 Salaries of the members of the Board of Chosen Freeholders is set at $1.00 per year.

1800 Population of Middlesex County is 16,000.

1806 Solomon Andrews, inventor, perfects the dirigible in Perth Amboy.

1820 New Brunswick hosts the New Jersey cattle and agricultural fair.

1825 Queens College is renamed Rutgers College.

1826 Theodore F. Randolph, later to become Governor of New Jersey, is born in New Brunswick.

1830 Dr. Ezra M. Hunt, international leader in health care, is born in Metuchen.

1831 The *John Bull* the first steam locomotive in New Jersey, ran for a short distance near Jamesburg. It was put into service in 1832.

1832 First horse-drawn train traverses the state and passes through Middlesex County.

1834 Delaware and Raritan Canal is finished at a cost of $2,830,000. The last lock is in New Brunswick.

1835 A tornado severely damages New Brunswick. It crosses the Raritan River and causes damage in Woodbridge.

1846 A. Hall and Sons, a manufacturer of bricks and terra cotta, opens in Perth Amboy.

Highland Park Post 88, American Legion Drum and Bugle Corps, in 1932 posed in their uniforms that consisted of French blue cloth, black leather puttee, Sam Brown belt and a helmet. A very active and community minded organization, they sponsored a local Boy Scout Troop, a community night intended to foster neighborhood spirit, and a Christmas Eve celebration held at the Highland Park Soldiers Monument. Post 88 received its charter in July of 1921, at that time, the 13th post in Middlesex County. Meetings took place in a room over Hodges Garage, later at 127 Benner Street. Presently, Post 88 meets in a modest building that is their headquarters, at 808 Raritan Avenue. Courtesy, Highland Park Historical Society.

1847 H.W.Crosby establishes a factory to make tin cans and can food in Jamesburg.

1853 New Jersey Educational Association is founded in New Brunswick.

1864 Rutgers College becomes a land grant college.

1865 Abraham Lincoln's funeral train passes through New Brunswick.

1867 Salaries of the members of the Board of Chosen Freeholders are raised by 100% to $2.00 per year!

1868 Famous American landscape artist, Geoge Innes, makes his studio in Perth Amboy.

1869 First intercollegiate football game is played in New Brunswick, between Princeton University and Rutgers College.

1870 Thomas Mundy Peterson, first African American to vote under the 15th Amendment to the Constitution, casts his ballot in Perth Amboy.

1870 George S. Silzer is born in New Brunswick. He will enter politics and be elected Governor of the State.

1872 New Jersey State Board of Agriculture is formed in New Brunswick.

1872 The original St. Peter's Hospital is established but is in operation only 2 years. It later will be recreated in 1907 as St. Peter's General Hospital.

1877 Thomas Alva Edison invents the phonograph at his laboratory in Edison.

1879 Thomas Alva Edison invents the incandescent light bulb at his laboratory in Edison.

1880 George Washington Helme takes over the snuff factory of Appleby and begins the Helme dynasty and company town.

1880 New Jersey Agricultural Station is formed in New Brunswick.

1880 Christie Street in Edison

becomes the first in the world to be lit by electric light.

1882 Morgan Larson is born in Perth Amboy. An engineer by profession, he later is elected Governor of the State.

1884 Founding of New Brunswick City Hospital, later to be known as Robert Wood Johnson University Hospital.

1886 Joyce Kilmer, poet and author is born in New Brunswick, later to claim fame as the author of the poem *Trees*.

1886 Robert W. Johnson and James W. Johnson establish their business in New Brunswick, now Johnson & Johnson.

1889 Harry Tierney is born in Perth Amboy. He is later recognized as an outstanding musical composer.

1890 Population of Middlesex County is 18,000.

1891 Dr. Thurlow Nelson, noted marine biologist, is born in Highland Park.

1895 County park system is authorized by state enabling legislation.

1896 Harold G. Hoffman is born in South Amboy. Later he becomes Governor of the State.

1899 Spanish gunboat travels up the D&R Canal, having been seized by American troops, battle of Santiago, Spanish American War.

1900 Quadricycle is invented in Cartaret.

1902 Raritan Bay Medical Center is founded.

1912 First airmail flight takes

The Jersey Devil was "seen" numerous times, throughout central and southern New Jersey in the year 1909. Sightings were reported by local law enforcement officials, individuals and even politicians. New Brunswick took the remarkable step of placing policeman on trolley car runs, to assure protection of its citizenry. The Jersey Devil is New Jersey's most famous legendary character. Courtesy, Middlesex County Cultural and Heritage Commission

place between South Amboy (leaving from Star Field) and Perth Amboy.

1912 Theodore "Teddy" Roosevelt campaigns in New Brunswick.

1912 The Fellowship Farm Cooperative is established in Piscataway, a utopian community.

1913 Atlantic Terra Cotta Company in Perth Amboy produces architectural elements for Woolworth Building, largest structure in world.

1915 First vocational training school in the USA is opened in New Brunswick. The state would not create vocational schools until 1923.

1918 Morgan Company explosion shakes the County, it is a munitions plant in Sayreville.

1918 New Jersey College for Women is opened. It later becomes Douglass College, part of Rutgers, The State University.

1918 Raritan Bay freezes over. Cars and people ride and skate on the frozen water.

1925 Inauguration of night airmail service from Hadley Field in South Plainfield, air freight service will follow in 1927.

1926 Victory Bridge linking South Amboy and Perth Amboy is opened.

1928 Outerbridge Crossing opens, named for construction engineer Eugenius H. Outer-bridge.

1930 Population of Middlesex County is 200,000.

1930 The Rotolactor on the Walker Gordon farm is put into operation, milking 50 cows in a record breaking 12.5 minutes.

1934 The famous "Rutgers Tomato" is developed by the New Jersey Agricultural Experiment Station at Rutgers University.

1940 Edison Route #9 Bridge, now called the Driscoll Bridge, is erected and opens to traffic. It spans the Raritan River.

1941 Camp Kilmer, an Army installation, opens in Edison/ Piscataway as a staging area for WWII troops.

1942 Hamilton Street and Johnson & Johnson are closed off to the public by the US War Department, to safeguard its wartime manufacturing.

1943 Selman Waksman discovers the first broad spectrum antibiotic—streptomycin, for which he is later awarded the Nobel Prize.

1952 New Jersey Turnpike opens.

1954 Raritan Township votes a name change to Edison Township in honor of its most illustrious former resident, Thomas Alva Edison.

1956—1957 30,000 Hungarians escape political oppression and the Hungarian Revolution, arriving in USA through Camp Kilmer in New Brunswick.

1959 The last passenger service over the historic Camden/Amboy Railroad is run, when a single-car train makes the trip from Jamesburg to Perth Amboy.

1966 Middlesex County College opens to the first students, having been created by the Freeholders in 1964.

1970 University of Medicine and Dentistry of New Jersey is created.

1971 East Jersey Olde Towne, Inc. a nonprofit organization is formed and begins efforts to create an historic village in Piscataway.

1975 Madison Township changes its name to Old Bridge Township.

1976 The five railroads serving Middlesex County are consolidated under the plan to create Conrail.

1980 Town of Cranbury is placed on the State and National Registers of Historic Places.

1983 County wide celebration in honor of the Middlesex County Tercentennial.

1983 Johnson & Johnson world

wide headquarters opens in New Brunswick, designed by internationally acclaimed architect I.M. Pei.

1985 By this year, there are 324 miles of county roads (as opposed to state or local) within Middlesex County.

1987 New Jersey Museum of Agriculture opens in New Brunswick.

1989 East Jersey Olde Towne Village is acquired by Middlesex County. It is restored and opens in 1997 under the Cultural & Heritage Commission.

1990 Population of Middlesex County is 671,780.

1990 US Route #1 between Princeton University north to Rutgers, The State University is dubbed the "high tech corridor."

1993 Helme Snuff Mill (now owned by the General Cigar and Tobacco Company) in Helmetta is closed.

1997 Restoration of the landmark structure, Cornelius Low House, by the Middlesex County Cultural and Heritage Commission.

1998 Ferry slip in Perth Amboy is restored and reopened.

1998 Raritan Bay Waterfront Park is opened to the public. In 1999 it receives two awards for design excellence.

2000 Population of Middlesex County estimated to be 721,000.

BIBLIOGRAPHY

Archibald, Alice J. *The Black Community in New Brunswick.* Pamphlet, 1980, available at the New Brunswick Public Library.

Benedict, William H. *New Brunswick in History.* New Brunswick, N.J.: n.p., 1925.

Cawley, James and Margaret. *Along the Delaware and Raritan Canal.* Rutherford, N.J.: Fairleigh Dickinson University Press, 1970.

The City of New Brunswick. 1908. Reprint. New Brunswick, N.J.: Clark's Bookstore, 1979.

Charter of the City of New Brunswick of December 30, 1730 and Early Ordinances of the city. No. III. New Brunswick, N.J.: Historical Club Publications, 1912.

Clayton, W. Woodford. *History of Union and Middlesex Counties, New Jersey, with Biographical Sketches of Many of their Pioneers and Prominent Men.* Philadelphia: Everts and Peck, 1882.

Coad, Oral S. *New Jersey in Travellers' Accounts—1524-1971: A Descriptive Bibliography.* Metuchen, N.J.: Scarecrow Press, 1972.

Cohen, David Steven. *The Folklore and Folklife of New Jersey.* New Brunswick, N.J.: Rutgers University Press, 1983.

Colon, Otilio. *A Brief History of the Hispanic Community in New Brunswick: 1948-1980.* Typescript, 1980, available at the New Brunswick Public Library.

Cook, James G. *Edison—The Man Who Turned Darkness Into Light.* Pamphlet, 1978, published by the Thomas Alva Edison Foundation, Inc.

Cunningham, Barbara, ed. *The New Jersey Ethnic Experience.* Union City, N.J.: Wm. H. Wise & Co, 1977.

Cunningham, John T. *Colonial New Jersey.* New York: Elsevier/Nelson, 1971.

———. *New Jersey: A Mirror On America.* Florham Park, N.J.: Afton, 1978.

———. *The New Jersey Sampler: Historical Tales of Old New Jersey.* Upper Montclair, N.J.: N.J. Almanac, 1964.

———. *This is New Jersey.* 3rd ed. New Brunswick, N.J.: Rutgers University Press, 1978.

Demarest, William H.S. *The Anniversary of New Brunswick, New Jersey, 1680-1730-1930.* New Brunswick, N.J.: J. Heidingsfeld Co., 1932.

Gerlach, Larry R. *Prologue to Independence: New Jersey in the Coming of the American Revolution.* New Brunswick, N.J.: Rutgers University Press, 1976.

Heusser, Albert H. *The Footsteps of Washington: Pope's Creek to Princeton.* Paterson, N.J.: n.p., 1921.

Hill, H. Solomon. *Negro in New Brunswick, N.J. As revealed by a study of one-hundred families.* Master's thesis, Drew University, 1942.

History of the Jews of New Brunswick, N.J. and Its Environs. Unpublished paper, assumed to be written by Rabbi Nathaniel M. Keller, available at the New Brunswick Public Library.

Hoagland, Stewart. *New Jersey Historical Profiles: Revolutionary Times.* Somerville, N.J.: Somerset Press, 1973.

Hoffman, Robert V. *The Revolutionary Scene in New Jersey.* New York: American Historical Company, 1942.

Illustrated History of the New Brunswick Fire Department. New Brunswick, N.J.: Washington Engine Co., No. 1, 1909.

Josephson, Matthew. *Edison: A Biography.* New York: McGraw-Hill, 1959.

Journal of the Medical Society of New Jersey. Vol. 81, No. 9. September, 1984. Includes study of herbal medicine among the Lenni Lenape.

Listokin, Barbara Cyviner. *The Architectural History of New Brunwick, New Jersey, 1681-1900.* New Brunswick, N.J.: Rutgers University Art Gallery, 1976.

Some South Plainfield residents can recall the R.B. Manning and Bros. store on Front Street as typical of many local groceries. Inside was a pot-bellied stove and lots of penny candy. Although the store had electricity by 1910, when this photo was taken, sidewalks had not yet been installed. The structure, which still stands, is now a private residence. Courtesy, South Plainfield Historical Society

Makar, Janos. *The Story of an Immigrant Group in Franklin, New Jersey.* Translated by August J. Molnar. New Brunswick, N.J.: Standard Press, 1969.

Master Plan, City of New Brunswick, N.J. A Report Prepared by The City Planning Commission and Planning Consultant Russell Van Nest Black. January, 1947.

McCormick, Richard P. *New Brunswick During the Revolution.* Typescript of Speech, 1976, available at the New Brunswick Public Library.

————. *New Jersey From Colony To State, 1609-1789.* N.J. Historical Series, Vol. I Princeton, N.J.: Van Nostrand, 1964.

McKelvey, William J., Jr. *The Delaware and Raritan Canal, A Pictorial History.* York, Pennsylvania: Canal Press, 1975.

Miers, Earl Schenck. *Where the Raritan Flows.* New Brunswick, N.J.: Rutgers University Press, 1964.

Miller, Lynn F. and Olin, Ferris, eds. *Women's Spheres: Celebrating Three Centuries of Women in Middlesex County and New Jersey.* New Brunswick, N.J.: Middlesex County Cultural and Heritage Commission, 1983.

New Brunswick and Its Industries: A Synopsis of the History of the City with Special Reference to Its Trade and Commerce, Plain Presentment of Its Claims as a Place of Residence and of Manufacturing. New Brunswick, N.J.: A.E. Gordon, Times Printing House, 1873.

New Jersey: Unexpected Pleasures. Princeton, N.J.: United Jersey Banks, 1980.

Patt, Ruth Marcus. *The Jewish Scene in New Jersey's Raritan Valley.* New Brunswick, N.J.: Jewish Historical Society of Raritan Valley, 1978.

————, ed. *The Tercentennial Lectures.* New Brunswick, N.J.: City of New Brunswick, 1982.

Pierce, Arthur Dudley. *Smugglers' Woods: Jaunts and Journeys in Colonial and Revolutionary New Jer-

The steamboat New Brunswick *was launched in 1879 by Captain Adams, who founded the New Brunswick, Amboy and New York Steamboat Company. The vessel carried both freight and as many as 1,000 passengers. She was 176 feet long with two passenger decks. Courtesy, Special Collections and Archives, Rutgers University Libraries*

sey. New Brunswick, N.J.: Rutgers University Press, 1960.

Puskas, Julianna. *From Hungary to the United States (1880-1914).* Translated by Maria Bales. Translation revised by Eva Palmai. Budapest: Adademiai Kiado, Budapest, 1982.

Schmidt, George P. *Douglass College: A History.* New Brunswick, N.J.: Rutgers University Press, 1968.

Seamon, Terrence H. *Buccleuch: A History in New Brunswick.* New Brunswick, N.J.: Department of Parks and Recreation, 1978.

The Story of Dunellen. Federal Writers Project, Works Progress Administration, American Guide Series, 1937.

Thompson, Robert T. *Colonel James Neilson: A Businessman of the Early Machine Age in New Jersey.* New Brunswick, N.J.: Rutgers University Press, 1940.

Trends, Issues and Priorities in the Revitalization of New Brunswick, New Jersey. Columbia, Maryland: American City Corporation, 1975.

Van Dyke, J.C. *The Raritan: Notes on a River and a Family.* New Brunswick, N.J.: n.p., 1915.

Van Eerden, Bernard. *A Dutch Village: The New Brunswick Story.* Typescript, 1976, available at the

New Brunswick Public Library.

Veit, Richard F. *The Old Canals of New Jersey: A Historical Geography.* Little Falls, N.J.: New Jersey Geographical Press, 1963.

Views of New Brunswick, N.J. Portland, Maine: L.H. Nelson Co., 1925.

Wachhorst, Wyn. *Thomas Alva Edison: An American Myth.* Cambridge, Massachusetts: MIT Press, 1981.

Wall, John P., comp. *New Brunswick in the World War 1917-18.* New Brunswick, N.J.: S.M. Christie Press, 1921.

Wall, John P. and Pickersgill, Harold E. *History of Middlesex County.* 3 vols. New York: Lewis Historical Publishing Co., 1921.

Weiss, Harry B. *The Personal Estates of Early Farmers and Tradesmen of Colonial New Jersey.* Trenton, N.J.: New Jersey Agricultural Society, 1971.

INDEX

*The **Eagle Hook and Ladder Co. #1,** Metuchen, had recently lost one of its members when this photo was taken in 1890. Despite the dangers, the firefighting companies of Middlesex County displayed great esprit and stood ready to assist in time of need. Courtesy, New Brunswick Chamber of Commerce*